# The Biopolitics of Care in Second World War Britain

# THE MASS-OBSERVATION CRITICAL SERIES

*The Mass-Observation Critical Series* pairs innovative interdisciplinary scholarship with rich archival materials from the original Mass-Observation movement and the current Mass Observation Project. Launched in 1937, the Mass-Observation movement aimed to study the everyday life of ordinary Britons. The Mass Observation Project continues to document and archive the everyday lives, thoughts and attitudes of ordinary Britons to this day. Mass-Observation, as a whole, is an innovative research organization, a social movement, and an archival project that spans much of the 20th and early 21st centuries.

The series makes Mass-Observation's rich primary sources accessible to a wide range of academics and students across multiple disciplines, as well as to the general reading public. Books in the series include re-issues of important original Mass-Observation publications, edited and introduced by leading scholars in the field, and thematically oriented anthologies of Mass-Observation material. The series also facilitates cutting-edge research by established and new scholars using Mass-Observation resources to present fresh perspectives on everyday life, popular culture and politics, visual culture, emotions, and other relevant topics.

## Series Editors

**Jennifer J. Purcell** is Associate Professor of History and Chair of the History Department at Saint Michael's College in Vermont, USA. Using Mass-Observation diaries and directives, her first book, Domestic Soldiers (2010), seeks to understand the day-to-day lives of six women on the home front during the Second World War.

**Benjamin Jones** is Lecturer in Modern British History at the University of East Anglia in Norwich, UK. He is the author of The Working Class in Mid-Twentieth-Century England (2012), which was positively reviewed in Sociology, American Historical Review, Journal of Modern History, Journal of British Studies, The Historical Journal, Economic History Review, Contemporary British History, Twentieth Century British History, and Planning Perspectives.

## Editorial Board

Fiona Courage, Head of Special Collections, University of Sussex in Brighton, UK
Lucy Curzon, Associate Professor of Contemporary and Modern Art History, University of Alabama, USA
Claire Langhamer, Professor of Modern British History and Director of Research and Knowledge Exchange in the School of History, Art History and Philosophy, University of Sussex, UK
Jeremy MacClancy, Professor of Anthropology, Oxford Brookes University, UK
Kimberly Mair, Associate Professor of Sociology, University of Lethbridge, Canada
Rebecca Searle, Lecturer in the Humanities, University of Brighton, UK
Matthew Taunton, Lecturer in the School of Literature, Drama and Creative Writing, University of East Anglia, UK

## Published Titles

*The Biopolitics of Care in Second World War Britain*, Kimberly Mair (2022)

# The Biopolitics of Care in Second World War Britain

Kimberly Mair

BLOOMSBURY ACADEMIC
LONDON • NEW YORK • OXFORD • NEW DELHI • SYDNEY

BLOOMSBURY ACADEMIC
Bloomsbury Publishing Plc
50 Bedford Square, London, WC1B 3DP, UK
1385 Broadway, New York, NY 10018, USA
29 Earlsfort Terrace, Dublin 2, Ireland

BLOOMSBURY, BLOOMSBURY ACADEMIC and the Diana logo are trademarks of
Bloomsbury Publishing Plc

First published in Great Britain 2022
This paperback edition published 2023

Copyright © Kimberly Mair, 2022

Kimberly Mair has asserted their right under the Copyright, Designs and Patents Act, 1988,
to be identified as Author of this work.

All rights reserved. No part of this publication may be reproduced or transmitted in
any form or by any means, electronic or mechanical, including photocopying,
recording, or any information storage or retrieval system, without prior
permission in writing from the publishers.

Bloomsbury Publishing Plc does not have any control over, or responsibility for, any
third-party websites referred to in this book. All internet addresses given in this book
were correct at the time of going to press. The author and publisher regret any
inconvenience caused if addresses have changed or sites have ceased to exist,
but can accept no responsibility for any such changes.

Every effort has been made to trace the copyright holders and obtain permission
to reproduce the copyright material. Please do get in touch with any enquiries or
any information relating to such material or the rights holder. We would be pleased
to rectify any omissions in subsequent editions of this publication should they be
drawn to our attention.

A catalogue record for this book is available from the British Library.

Library of Congress Cataloging-in-Publication Data

Names: Mair, Kimberly, author.
Title: The biopolitics of care in Second World War Britain / Kimberly Mair.
Description: London ; New York : Bloomsbury Academic, 2022. |
Series: The Mass-Observation critical series |
Includes bibliographical references and index.
Identifiers: LCCN 2021030077 (print) | LCCN 2021030078 (ebook) |
ISBN 9781350106918 (hardback) | ISBN 9781350106925 (pdf) |
ISBN 9781350106932 (ebook)
Subjects: LCSH: World War, 1939–1945–Social aspects–Great Britain. |
Mass-Observation (Project : 1937–1960?)–History. | Civil defense–Great Britain–History–
20th century. | World War, 1939–1945–Evacuation of civilians.
Classification: LCC D744.7.G7 M35 2022 (print) | LCC D744.7.G7 (ebook) |
DDC 941.084—dc23
LC record available at https://lccn.loc.gov/2021030077
LC ebook record available at https://lccn.loc.gov/2021030078

ISBN: HB: 978-1-3501-0691-8
PB: 978-1-3502-8209-4
ePDF: 978-1-3501-0692-5
eBook: 978-1-3501-0693-2

Typeset by RefineCatch Limited, Bungay, Suffolk

To find out more about our authors and books visit www.bloomsbury.com
and sign up for our newsletters.

# Contents

| | |
|---|---|
| List of Illustrations | vi |
| Imperatives: A Preface | vii |
| Acknowledgements | xxi |
| | |
| Introduction: Read, Listen, Obey and Keep a Good Heart | 1 |
| 1  Keeping Watch Over the Population | 43 |
| 2  Verminous Houseguests and Good Hosts: Evacuation Stories | 67 |
| 3  Lazy Dogs | 109 |
| 4  Confused Animacies on the Home Front | 135 |
| 5  Careless Homes Cost Lives | 153 |
| | |
| Notes | 171 |
| Bibliography | 201 |
| Index | 211 |

# Illustrations

| | | |
|---|---|---|
| 0.1 | Coughs and sneezes spread diseases, Poster issued by the Central Office of Information | 31 |
| 1.1 | Careless Talk campaign, Poster issued by the Central Office of Information, artist Feibush, c. 1939 | 60 |
| 2.1 | She's in the ranks too, Poster issued by the Central Office of Information | 91 |
| 2.2 | Don't do it, Mother, Poster issued by the Central Office of Information | 94 |
| 4.1 | Animals, in the service of Man, Poster issued by the National Savings Committee, c. 1945 | 143 |
| 5.1 | We've great things to do, keep on Saving, Poster issued by the National Savings Committee, c. 1944 | 161 |

# Imperatives: A Preface

The BBC drones on about coming attacks from the sky, food shortages, evacuation and loss of life. Perhaps these things have already taken shape in your dreams. In waking hours, as you fold your linens, you try to tuck images of war into the tidy creases, but you are frequently addressed with exhortations to act always in anticipation, to carry out 'methodically the preparations recommended to you'.[1] The images unfurl with the cloth you spread over the table and the sheet over the mattress. Sometimes you can see them from the back window, as though they were stuck to the underclothes hanging on the line, shedding radiant heat on thirsty gardens. They take up room in the pantry, occupying the spaces that your shopping should promptly fill.

In the coming war, the fortified household will be the primary line of defence and as crucial to the nation as the army: 'If the emergency comes the country will look for her safety not only to her sailors and soldiers and airmen, but also to the organised courage and foresight of every household.' Begin by selecting a room, perhaps a spare one, for refuge purposes. If your dwelling consists of only one room, then it must be prepared as a refuge room, 'So do what you can.'[2] Reinforce the ceiling. Seal all cracks. Do not use your attic or top-level rooms for refuge, but apply two coats of limewash to any woodwork there, and the flooring should be covered with iron sheets, asbestos wallboard or sand. Any upper floor should be equipped with a Redhill sand container, or a bucket full of sand and a long-handled shovel in case there is a need to contain an incendiary bomb.[3] Be rest assured that a Redhill container is so sturdy that, should you need to, you can simply deposit a burning magnesium bomb into it and then carry it a safe distance from your home.[4] Gather the following items downstairs in your refuge room: chamber pot, wash basin, hand-pump, pick axe and a long-handled shovel. If you could see the future in advance, you would know to expect that these items will furnish your domestic surroundings for a stretch of years.

Shroud doorways with blankets pulled over felt-covered sheets of wood to prevent gas seepage, and do not forget to seal the fireplace. Cover all windows in the entire household with thick black fabric, paper or paint to blacken out interior light from the air bomber's keen, searching eyes.[5] Later, you might sit, huddled with your loved ones, in a darkened room just a bit too small, practicing with your gas masks, trying not to listen to the airplane's 'steady deadly tenor' as it asks: '"Where are you? Where are you?" overhead'.[6] Cover all windows with sheets of celluloid to contain shards of glass in case your windows are shattered by an explosive blast.

Learn how to care for and wear a respirator properly; it is 'your second line of defence'.[7] If you have a baby, practice putting on its mask with yours already on, but, if you care for more than one infant, you have a predicament because you are not going to be able to do this alone. With slightly older children, drills that consist of putting on and removing a gas mask can be a fun game.[8]

\* \* \*

Anticipation of the next war stretched back years before it became instrumentalized in the flood of cautionary instructions to which British civilians eventually became accustomed. Expectation and dread hung on the same notion that organized H.G. Wells's speculative future-history, *The Shape of Things to Come*: '[t]he new war was like no war that had ever been before', with the Great War having taught that 'the extreme slowness with which the realization of even the most obvious new conditions pierces through the swathings of habitual acceptance'.[9] Labouring under the spectre of this new war, the interwar government considered abstract provisions for wartime evacuation of vulnerable populations from out of high risk areas, particularly those that contained aerodromes and docks, munitions works, central utility service sites and dense populations.[10] Although this scheme was sketchy and only began to take concrete form in 1938, official considerations for it can be traced at least back to 1931.[11] At that time, it was speculated that attacks could 'paralyse London's public services, putting out of action all the main line railway termini and a considerable part of the gas, telephone and water services, closing the underground railways, and destroying or damaging half the important electric power stations'.[12] The Committee of Imperial Defence had been advised that, upon declaration of war, aerial bombings targeting urban centres could be expected. Further, an air strike on the city of London could last for up to sixty days, having the grave potential of up to 600,000 deaths and more injuries.[13]

It is possible that you have not heard these grim numbers. Nevertheless, you know that the new war will favour the sky as its strategic terrain. Though the sky promised 'freedom's realm, where travel would go on unimpeded by rails, roadblocks, or stationmasters' and the coming of what Alfred W. Lawson, purported inventor of *the idea* of the airliner, called the '"alti-man," who would be born in the air and live his whole life up there',[14] Sven Lindqvist suggested that the fear of the new superweapons that the airplane could wield did not extend to their vehicle. No, the airplane brought awe. Its rapid ascendance would have been only the stuff of dreams and fantasy for those who had died not so very long ago. That is what Graham Greene's protagonist Arthur Rowe thought when he considered how the blitz would appear to his mother, who 'died before the first great war, when aeroplanes – strange crates of wood – just staggered across the Channel'. Instead, in Rowe's own dream, he informed his dead mother that '[t]his isn't real life any more', and London was being broken into ruins, including the places they went together. 'You remember St Clement's – the bells of St Clement's.'[15] Perhaps, as Lindqvist observed, some people thought that air war would distribute its dangers more democratically, or that it was more noble than other means of waging war. Thus, fighter pilots could be regarded 'as the duelists of the air, modern knights engaging in a heavenly tournament'.[16] Rowe failed to see the romance of chivalry in it. To him, the blitz experience followed the genre of the thriller, 'but the thrillers are like life', he told his mother in the dream, 'more like life than you are, this lawn, your sandwiches, that pine'.[17]

Yet Susan Grayzel's analysis of responses to aerial bombing on Britain during the First World War suggested much less admiration than Lindqvist observed (though he based his attribution on the apparent eagerness to use the air strategy, as well as Secretary of the Air Ministry, James M. Spaight's appraisal of Churchill's orders to bomb German cities as 'a splendid decision'[18]). Drawing attention to the sarcastic cultural representations of bombers as knights waging battle from the sky, Grayzel demonstrated that air war was publicly considered neither democratic, nor moral. Rather, attacks from the air were described as atrocities aimed at the unarmed, the sick, the sleeping child and the helpless. Responses emphasized that the targeting of civilians was inconsistent with the codes that guided international war.[19] In the aftermath of a zeppelin raid on London in June 1915, one of one-hundred attacks from the air between 1914 and 1918,[20] observers and newspapers questioned whether the dead could even be considered the casualties of war. Grayzel remarked, 'It is clear from the press coverage of the inquests held for those killed by this zeppelin raid that many felt them to be victims not merely of war but of something entirely illegal, of "murder".'[21]

After the First World War, dire speculations about the potential of enhanced air war were rhetorically entangled with internal pressures to expand and innovate Britain's domestic aviation industry. In 1922, former RAF officer General P.R.C. Groves wrote serial instalments of 'Our Future in the Air' for *The Times*. Brett Holman has observed that in these articles Groves popularized the notion of the 'knock-out blow' from aerial attack, while asserting that German commercial airpower, given its potential for conversion, posed a stark threat despite the disarmament of Germany under Versailles. While 'converted airliners did not make very effective bombers and were of little consequence during the Second World War', Holman argued that the perception of this threat was effective and made the commercial bomber 'a rhetorical weapon in the battle to make Britain airminded'.[22] Such foreboding, as well as hope, about the seemingly open possibilities of rapid technological advancements in aeronautics for the devastation of civilian life was not limited to the speculations of industry, military and government. These themes were also animated in interwar fiction and hinted that the dreadful strain and apprehension, often attributed to the week before the Second World War broke out, merely followed from an anxious anticipation that had long lingered in the background like the smell of buildings turned to ashes that adhered to days long before those last ones of August 1939.

Consider, for instance, Cicely Hamilton's 1922 foreboding novel. *Theodore Savage* captured the intertwinement of bureaucratic and aeronautic technologies, which, perhaps more than war itself, eradicated Britain and seemingly all of what might be understood as 'civilization' too. While the protagonist's office at Whitehall is made endlessly busy by the palpable threat of an imminent war designed on all sides for 'the perfection of scientific destruction' through the 'displacement of population, not victory in the field',[23] its abstract remoteness from the routines that sustain civilian life render the government unprepared for the panicked migrations of its own hordes driven to restless flight by relentless bomb and gas attacks from the air. Thus, the shape that novels like this gave to fears of the next war would perhaps invite relief when met with the formalized programme of Air Raid Precautions (ARP) and its flood of imperatives. After all, the fictional Whitehall in Hamilton's novel failed to plan for the inevitable displacements of the domestic population and, therefore, protected neither its citizens nor its own bureaucratic and military machinery.

Theodore Savage, a government clerk, who seemed far removed from the implications of his office routines that appeared to have no objectives, is finally assigned to defend – from roaming, starving, voracious herds of persons displaced by enemy air attacks – a small camp storing limited provisions, supplies and weapons. Yet, eventually, neither troops nor messengers arrive at the camp to retrieve provisions. Operations have apparently ceased. Presumably, under this kind of war, not even the military, which soon gave up trying to save the nation and its people, can save itself. When the outpost is bombed, Savage is himself displaced to wander in fear. He is afraid less of air war than of those others he once counted as his fellow citizens. They now roam hungry and terrorized in a geography no longer marked by peoples, place names, habits, traditions, or architectures that resemble those of the Britain they once knew. Of the small numbers who endure, surviving mostly on the meat of rats, insulated tribes spring up alongside a new religion that abhors science and its heretical machines. In this new world that renounces the last one, the practice of science is punishable by death. It appears that no children survived, and the women who did were stripped of any political function and restricted to activities that ensure the reproduction of life.

Hamilton's depiction of the end of civilization through air war describes '[a] people retracing its progress from chaos retraced it step by step', stressing the retreat from socialized habits to animality and the laws of 'beast-right'.[24] While people feed from the animals previously deemed vermin and unfit for consumption, a robin perches upon the exposed breast-bone of a human corpse lying in the road of a village still home to the decayed remains of those gassed within it. It is the birds and animals who have inherited what is left of the homes and villages that human survivors, scrambling and scratching the scorched landscape for the barest means to support themselves, avoid lest they make themselves visible and vulnerable to other survivors.

If that was only fiction, informed speculation offered no comforts in describing London under air attack as

> one vast raving Bedlam, the hospitals will be stormed, traffic will cease, the homeless will shriek for help, the city will be in pandemonium. What of the government at Westminster? It will be swept away by an avalanche of terror. Then will the enemy dictate his terms, which will be grasped at like a straw by a drowning man.[25]

The Spanish Civil War punctured the dramatizations of both fiction and planners' speculation by bringing to life the terror of air war destruction of far greater magnitude than what was possible during the First World War's zeppelin and air attacks. The image of a dead child on the iconic Republican Ministry of Propaganda poster, 'Madrid – The "Military" Practice of the Rebels', was distributed in English with the additional appeal: 'If You Tolerate This – Your Children Will Be Next'.[26] While it sought to recruit support for the Republican cause in Spain, its circulation in Britain reinforced anticipations with sharp imagery that underlined the significance of rapid advancements in aeronautics technologies that would expand the geographical coordinates of the next war.

Coverage of Spain's devastation re-sparked a public conflict between anti-war British scientists, such as John Desmond Bernal and J.B.S. Haldane, who coalesced as the Cambridge Scientists Anti-War Group (CSAWG), and the British government over the inadequacy of precautionary planning; the group had previously launched letter campaigns in response to the Incitement to Disaffection Bill in 1934 and against aeronautical research to be conducted at the University of Cambridge in 1935.[27] Members of the CSAWG conducted experiments, sometimes in residences, on explosives, incendiary bombs, gasses and the adequacy of gas masks. Their 1937 book *The Protection of the Public from Aerial Attack* charged that government precautions were inadequate. A key point was that the instructions to prepare a gas-safe room in one's dwelling would not result in a gas-tight space and, furthermore, a great number of people simply could not afford to do so. In a published response to the book, General C.H. Foulkes accused the group of trying to induce panic and retorted that 'in many of the poorer homes completely gas-proof shelters can only be provided with great difficulty; but that is no reason why the remainder should not be protected'.[28]

A Mass Observation bulletin published in April 1938 provides an indication of the perceived significance of circulating representations of the conflict in Spain for the public, as it prompted volunteer social observers to 'bring the word SPAIN casually into the conversation and record the response or absence of response. Try this experiment with different kinds of people. In each case, give time, date, and place. Give in not more than ten lines, your own thoughts about Spain.'[29]

Photography produced during the Spanish conflict rendered a much more complex battlefield than was previously known in Britain, one that subsumed not only trenches, but homes and schools. A reporter notably referred to Spain's civil war as 'this most photogenic war,'[30] and an early edition of the *Picture Post* included a feature on Robert Capa's photography of field battle in the streets of Spain. By capturing a dying man as he dictated his final letter, one of Capa's photographs threatened to strike the viewer physically.[31] Early in 1939, the *Picture Post* presented a photograph of a main artery in Barcelona that had been bombed. The attack brought down six-story buildings on both sides of the street, and it reportedly took two weeks to clear the way for transport and military activity. The photograph's caption asked rhetorically: 'Could this happen in Piccadilly Circus?'[32]

Furthermore, Winston Churchill had vividly and gruesomely painted the threat by describing London as 'the greatest target in the world, a kind of tremendous, fat, valuable cow, tied up to attract beasts of prey'.[33] Cautionary imagery reinforced a public consciousness of the new coordinates of war already demonstrated, as Grayzel argued, in the first air raid on British civilians during the Great War.³⁴ The pressures that reshaped the relationship between state and civilians were sharpened further in interwar planning, which was marked by pessimistic anticipations of the coming war. Yet for all the speculative predictions and preliminary discussions that preceded the war, many plans remained sparse, subject to contention, fragmented between different departments, and only took shape in the months just before the start of the Second World War.

The Home Office was tasked primarily with wartime planning from 1929. When the ARP Department was established in 1935, it responded in part to criticisms of disorganized planning,³⁵ by formalizing and redistributing functions previously held by other bodies, some of which had been done under a subcommittee of the Committee of Imperial Defence since 1924. One of the first information leaflets issued by the new, but apparently understaffed, ARP Department provided instruction on preparations for gas warfare. But Richard Titmuss has pointed to two obstacles to Home Office war planning under Sir John Anderson, Lord Privy Seal: lack of financial resources and the need to control access to information under a ban which operated until after the Munich Crisis.³⁶

In June 1939, the office of the Lord Privy Seal prepared a public information leaflet 'Public Defence: Some Things You Should Know if War Should Come'. Among other instructions concerning gas masks and evacuation, citizens were made responsible for collecting a small store of food to be kept for an emergency, as well as materials needed to blackout their windows at home.³⁷ Much of the information provided in this initial draft document remained very general, as the interdependency of government departments made each reliant on the other's policy provisions before the full implications for public information could be worked out. During preparations for the material, the Lord Privy Seal had expressed that the status of ARP planning and guidance for the public seemed to be behind that of other nations. He cited Poland's ARP instructions. 'I am very anxious about our backwardness in this direction,' he wrote in a letter. 'What is now wanted to meet the changing mood of the public is a constant flow of information and instruction, through the press, the pulpit, the platform and by means of leaflets, films, posters and exhibitions.' Softening the criticism in his note, he acknowledged that, of course, 'publicity cannot come before administration', but he urged more cooperation between departments, as the public needed, and demanded, information, particularly about evacuation.³⁸ At this stage, the material carefully navigated the gaps in the public information it could provide. It did, however, clearly articulate that civilians had duties to the very life of the nation that they were expected to uphold in the anticipated emergency: 'All who have work to do, whether manual, clerical or professional, should regard it as their duty to remain at their posts, and do their part in carrying on the life of the nation.'[39]

A letter received at the Lord Privy Seal's office requested clarification concerning the apparent tension between the preservation of individual personal safety and what appeared to be a call from the government for the citizen to internalize a sense of duty equivalent to that of a direct combatant. The response reinforced that it will be the duty of each citizen to remain at their post, as 'the life of the community must be maintained'. Whether a citizen was to choose the duty of remaining or self-preservation through flight from their post was a matter of personal conscience.[40]

\* \* \*

You are at home, you say? *That is your post.* You will have other posts too. As a citizen, you will be enlisted as a volunteer or conscripted 'to support the military, in civil defence, and to produce the necessary goods and services for military battle, and survival at home.'[41]

But I digress, and you look tense. There is no need. Please, take a seat and a moment to gather yourself. You agree this is necessary and, 'yes, I'll have a cigarette – that excuse to breathe long and deeply'. But as you fumble with that beaten packet of Churchman's, out falls the latest instalment of collectable cards, No. 29, to show you how to remove the civilian respirator. Not again.

\* \* \*

As war appeared imminent, the Ministry of Information issued three now iconic red posters intended to build morale. The posters 'Freedom is in Peril, Defend it with All Your Might', 'Your Courage, Your Cheerfulness, Your Resolution Will Bring Us Victory' and 'Keep Calm and Carry On' consisted of bold white lettering on a vibrant red background; the only image was a silhouette of a crown at the top. The 'Keep Calm' poster, now so commonly remixed in digital memetic communications, was kept in reserve and never used. At the time, Mass Observation studied the effectiveness and public reception of the 'Freedom is in Peril' and 'Your Courage' posters. Those interviewed described the posters as old-fashioned, too official and conservative. The crown depicted at the top seemed to underline the clear distinction between the referents of You and Us on the 'Your Courage' posters, and visually reinforced the top-down direction of the instruction given. As one Mass Observation national panellist put it, 'All due respects to our Monarch, but I always associate the crown when used on a public announcement as a command, something connected with laws and acts.'[42]

Further, Mass Observation noted that specific word-choices of the 'Your Courage' poster illustrated the social distance between those making the announcement and those addressed by it. For instance, they identified that four of the words, resolution, might, freedom and peril, were rarely used in everyday speech. Of these, resolution was the most opaque word, as people found it difficult to operationalize contextually when asked to do so: 'Some people'll want a bloody dictionary.'[43] Meanwhile, Mass Observation found that the 'Freedom is in Peril' poster was perceived to be too abstract. First, the concept of liberty resonated with interviewees more than freedom did. Second, interviewees questioned whether they were indeed free and critically challenged any assumption that peril to freedom arose from sources external to the nation. Third, respondents thought it was unclear what one ought to do concretely to defend freedom.[44]

Though most people preferred 'Your Courage' over 'Freedom is in Peril', citing that the former had more of a tangible recommendation in it, Mass Observation found that the second-person address, using the possessive pronoun 'your' had a negative impact upon identification, despite the clear intention to establish personal appeal through direct address. Mass Observation argued that, in contrast, 'Your Courage' produced impersonal distance between the message and its receiver. This is illustrated in responses such as: 'Somebody will be a bit happier for it, I suppose, but it won't be me'; 'I don't take much notice of them myself, I'm sure there is a class that does'; 'It gives a sense that they can do something, I suppose. Personally it leaves me untouched'.[45] The latter comment, in which the respondent expresses approval on the basis that the poster gives 'them' rather than 'me' a sense of purpose, is particularly striking in its support of Mass Observation's argument that the second-person construction produced dissociation in viewers. Here, Mass Observation exhibited adeptness with social psychology, as it analysed the potential for misrecognition by stressing that 'to myself I am "me"', therefore, the word 'you', especially when used in an impersonal and abstract form, does not immediately achieve identification: 'I recognize that it means somebody, and therefore unconsciously associate it not with me but with people who are not me or mine, but vague YOUs, people of [an]other class or other intelligence'.[46]

Mass Observation extended this problem to the use of 'you' so often deployed in ARP instructions. In elaborating their critique, Mass Observation referred to the official instruction given in an ARP leaflet: 'You should carry about with you your full name and address clearly written.' This prescription anticipated the untimely death of its reader and the need for officials to identify civilian remains with expediency in an emergency. Mass Observation described the use of second-person address in this instruction as inherently violent. Here, there was no softening of words in Mass Observation's determination that the leaflet thus addresses 'the YOU as [a] corpse'.[47]

If Hamilton's novel *Theodore Savage* indirectly warned about what happens when civil defence provisions are not prepared, Lewis Mumford's 1938 non-fiction work, *The Culture of Cities*, which offered imagery just as harrowing, warned readers about anticipation. His insistence that 'Fear vomits: poison crawls through the pores', prompted Paul K. Saint-Amour to reflect, 'for Mumford, the violence most particular to the air raid arrives along the temporal vectors of preparation and expectation. What wounds is not the [spatial] expansion or extent but sequence: the series of protocols – sirens, searchlights, gas masks, scrambling, anti-aircraft guns, engines, bombs – whose terminus is the catastrophe'.[48] Saint-Amour has argued that, in the 1920s, 'the memory of one world war was already joined to the specter of a second, future one', a total war whose promised arrival threatened to foreclose the future. In this, the weaponization of the air is not the main concern for Saint-Amour. Instead, he foregrounded the weaponization of anticipation, the emotional injury it wields, and the simultaneous spilling of both 'doom and refusal'.[49]

From the bureaucratic use of the imperative as a grammatical structure that insists upon action, to the minimization of the difficulty of the instructions or the consequences of failure, fear wrestled with a stubborn sense of unreality. 'This was the problem of the Public Information Leaflets,' a Mass Observation report noted in October 1939, 'they had to get people to act, without disturbing their peace of mind, so essential for the calm carrying on of the nation's work.'[50]

There was resistance. In those months before the war, many people refused to read the instructional leaflets, others forgot what they read. Still more, there were those who devised convoluted mechanisms for filing them away for later – thus, simultaneously tidying sideboards and sublimating apprehensions delivered straight to the door with the onslaught of urgent protocol brochures. One man admitted to a mass observer, 'I give them to the kid to play with.' Another asserted:

> I have taken no steps whatsoever with regard to the present crisis. I do not think there will be a war over the Danzig question; and I regard all the precautions now being taken as unnecessary and wasteful both of time and money. I derive no inconsiderable amusement from the newspaper reports of 'practice

evacuation', sandbagging [b]anks, laying in stocks of food and gas mask distribution.⁵¹

Finally, from an ARP warden: 'I have not read the leaflets – I feel a bit guilty about this ... I shall take more interest in them when war does start.'⁵²

Mass Observation determined that these reactions demonstrated 'special resistances, social, psychological and political, which have developed against this kind of literature'.⁵³ In different ways, 'doom and refusal' accompanied each other or took their turns. They can be felt together in the thoughts of George Bowling, the protagonist in George Orwell's *Coming Up for Air*. Just before disappearing on a (final?) trip to see his childhood home in Lower Binfield, Bowling oscillates tentatively: 'Is it going to happen? No knowing. Some days it's impossible to believe it. Some days I say to myself that it's just a scare got up by the newspapers. Some days I know in my bones there's no escaping it.'⁵⁴

In the days just before war was declared, a Mass Observation diarist, Pam Ashford, wondered if war will happen and began to stockpile as she fretted about what would become scarce if there was a war. Will I have enough lingerie if I cannot do laundry? She shopped and she sewed ritualistically in the days before the war. At the outset, she deliberated about the status of her shopping, 'hanging between two decisions, one that buying is patriotic foresight, and the other that it is a dirty form of hoarding'.⁵⁵ When Mr Mitchell at her office chided her for hoarding, she insisted that her preparations for a potential war could not really be defined as such. But later, she continued to buy just a few things each day after work – torches, batteries, sewing supplies, tins of food and butter substitutes. It is, she thought, justified in her particular case: 'It's not shortage of essential foods that I dread but queues ... I don't want Mother to have to stand about more than can be helped. If need be, I would rather live off the tinned stuff and let the Govt. rations go.'⁵⁶

George Bowling was half right; 'The old life's finished ... There's no way back to Lower Binfield',⁵⁷ and Pam Ashford, who admitted to being 'sorely perplexed as to the line of demarcation between "hoarding" and "genuine foresight",⁵⁸ would need her stockpile. On 3 September 1939, she wrote:

> To-day is just like an 'ordinary' Sunday but somehow it is not an 'ordinary' Sunday. We have had our meals at the same time ... Then there has been the usual Sunday ironing and mending for to-morrow. It has been just like an 'ordinary' Sunday, but all the time there is the thought 'This is the last of the ordinary Sundays'. It is now 7 o'clock. I am just going out for a walk, and unless

something quite unexpected happens there will be nothing more to put down for to-day in the diary. This has seemed such a long, long, long day.[59]

On this ordinary Sunday, Chamberlain had declared war on Germany. Even if all activities, meals, ironing and mending, were ordinary, the time stretched out into a numbing blur so that Ashford opted to adjourn the day at only seven o'clock to hope for sleep to encroach. Similarly, artist Julian Trevelyan, who had arrived at Waterloo earlier that day, as the first false air raid sirens wailed, felt that the earth itself might open, 'But the sun still shone, the tugs still chugged on their way, and the porters still expected a tip.' Despite the expectation of immediate air raids in areas designated as high risk, they did not occur for another eight months. While interiors, clothing, food and various practices changed, the period was known as the Phoney War, or sometimes the Bore War. Perhaps the earth had not split open that Sunday after all, as Trevelyan expected. Nevertheless, 'an epoch for each of us had ended and a new one was to begin'.[60]

From then on, every act, no matter how mundane, was urgent and infused with consequence for the nation. Posters, notices and instructive leaflets multiplied with breathless imperatives extending to every aspect of quotidian life so that, as Jennifer Purcell has observed, it was felt that 'Every moment and every action counted: turning over your flowerbeds to vegetables, using less hot water, scraping the margarine paper till all the grease was gone, saying "no" to a new pair of shoes ... shivering on a cold December morning. The war lurked behind every act on the home front.'[61] Each message underlined individual responsibility: 'Your safety, and the safety of those for whom you are responsible, may depend upon you.'[62] But those efforts extended to the safety of the nation. Blackening your windows, carrying your gas mask and knowing how to navigate around your neighbourhood in the dark demonstrated responsibility for the nation, something you would be called to do at every turn. The imperatives were everywhere: Care for evacuees and join the ranks; it's a national service.[63] 'Serve to Save through ARP.'[64] Take care about the things you say, 'When you go out don't crow about ... the things you know about'[65] and 'Keep it under your hat!'[66] because 'You never know who's listening!'[67] Before sleeping, always asking: are 'all windows and inner doors open?'; are the buckets of water and sand ready?; are my 'gas mask, clothes and torch handy?'[68] Official imperatives stopped short of *Picture Post* author Tom Wintringham's call to take lessons from Spain and prepare for invasion, giving do-it-yourself pointers to civilians, such as, a mattress affixed to the roof of an automobile could help to stop a racing bullet.[69]

Imperatives concerning ARP changed the home and daily routines, but soon imperatives concerning the intensified needs for conservation and post-war reconstruction messages joined them. It was not just a matter of saving the beauty that lay '[u]nder the sunshine of a lovely summer, the fields and woods of Britain – the fields and woods we are all fighting to protect'.[70] It was about saving for a future that will be 'worth saving for'.[71] 'Use Spades Not Ships – Grow Your Own Food.'[72] 'Help Win the War on The Kitchen Front' by avoiding waste.[73] But also save waste, keep it dry and sorted and leave it for council collection, but kitchen scraps can feed the hens and pigs that you could be keeping.[74] 'Cook with care and save fuel,'[75] but that's not all; housewives, you can learn 'to protect cold water tanks and pipes ... improvise draught excluders ... lag hot water pipes and tanks ... use substitute fuels correctly ... make briquettes at home' and more.[76] Don't be a squanderbug.[77] Rather than spending clothing coupons, take out your sewing needles and mend. For children's wardrobes, leave room for growing.[78] Patch your towels and ... .[79]

So many tasks to be abruptly punctuated by sirens ordering you to take shelter immediately. 'Do you not find it a terrible waste of time going to the shelter during the day?' a woman asked the other members of her correspondence club, 'I just carry on with my work here as I simply couldn't get through the duties and meals if I didn't!' Another responded in the margin, 'I don't go unless I hear gun fire (there's a warning on now, but I'm at the dining table) and then I do mending, silver, letters etc. which I save up for such times.' 'For my part,' a third replied, 'I go on from day to day, cooking, washing, shopping in between the sirens, canteen on Mondays, first aid on Thursdays, Recorder practice on Fridays, my only relaxation.'[80]

Several decades after the war's end, Tom Harrisson, one of Mass Observation's founders, boldly speculated that a considerable amount of wartime suffering had stemmed from the coupling of air-power and a 'fear-fantasy' fostered in government officials, leaving them to believe that attacks from the air would unleash apocalyptic-like scourges upon civilian populations, leaving them to 'be killed, shell-shocked or reduced to panic. It was presumed that they would not be able to stand up to the experience. Thus, the properly motivated, disciplined armed forces of traditional war would be threatened by collapse on the home front, fatally stabbing them in the back.'[81] If, as Michal Shapira has remarked, military discourse on air war and the shellshock of the First World War contributed to the assumption that 'fear and anxiety' were 'the normal reactions to total war,'[82] Harrisson suggested that leaders understood civilians as internal threats to the war effort. Therefore, provisions for war in the form of new instructions and habits simultaneously constituted both resocialization and the home front itself.

Despite Harrisson's critique of the problems that 'fear-fantasy' brought, concrete suffering endured on the home front. As Jose Harris has noted, bombings took 62,000 civilian lives and destroyed a quarter of million homes. The numbers of physical injuries and damage to homes vastly exceeded these. Further, '[t]wo and a quarter million were made homeless by the worst period of aerial bombardment (August 1940 to June 1941)'.[83] These striking figures, however, can only take imagination so far in accessing the kind of experience Elizabeth Bowen described in retrospect:

> I felt one with, and just like, everyone else. Sometimes I hardly knew where I stopped and somebody else began. The violent destruction of solid things, the explosion of the illusion that prestige, power and permanence attach to bulk and weight, left all of us, equally, heady and disembodied. Walls went down; and we felt, if not knew, each other.[84]

Amidst such duress and destruction, fear's mobilization of foresight through endless instructions that precipitated the organization of everyday life for total war may have served a critical (if sometimes absurd) role. Hence, Harrisson's post-war reflection emphasized what Mass Observation had argued from the early days of the war, that the official preparations and the imperatives set out for civilians on the home front, the 'precautions taken, things done and left undone', were complicit in the wartime suffering experienced in Britain during the Second World War.[85]

# Acknowledgements

The author and publisher gratefully acknowledge the permission granted to reproduce the copyright material in this book.

Care can be oriented towards an ideal, a convention, a person, a movement, an object or an image. It can be wound up in confused territories of the intimate and the social structure's inculcated investments, such as the demand that forms of life and being be readily socially legible. I wrote this book while grappling with a word that I really like, as care is a beautiful word that makes me think of colourful threads of attachment. Like most words, care renders many contradictions and troubling connotations. It is an untidily folded word. Care is always about attachment, but not always the warming kind, and sometimes the threads it casts get caught and fixed upon the wrong sides. I have tracked many of these threads in this project, but the threads of care cannot easily be untangled, especially in the context of care's mobilization in public civil defence strategies enacted in private homes and gardens. This space, however, is dedicated to the positive and personalized forms of care that I have been so fortunate to receive from those who have gifted attention to my thinking, writing and career, as well as to my heart in everyday experience.

But, first, I wish to acknowledge institutional forms of support for this project that have mattered greatly to me personally and note individuals working under these auspices who have in their care gone beyond those structural parameters to foster the development of this book in meaningful ways.

Funding support that made this project possible came from an Insight Development Grant from the Social Sciences and Humanities Research Council of Canada, as well as an Internal SSHRC Grant and a Community of Research Excellence Development Opportunities Grant facilitated by the Office of Research Services at the University of Lethbridge. In the funding proposal stages, Mary Butterfield and Hector MacIntyre were sources of advice, encouragement, kindness and good humour. As an aside, one of my favourite storytellers and a former colleague, Heidi MacDonald, also gave me crucial advice (and chocolate from her not so secret stash) early on.

It goes without saying that I have depended greatly upon the Mass Observation Archive (MOA) of the University of Sussex Special Collections, now housed at The

Keep in Brighton. I found much to wonder about in those boxes. The joy that the collection engendered was magnified by the amazing people who care so much for these documents and for the ongoing work of MO. Special mention goes to Jessica Scantlebury, who always showed interest in my project and made many helpful suggestions, but also to Kirsty Pattrick, Suzanne Rose, Fiona Courage and the MOA Trustees for their support of my book project within this series. As an extension to this, this book would not be in current form if not for access through Matthew Adam Digital, I have special appreciation for Alex Butler, whom I met in Providence. This project has also depended upon the collections held at the National Archives in Kew and the Imperial War Museum in London. Many thanks to Matthew Watson who graciously shared his time and gave me a tour and behind the scenes access to artwork connected with MO at the Bolton Library and History Centre. I will always remember fondly my experiences photographing litter and MO pub crawling with the Worktown Observation Centre organized by Caroline Edge.

Anonymous reviewers of the prospectus and writing samples both challenged and freed me from some of my own early impositions on this text. Special thanks to Rhodri Mogford and Laura Reeves of Bloomsbury Press for ushering this book through the publication process and to Juliet Gardner for attentive care in copy-editing the manuscript.

Due to the kind cooperation of both Wiley and Bloomsbury, a previous and shorter version of the preface was published previously in March 2020 as 'The "Last of the Ordinary Sundays": How to Prepare for the Air War'. *Journal of Historical Sociology* 33, no. 1 (2020): e1-e10. Both versions benefitted from the comments of generous listeners at Structures of Anticipation at SB Contemporary in Windsor, especially Craig Campbell, Derek Sayer and Yoke-Sum Wong, and close readings from a local writing group: Luke Dani Blue, Helen Connolly, Nicole Hembroff, Annie Martin and Elaine Storey.

I owe debts to Nathan Wong and Jake Vinje for their assistance in provisionally coding and organizing hundreds of sometimes blurry digital photographs of faded documents prepared on war-era paper. Some time ago, Greg MacDonald carried out an initial review of literature for this project, and Tanner Layton prepared my endnote library, which someday I promise I will actually use. Beyond this, my thinking and reading have been enhanced by the diverse range of work being done by graduate students I supervised over the course of writing the book: Jake and Tanner, as noted above, but also Victoria Holec, Harley Morman and, near the end, Tyler J. Stewart.

I am grateful for those with whom I have been able to share enthusiasm about MO. Ben Highmore, and his wonderful books, sparked my curiosity and set me out to my first visit to the MOA. Jenna Bailey, who has done very exciting work with ancillary archives from the same period, has helped to bring other MO people into my life. I have cherished time and many lovely conversations with Lucy Curzon in Brighton and Providence. Lucy put me in touch with Jen Purcell, for whom I have a deep gratitude. Jen has been a consistent source of encouragement and guidance during the writing of this book, she invited me onto the editorial board of the Mass Observation Critical Series and has generously given her time to support me. Natacha Chevalier, who insists that I am not really a sociologist but a historian, has given me warm hospitality in Brighton and London and conversation that always picks up as if no time has passed whenever I cross the Atlantic – also board games and vintage sewing patterns too!

Many local friends and colleagues have supported me by showing interest in this work along the way, among them are: Athena Elafros, Trevor Harrison, Michelle Helstein, Jan Newberry, Gülden Ozcan, William Ramp and a special thanks to Christopher Churchill for bringing Lindqvist's wonderful book *A History of Bombing* to my attention. I have much appreciation for the enduring warmth of Muriel Mellow, from whom I have learned a great deal just by being in proximity to her in the Sociology Department. Jason Laurendeau has consistently given both personal and institutional support to me and my work. If it were not for his advocacy for the preservation of my time, this book would perhaps not exist yet. I deeply value conversations with Sean Brayton about work that undermine the imperative to enact neoliberal forms of care about it. I always feel as though my friend Shane Gannon is near me even when he isn't – although it's not that far. Tom Perks, a long-time friend and next-door office neighbour, has been a source of encouragement and daily good humour. At a time when I was particularly burdened with a negative sort of care, Catherine Kingfisher, as an anthropologist even in friendship, reminded me of the power of ritual. Kara Granzow – I treasure so many things, including intermittent outrageous statements that make me laugh, only to find she is not even joking. I love that! To two, and many more, decades of revelling together in all things 'oddinary'.

I would not be the same if it were not for the breath-taking writers, thinkers and dear friends of the infamous Alberta School: Craig Campbell, Karen Engle, Lindsey Freeman and especially Yoke-Sum Wong and Derek Sayer. On an ongoing basis, Cody Adams, Geoffrey Chappell, Cole Dempsey, Jean-Pierre Marchant and Thuyvi Nguyen have brought me far more happiness and sense of comradery than they will ever know. Harley Morman, Luke Blue and Migueltzinta Solís have surrounded me in all kinds of care – the gifts of blunt insights, road trips and writing retreats, meta-stories and so much laughter. And Jarrett Duncan for a presence that quells the burden of all kinds of troubles, whether in Lurnslye, Havermill, Delberz or here.

My family, Nonie, Eric, Gina and Rain, have cared for me forever, and has taught me with the deepest resonance and across geographical distance what it feels like to be the fortunate recipient of an everyday form of care.

Every effort has been made to trace copyright holders and to obtain their permission for the use of copyright material. However, if any have been inadvertently overlooked, the publishers will be pleased, if notified of any omissions, to make the necessary arrangement at the first opportunity. The third party copyrighted material displayed in the pages of this book are done so on the basis of 'fair dealing for the purposes of criticism and review' or 'fair use for the purposes of teaching, criticism, scholarship or research' only in accordance with international copyright laws, and is not intended to infringe upon the ownership rights of the original owners.

# Introduction: Read, Listen, Obey and Keep a Good Heart

*READ THIS LEAFLET CAREFULLY*
*Listen carefully to all broadcast instructions*
*Obey promptly any instructions given*
*KEEP A GOOD HEART: WE ARE GOING TO WIN THROUGH*[1]

During the crisis of the Second World War, official Air Raid Precautions made the management of ordinary, daily life in Britain a moral obligation of civil defence by introducing new prescriptions for the care of homes, animals and persons displaced through evacuation. Government publicity campaigns and brochures communicated new instructions for care formally, while the circulation of wartime rumours negotiated these instructions informally, and gossip that circulated around individual conduct unevenly reinforced and contested such instructions. Together, formal and informal directives on caregiving reshaped everyday habits and supported the construction of a responsible and good social subject committed to the war effort specifically and to the population's interests generally through strategies of 'passive civil defence' that targeted the home and community.[2] Mass Observation played multiple roles as investigator, mediator and agent in this complex arrangement, but with a critical difference since it also targeted politicians and decision-makers to foster more compassionate forms of governance during the war.

From its inception in 1937, Mass Observation had mobilized a participatory movement dedicated to the study of everyday life and the mapping of public feelings, animated by its founders' vision for a dynamic public sphere. Mass Observation studied in minute detail the beliefs and practices that enable the tracing of shifting norms of care for homes, animals and displaced persons. Making its own critical interventions into public discourse, Mass Observation often reversed the direction of the imperative logics that organized civil defence, asking those who occupied positions of power to do what it asked of the people: to listen and to keep a good heart. This book examines how the Mass Observation movement recorded and shaped the logics of care that became central to the daily routines of civil defence in the homes and neighbourhoods that mediated shifting conceptions of good citizens, population security and the evaluation of worthy life in the Second World War.

Susan Grayzel has argued that Germany's first air raid on British civilians in 1914, and other attacks during the course of the First World War, brought the home and the state into a new relationship and 'shattered this sense of separateness between the two fronts' of the home front and the frontline.[3] Thus, Grayzel located the initial contours of the civil identity that was called upon and shaped during the Second World War in these earlier experiences, which had already begun forming the conception of a citizen who was at once both democratized and militarized. The state, conceiving the anticipated war as one in which neighbourhoods would constitute a critical front, mobilized individual agency, resilience and care in a military conflict that came to be framed as the People's War. If the war would essentially be won or lost on the home front, then the rhythms of intimate quotidian life would need to be revised and, as Lucy Noakes has observed, new modes of citizenship that linked Air Raid Precaution (ARP) participation with duty would need to be fostered and maintained.[4]

The evacuation of children, expectant mothers, teachers, the elderly, the disabled and civil servants in September 1939 initiated a flooding of urban dwellers into the countryside. From the war's outset, the uncomfortable meeting of town and country heightened vast social, cultural and economic class divides in the nation, rather than fostering tighter social ties and bolstering wartime morale as was initially hoped.[5] This first official evacuation sparked the circulation of rumours that described ill-mannered, verminous and destructive house guests in reception areas. The rumours spread in many different generic forms and had multiple interpretative effects, but insofar as many of them expressed anxieties about physical and cultural contagion through judgements about manners, cleanliness and morality, they helped to sketch a provisional image of the responsible wartime subject against which the troublesome evacuee was described. Alarmist tales that described evacuees from the towns as so 'animalistic' that they did not know how to use a knife and fork and were prone to smashing fine china, breaking furniture and urinating in gardens led to calls for the building of camps to house them;[6] these calls were echoed as Germany's army continued to encroach upon other European territories, and refugees sought asylum in Britain.[7]

Notwithstanding the social tensions that arose from it, the evacuation scheme was premised upon a logic of care oriented towards the security of the population.

But what kind of care did the official plan enact? Care, as a noun, denotes provision and attention. As a verb, care suggests feeling relations, potentially one-directional, of concern or affection. Care also feels like a good word, perhaps most often suggesting warm attentiveness. Less often, it seems, the word care is tacitly acknowledged for its cooler capacity to refer to the circumstance of being encumbered with worries or troubles.[8] Thus, we are sometimes advised by well-wishers to let go of our cares. Or, we are bidden to take care, which, upon reflection, seems to exhort that we take our burdens with us and release our company from them; though both expressions are given with good intentions. The fact that there can be warmth and beauty in acts of caregiving does not elide the fact that care is often born of asymmetrical relations, a point that Didier Fassin has underlined in relation to humanitarian efforts.[9] More emphatically, Yi-Fu Tuan, in his elaboration of the making of pets – from the histories of animal domestication, to the building of gardens and even the social positioning of women and children – insisted that the relation of care is usually forged in 'bonds of inequality'.[10] Thus, Tuan's underlining of the connection between care and condescension does not let the carer dwell too long or comfortably in feelings of goodness but locates care in the uneasy tension between domination and affection, two relations that appear differently intonated but are nevertheless intertwined.

Central to this book's treatment of the notion of care is the distinction that Lisa Stevenson has made between anonymous and everyday forms of care. Stevenson described anonymous care as bureaucratic and 'primarily concerned with the maintenance of life itself'.[11] Since it concerns the population, this form of care is anonymous, targeting categories, not unique persons. Therefore, this form of care can be indifferent because it neither requires nor fosters the personalized bonds that animate everyday forms of care.[12] The state's plan for the September 1939 evacuation, officially known as 'Operation Pied Piper', exercised a bureaucratic form of care for maintaining life on a general level that was centred on the military objective to thin out the population by removing the weakest of those located in what were perceived to be potential aerial attack hot zones. Although it did not use these terms, Mass Observation made a distinction that complements Stevenson's in its critique of the official evacuation scheme and other civil defence planning. Mass Observation argued that the initial evacuation scheme may have looked good on paper but it 'under-estimated the differences' that would exacerbate social resentments and misunderstandings,[13] and thus the plans were made with 'little regard for social consequences'[14] and treated 'citizens as mathematical units, all alike'.[15] Mass observers embedded themselves in reception areas, blitzed towns and public shelters to seek out ways of activating everyday forms of care, which, in turn, they attempted to translate into policy recommendations.

Meanwhile, domestic animals, particularly dogs, were implicated in many of the everyday practices that needed adjustment during the war. Thus, their care was subject to revision under wartime imperatives concerning a range of precautions, from blackout procedures to food rationing, that introduced new norms to which an ostensibly good national subject conforms. The onset of war brought a sharp rise in the destruction of dogs and cats, with 80,000 pet corpses reportedly interred in London's East End in only one night.[16] This, along with the widespread social disapproval expressed towards urban dwellers keeping supposedly unproductive dogs during the war, provoked rhetorical interventions from animal advocacy groups, entrepreneurs, popular media, as well as from Mass Observation.[17]

The differential value of animals as companions and labourers was debated explicitly with respect to the former's worthiness to receive food and protection from the threat of air raids. The appropriation of the rhetorically forceful concept of morale appears to have had some efficacy in abating social disapproval towards those who kept pets in densely populated towns during food rationing,[18] although the proposed relationship between pets and morale was contested. Further, the presumed autonomy or dependence of companion animals contributed to divergent expectations for dogs and cats, a point to which I will return later. Dogs who did not work are of interest because they aroused a considerable amount of social disapproval during the war. Mass Observation's research concerning dogs in wartime captures the intricacies of the contradictory public discourse and illustrates that social disapproval had multiple targets. For instance, one man's assertion that 'whatever way you look at it you must have a house and a bit of a garden before you can keep a dog ... It's not so bad having a dog in the suburbs, but if you are a dog lover I don't think it is fair to have a dog during the war' targets caregivers' sense of fairness towards their dogs' comfort. This is echoed in another man's remark: 'I wouldn't keep a dog in London in any time. I don't think it is fair to the dog or your neighbours.' A woman responded to the Mass Observation investigator's prompt with a different target in mind, expressing the lack of legitimacy of an authority who would demand that carers give up their pets – a step she anticipated the government might take: 'I don't see how the [government] can be justified in asking people to give up their pets – not that they have yet, but I can well believe that they might.'[19]

Official government documents give only the surface impression of stable discourse on the status of companion animals during the war, but informal public discourse and Mass Observation research that captured some its contents are rich with sharp contradictions that inform how biopolitical concerns about the vitality of the population were articulated within the routines of everyday life during the war. More significant perhaps is Mass Observation's critical interventions into this discourse. Central among them concerns how the degree and nature of a companion animal's utility became a recurrent and explicit device brought to bear by both animal advocates and those who in contrast believed that keeping pets during wartime was harmful to the war effort and to the animals themselves. Depending upon the respective positions of those that investigators approached, utility was variously defined. Utility could refer to productivity, such as the vital work of a farmer's dog, but utility seems to have had so much salience in common sense narratives that the utility of a companion animal could also be effectively animated in relation to morale building.

The morale support that could be offered by companion animals became a crucial point forwarded by people and organizations that defended animal life during the war. Mass Observation itself drew from their studies to produce and mobilize a version of this argument in defence of non-working animals. Though they did not explicitly construct morale as a function of animal utility, they nevertheless challenged assumptions about the seemingly lazy companion animals by characterizing them in terms of the production and support that they could provide for their caregivers' morale and further advocated this construction as a rhetorical strategy: 'the great point to stress in dog propaganda now is the emotional, companionship, and blitztime morale support angle'.[20] Mass Observation's analysis also responded to the common suggestion that people who kept pets during wartime were selfishly unwilling to sacrifice their animals for the war effort. It did this by reversing the object of sacrifice from animal to human. For instance, by interpreting expressions of support for keeping pets in wartime as the recognition of acts of 'self-sacrifice', Mass Observation positioned the human who enacts this care, despite all the difficulties, as the object of secular sacrifice for the good of the animal.

The respective discourses surrounding pets and displaced persons together reveal shifting social expectations with respect to caregiving that seem to underline the implications of moral regulation on notions of citizenship as realized in intimate routines of everyday life.[21] For instance, rumours that explicitly repudiated the improper socialization of evacuees also produced a salient image of the host as a good wartime citizen, who was imagined to be impervious to the cultural invasion of the ostensibly ill-mannered, dirty and destructive house guest. Although the work of the Mass Observation movement shows that this image that tended to pair the host with the performance of civic duty and selflessness was indeed contested. There were evacuees, mothers who remained at home and teachers who had difficult and painful evacuation stories of their own to tell regarding neglect and abuse in reception homes and communities.[22] Simultaneously, explicit contestations over the value of pets, conceived as animals who do not work, placed attention on the animal companion caregiver, whose responsible use of limited provisions or personal sacrifice to both human and non-human subjects could be judged.

Two related questions have guided my investigation into Mass Observation's use and contestation of the logics of care that organized civil defence. First, in what ways did formal and informal civil defence imperatives of care communicate or contest specific expectations for good wartime citizens and distinguish them from others? Second, what were the implications of shifting social expectations for those whose dependency was perceived to be inconsistent with the moral obligations of civil defence? Finally, the book will attend to a third broader question: How can the assignment of security responsibilities to the home front through imperatives of care in the civilian home be understood in relation to the biopolitical concerns of modern nation states focused on the protection of the population's strength? Put another way, this question anticipates care's potential as a weapon that can be wielded against perceived threats.

The Second World War's legacy as the People's War, during which, as the narrative suggests, the resilience and cooperation of the British brought them together and ensured their victory despite disparities and differences, has been a matter of much scholarly debate that has unsettled acceptance of Paul Addison's image of enduring political consensus engendered by the crisis, as elaborated in his book, *The Road to 1945*.[23] Addison argued that 1940 gave rise to 'egalitarianism and community feeling' as 'the pervasive ideals of social life' that contributed to the making of the post-war welfare state[24] that would carry on – at least until the Thatcher years. Despite the apparent willingness of politicians across partisan lines to rally around William Beveridge's 1942 report 'Social Insurance and Allied Services' and its recommendations concerning education, family allowance and industry, as Stephen Brooke argued, recent scholarship traces 'as many differences between the parties as points of agreement' regarding the path that would lead to desirable reconstruction.[25] By illustrating the dramas in parliament and beyond, Jose Harris has effectively countered the script that has the Beveridge Plan received as 'a sort of Magna Carta'.[26] While a much earlier key text, Angus Calder's *The People's War*, elaborated the implications of scheme failures and national struggles and conceded that, for instance, the September 1939 'evacuation dramatized [the nation's] disunities'.[27] Calder nevertheless held that 'it was the first of those social developments from the imperatives of military and civil defence which scrambled the people together and acquainted them with each other as never before'.[28] Yet, Harris has remarked, 'Much has been said about the war's reinforcement of the global trend towards collectivism. By contrast, surprisingly little has been said about the opposite effect: its strengthening and legitimation of a highly privatised and unstructured psychological individualism – an individualism that was explicitly opposed to fascism, but that also presented definite boundaries to collectivisation of all kinds.'[29]

Further, Harris contended that the class structure, while 'dented', remained intact, and 'many archival sources suggest that throughout society those most vocally pressing for structural change were often those least willing to contemplate changes that would affect their own interests'.[30] Selina Todd has observed that '"Fair shares" and "equal sacrifice" were the watchwords of civilian life, but some were more equal than others'.[31] Todd pointed to the ways in which rationing was uneven in practice because it assumed all needs were the same. Additionally, for many working-class families, there simply was neither the space nor the resources to put up their individual Anderson Shelters, and public shelters in working-class areas were often unsafe and overcrowded. Todd also highlighted that, while the majority of evacuated children were working class, 'So were most of their hosts, who received a paltry allowance on which to keep their new charges.'[32] Despite these challenges arising from the class structure, Todd emphasized,

> Britain at the end of the war was certainly not an equal country, but the gaping social chasm of 1939 had narrowed slightly in favour of wage-earners ... Those responsible for this change were the workers on the home front and the troops now returning from abroad – those whom Ernie Bevin called 'our people', and who had now become *the* people.[33]

Some of the calls for reform that arose from reactions to evacuation had ambivalent implications that concern the subjects treated in this book. If an image is permitted: war seemed to have produced a space upon which a double battleground could emerge. The subordinate battleground was one in which struggle turned inward; it was one upon which cultural sensibilities, social class and established order were at stake. Anticipating the currents of change that would shape post-war Britain, and feeling that his 'whole class is being assailed', Harold Nicolson, Member of Parliament, author, and for a brief time Secretary to the Minister of Information, wrote in his diary on 13 January 1940:

> I have always been on the side of the under-dog, but I have also believed in the principle of aristocracy. I have hated the rich but I have loved learning, scholarship, intelligence and the humanities. Suddenly, I am faced with the fact that all these lovely things are supposed to be 'class privileges'... We imagine that we are fighting for liberty and our standards of civilization. But is it perfectly certain that by these phrases we do not mean the cultured life which we lead?[34]

Nicolson, a member of the waning aristocracy, was alone neither in his assured sense that the war would bring sweeping, levelling social change, nor in feeling an ambivalence about it that weighed far towards a melancholic attachment to an elitist notion of culture somewhat reminiscent of Matthew Arnold appealing to Swift's 'sweetness and light'. According to David Cannadine, Nicolson held racist attitudes and somehow rationalized a distinction between his own dislike of Jewish people and antisemitism.[35] As for levelling, Penny Summerfield's analysis of income, spending and the structure of labour during the war – all temporary – effectively challenges assured claims of wartime class levelling that ostensibly succeeded into the 1950s.[36]

In *Which People's War?*, Sonya O. Rose examined the contradictions inherent to the productions of national identity and conceptions of citizenship in Second World War Britain and thus 'exposes the fragility of a unitary national identity',[37] noting that the post-war, popular imaginary of the People's War consensus obfuscates the hegemonic character of constructions of nationhood at the time, which were 'not total'.[38] Troubling the popular image of consensus, of which, according to Rose, Addison's text provides a key example, she asks 'who was included and who was excluded' in the contested constructions of the nation and its citizens that 'made the "common man" central to the nation at war, celebrated diversity, implicitly advocated tolerance, and recognized Britain as a class- and gender-divided society but denied that it mattered to national unity – to the image of Britain as essentially one people'.[39] Rose argued that the relatively homogenous and heroic presentations of the British during the war 'did not have singular meanings – they differed by gender, for example, and were inflected by issues of class difference, the significance both of British imperialism and racial difference as well as regionalism to ideas about the nation'.[40]

Elaborating upon the discursive framework of citizenship that was evoked in the constructions of national identity during the war, Rose noted the contradictions of a liberal, universal notion of citizenship. Drawing from the work of Uday Mehta, Rose underlined the significance of notions of 'civic virtue' assumed to be characteristics possessed by, or developed in, individuals recognized as 'good citizens'. Rose observed, 'Independence and rationality are two such characteristics that have been the basis for the exclusion of non-whites, the economically indigent, and women.'[41] Given that so many of the home front imperatives targeted the kitchen and the household, it was possible to present them as affecting everyone all the same. For instance, Marc Wiggam argued that the blackout, its justification and practices, was more than a defence strategy. Insofar as it contributed to the perception of home front unity by 'framing the relationship of individuals to the nation and each other and a manifestation of wartime priorities which everyone was affected by and which everyone had to adhere to', he insisted that it did crucial ideological work in the production of assent to the notion of wartime unity.[42] What it meant in real terms to participate in the blackout measures and to follow other imperatives could not have been equal across social groups, and since they primarily addressed women, these prescriptions asked for different commitments within social groups as well. Indeed, the instructions to civilians that were the most disruptive to the daily patterning of life – shopping, cooking, care of children and animals and so on – were activities that were disproportionately assigned to the domain of women's work.

Though wartime nevertheless brought women out from the home into manufacturing and a vast range of service, the struggle for women's acceptance into the Home Guard, for instance, demonstrates some resistance to the blurring of boundaries that governed gender. Addressing the emotional debates about arming women, Summerfield and Peniston-Bird quoted a letter written by MP David Robertson, who asserted that 'a woman's duty is to give life and not to take it'.[43] Nevertheless, they insisted, 'In the social and cultural borderlands in which new indicators of the limits of masculinity and femininity were generated, old definitions of what it meant to be a man or a woman were at the same time strengthened, weakened and preserved intact.'[44]

As women were drawn from the home for war work, the realms of leisure in which they could participate were also extended, as Claire Langhamer has shown. Langhamer observed that the war provided material and discursive opportunities that bolstered 'women's own notion of legitimate leisure reward for war work well done'.[45] She argued that women's increased attendance in pubs during the war 'provides evidence of women challenging gendered leisure norms,'[46] and, although attitudes towards women's participation in pub life shifted and remained contradictory, the shift illustrates that a significant transformation of the cultures of pleasure for women occurred during the war.

Despite these critical shifts, domestic work was crucial for the defence of the home and neighbourhood. The profoundly gendered perception of this vital work contributed to, and perhaps heightened, the tensions that seem to have been inherent to the ways women were addressed and portrayed in wartime discourse. Jennifer Purcell has observed, 'Messages aimed at women on the home front in wartime were contradictory; one discourse elevated the traditional femininity associated with wives and mothers while another urged women to compromise that femininity in paid war work or military institutions.'[47] Purcell highlighted the under-acknowledged force of messages that elevated traditional femininity. For women engaged in civil defence within the home, these messages 'raised the status of housewifery'[48] and enabled some women, such as the Mass Observation diarist Nella Last, to understand themselves as 'domestic soldiers', defining their work as complementary to that of the soldier's. As Summerfield and Peniston-Bird point out, the word 'home' was used forcefully during the war 'to stand for both dwelling place and nation, and if women were the cornerstone of one, then by analogy they were at the heart of the other'.[49]

Since the war would centre so much upon the civilian home and pose unprecedented dangers to children, Laura King has argued that 'the state developed a necessarily more direct relationship with children'[50] during the Second World War, when children were recognized not so much in terms of their present state but as worthy investments insofar as they were conceived to be 'future citizens'.[51] While the language of children's potential for participatory citizenship had unifying effects during the war, she observed that not all children were perceived to have the same role to play in the future to come. King noted that product advertising emphasized this future citizen as white, male and middle class – from these categories would arise future leaders and those tasked with post-war reconstruction. In contrast, charitable organizations often presented children who needed saving, 'These children were positioned differently; less likely to shape Britain's future, charities sought funding to ensure these children would be useful in some capacity.'[52] In their promotion of War Savings, the government drew heavily upon the child's futurity and thus the nation's. King cited the cover of the *Daily Mail* which pictured a young, smiling girl and appealed: 'Is she to bloom gently and sweetly into lovely English womanhood, or is she to become just another pinched, frightened little scrap in a slave State[?]'.[53] While messages circulated about inculcating the virtues of citizenship and usefulness into children, many children aged five to eighteen were heavily engaged in paid and unpaid war work in salvage, household, savings and agricultural labour – a fact that Berry Mayall and Virginia Morrow have stressed remains under-acknowledged.[54]

But there was always more work to be done, since being a good wartime citizen had not only to do with usefulness. 'Being a "good citizen"', as Rose has remarked, 'had to do with actively expressing a commitment to the nation by voluntarily fulfilling obligations and willingly contributing to the welfare of the community.'[55] The good citizen, therefore, must be emotionally resocialized. The mobilizing concept of morale in wartime Britain provides a window through which processes of emotional socialization can be accessed. Even though the concept had not been well-defined, it was nevertheless a rhetorically forceful instrument that had a curiously rich range of connotative meanings and suggestive demands.

To provide one example, the wartime civilian was understood to require some sensorial resocialization in anticipation of sensorial reconfigurations from the effects of the blitz, profound changes in habits of eating, sleeping, engaging with changed environments and so forth. Indeed, sensorial re-ordering or re-education was on the agenda of anticipatory planning during the interwar years. Officials considered it important that the public develop immunity to the sounds of war. 'Noise can be very intimidating, and it is of course liable to upset people's nerves,' according to a document drafted in the Home Office. 'But people can certainly, by doing a little mental self-training in advance, render themselves less likely to be upset by the din of explosions and gunfire.'[56] Recommendations regarding the necessity of reshaping the individual to be able to endure the encroachment of war on the sensorium were made with the intention to prevent panic, or the effects of shellshock that combatants had experienced in the previous war. These recommendations may have had unintended implications. Amy Bell's analysis of civilian diaries, advertising, psychologists' notes and literature considered how negative emotions, primarily fear, were indirectly expressed under 'London's wartime emotional regime,'[57] which was formally organized around the state's poorly defined mobilizing concept of morale. Bell thus countered the stoic image suggested in the appeal to the People's War narrative by tracing the symptoms of civilian fear, which she argued had to be repressed or displaced onto the air raided, ravaged built environments of the capital city.

Tensions quite rightly emphasized in scholarly literature highlight contradictions that I hope to retain rather than dispel in favour of a singular interpretation. The notions of care that reside at the heart of this book are indeed central to claims that the people of Britain pulled together during a war that endured far longer than anticipated and brought many intractable losses and heartbreaks.[58] Care for neighbour and nation compelled many acts of cooperation and giving that became commonplace on the home front. Further, while it is now perhaps a matter of contest to argue, as Richard Titmuss did in the wake of the war, that the Second World War, and evacuation more specifically, fundamentally transformed social policy,[59] crucial social questions never ceased to be raised and social agendas set. Such questions, many of which were not necessarily new ones, were revised and re-articulated with renewed urgency over the course of the war, an extended period when plans for both bare survival and an imagined future were simultaneously contested, negotiated and set into action.

Nevertheless, this book does not adjudicate the debate about the strength of home front morale or consensus. Rather, it examines how responses to the rapidly changing conditions of life under wartime civil defence tactics organized and supported sentiments of care and regimes of caregiving as materializations of shifting rationalities. Recent scholarship has observed that, since the asylum crisis at the end of the Cold War, the political status of vulnerable or stateless social subjects in the West is increasingly worked out through humanitarian care initiatives rather than in political arenas.[60] This shift suggests that compassion and care are overtaking political right in the governance of vulnerable subjects and dovetails with the historical process of the 'privatization of politics' that Matthew Hilton, James MacKay, Nicholas Crowson and Jean-François Mouhot (hereafter, Hilton et al.) have traced to the rise of the non-governmental organization (NGO).[61] In the analysis of imperatives of care in Second World War Britain and the Mass Observation movement's interventions at the crucial intersection where care and security meet, this book considers how proposed modes of care supported the encroachment, or flashes, of what Didier Fassin has called humanitarian reason. This book argues that civil defence indirectly made the home and civilian neighbourhoods discretionary sites in which informal asylum for vulnerable social subjects, whether human or not, would be deliberated, insofar as routines of caregiving became more explicitly tied with concerns relating to the protection of the population's strength – a decisively biopolitical concern. Before elaborating the concepts of humanitarian reason, biopolitics and the post-humanist critique presented by the notion of animacy hierarchies that will inform the argument, an introduction to Mass Observation will help to establish how and why it occupies multiple positions in this book, as both a dynamic repository of source materials that enable the tracking of the values and practices of everyday life and as a caring agent in Britain during the war.

## Mass Observation as source and agent

In January 1937, the letter page section of the *New Statesman and Nation* introduced Tom Harrisson and Charles Madge, who respectively described themselves as an ornithologist-explorer and a poet-newspaper reporter.[62] They recognized in each other's written contributions a shared critique of contemporary knowledge conditions. This chance occurrence brought about Mass Observation, dedicated to developing new methods through which ordinary and untrained individuals could participate as 'the cameras with which we are trying to photograph contemporary life' as felt and experienced in the everyday.[63] This innovative movement was founded by Harrisson, author of *Savage Civilisation*, a study of the cannibals of the Hebrides; Charles Madge, a poet, who also designed page layouts for the *Daily Mirror*; and Humphrey Jennings, the documentary filmmaker.

In setting the coordinates for their initial vision, they sought to gather the threads of the collective unconscious by documenting responses to events of symbolic significance, what Madge called 'symbolic situations'.[64] Their examples were two very recent events, the fire that destroyed the Crystal Palace and King Edward's abdication of the throne. Both events underscored 'the fundamental social division in Britain between modernity and tradition'.[65] On 30 January 1937, the founders announced Mass Observation's existence in a second letter to the *New Statesman*. Derek Sayer has described the perplexing mix of phenomena they proposed to study – from behaviour of people at war memorials to the private lives of midwives – as 'a gloriously surreal enumeration'.[66] Its provocative strangeness was probably simultaneously reflective and thought to be expedient for moving from the fifty volunteers they claimed to have already to the 5,000 they said that they wanted. Instead of quoting the list directly, however, I will quote a playful letter of reply to *New Statesman* from a midwife who communicated her preference not to have her private life observed:

> SIR, – I am not a very educated person and perhaps that is why I am rather alarmed at the letter signed by Mr. Harrisson, Mr. Jennings and Mr. Madge, in your issue of January 30th. I know it is very important to understand nowadays why everybody does everything, but I do not like the idea of 5,000 strangers observing my private life (which wouldn't be very private anyway by then), and I couldn't think of letting anyone observe my bathroom behaviour or my armpits, though I don't mind showing my eyebrows and my aspidistra to any or all of the fifty gentlemen already observing things.

I don't know what taboos are, but I'm sure I don't eat them, and none of the other things seem to apply to me; but I will be glad to help in any way I can except on the points above, i.e., armpits, bathroom and private life.[67]

In their book *Britain*, Harrisson and Madge critiqued an article published in *The Star* on 29 August 1938 that asserted that all of Europe was watching the crisis unfolding in Czechoslovakia: 'What is implied is that millions of people are on tenterhooks to know what is happening on the German border, in Foreign Offices and at Cabinet Meetings . . . But were they? How many were more tensely watching the racing news and daily horoscope? That is another kind of fact we shall not know without trying to find out.'[68] Mass Observation's investigations into the rituals of daily life can be understood in the context of the emergent twentieth-century popular cultural turn that redefined the concept of culture, which had previously excluded home, neighbourhood, public square and pub, while being wielded as an instrument to discipline the working classes.

The first half of the twentieth century brought attention to popular practices and sites, deeming them worthy of study. Mass Observation's contribution to this is astonishing for its breadth and depth and it preceded most of the prominent theoretical developments in cultural theory. Further, as Nick Hubble has pointed out, Mass Observation occupies an important place in the linage of British cultural studies.[69] In academia, the Centre for Contemporary Cultural Studies (CCCS) was established in 1964 at the University of Birmingham and was a central force for the establishment of Cultural Studies departments and programmes even on the other side of the Atlantic. Other developments in popular cultural studies with which Mass Observation shares affinities arose from the Frankfurt School of Critical Theory at the Institute for Social Research in Germany (although its scholars best-known to English readers fled from the Nazis to write from the United States) and the French cultural theorist and public scholar Roland Barthes.

The central point to underscore, however, is that Mass Observation was not only at the forefront of everyday life studies, taking the practices of popular culture seriously, it was critical of the practices without stripping them of their value as sites of informal knowledge and forms of communication. Ben Highmore and Hubble have both elaborated Mass Observation's positioning within the cultural theoretical development of everyday life and popular culture studies. Highmore located Mass Observation in the context of an avant-garde sociology and elevated it to its rightful place in cultural theory by treating it alongside Georg Simmel, Sigmund Freud, Henri Lefebvre, Michel de Certeau and Walter Benjamin – thinkers who also emphasized and defamiliarized the quotidian to theorize modernity.[70] When Hubble tracked the intellectual and literary contexts of the Mass Observation project and its role in transformative social reform through a broadening of social consciousness,[71] he, for instance, emphasized its collective, cultural level deployment of Freudian psychoanalysis, citing Freud's concept of parapraxis (popularly known as the Freudian slip) in Mass Observation's use of associations in its early directive prompts and so forth. But one of the central contributions that his study made arose from his orienting observation that Mass Observation can be approached in ways other than for the 'unparalleled' weight of the qualitative source material it offers from 1937 to 1949. Thus, Hubble's book situated Mass Observation within the fabric of European movements and thought, examining its approach as 'a therapeutic politics of everyday life'.[72]

From 1937, Mass Observation elaborated what they identified as superstition in popular songs, dance hall crazes, visceral reactions to margarine versus butter, ARP posters, use of pronouns in war propaganda, rallies, smoking habits, football pools and wrestling. Incidentally, wrestling was the phenomenon about which Barthes is best known for writing during the 1950s. Barthes worked directly from the cultural texts and images themselves to produce his well-known critiques, but Mass Observation used as its point of departure people's reactions and habitual behaviours for analysis, while still giving attention to the structural characteristics of cultural phenomena. Most crucially, however, Mass Observation stands apart from these developments in everyday life studies most notably for its involvement of a base of active volunteers and the participatory approach that was central to its study of popular culture and everyday life.

Therefore, Mass Observation has been defined as both a social research organization and a social movement, since it deployed volunteers all over Britain to observe the social habits of people in their ordinary day-to-day existences and to record the details of their own daily lives with the aim to produce 'a science of ourselves'.[73] One motivating impetus for this unusually dynamic organization, which remained active until it was incorporated as a market research company in 1949, was the founders' perception that the mass media and the academic social sciences were out of touch with the concrete lives, beliefs and behaviours of ordinary people. Mass Observation responded to a largely unrecognized knowledge gap arising from a class-divided social and cultural fabric, where the talk that happened at the pub or in the kitchen seemed to have no place of importance in public discourse.[74]

Today, the Mass Observation Archive (MOA), housed at The Keep in Brighton, constitutes a vast and rich collection of interviews, ethnographic data and ephemera pertaining to everyday life in Britain and attests to the success of Mass Observation as a social research organization. Perhaps most remarkable are the volumes of diaries and written replies to directive prompts people from all over Britain submitted over the course of years that preserve for us that which 'cannot be discovered elsewhere'.[75] As Sheridan, Street and Bloome have noted, the '"amateur" or non-élite writing' generated by Mass Observation brought visibility to literacy practices of everyday life while challenging the politics that reserve space in the public sphere only for restricted forms of writing produced by those whom institutions have legitimated as authors.[76] Mass Observation not only attached great value to everyday forms of writing, it provided unique platforms for its production, collection, analysis and use. It is this deep participatory dimension that makes it impossible to contain it under the restrictive parameters that define a research organization. When the MOA relaunched the national panel in 1981, it revived this participatory dimension of the Mass Observation research collaboration, or 'thought collective',[77] with an aim to produce material that 'describes the concrete and specific contexts of particular lives, details which are lost in large-scale summations'.[78]

As a social research organization, Mass Observation's diverse programme of methodologies was designed to capture the quotidian details of the everyday, phenomena not usually seen as worthy of tracking, but also to get at the aspects of social phenomena that elide consciousness. For instance, Mass Observation had often noted the gap between what people say they are doing and what they in fact do. This distance is not simply a matter of subjects feigning, although shame can indeed distort self-reporting, but the gap underlines that the relationship between intention and action is not necessarily a transparent one. Six months after the start of the war, Harrisson playfully addressed the readers of the *Sunday Graphic* in an interest piece composed in second-person prose that offers a good example. He introduced his subject matter as follows: 'you are rather inclined to think that life on the home front is very much the same as before. But you're wrong. Everything has changed. Here is what Mass Observation's 2,000 observers all over Britain have learned about you in wartime … and how your life has altered'.[79] After capturing the reader's attention thusly, Harrisson reported changes in how people spent their Sundays, what their wartime worries were, the sharp rise in marriages, the decline in automobile sales and how few still carried their gas masks. He insisted to his readers that two years ago you told Mass Observation what would be first to go if you had to economize, 'But I'm afraid those of you with less money haven't kept your word so well. You said the things you'd give up first of all were wireless and gramophone, drinks and smoking. My evidence suggests that you've done just the opposite!'[80]

Such evidence was derived from a diverse range of methods and documents that Mass Observation had developed to approach from a variety of perspectives and forms the social phenomena it studied. These included: diaries; personal written responses to directive prompts (for the national panel); short and long term participant observations in workplaces and communities; active eavesdropping; qualitative and quantitative surveys, interviews and observations; 'indirect' interviews (investigators initiated what appeared to be casual conversations with strangers; these were discreetly documented and treated as interviews concerning topics of interest to the organization); the collection of grey literatures and ephemera; the study of objects, such as advertisements, posters and even litter. Although not treated here, Mass Observation also produced documentary photography, collage and painting, which Lucy Curzon's study demonstrates as 'equally communicative' to their text-based production. Curzon stressed, however, that since the visual work draws from 'different systems of signification, including – for example – the indexical references of photography or the gestural marks of painting, the quality of its expression highlights nuance, even facts that are sometimes beyond what textual analysis is capable of generating'.[81] This is just one of the ways in which Mass Observation did more than seek facts. It sought new and transformative modes of seeing, making, feeling and communicating, which is why it has been understood as a social movement.[82]

A crucial aspect of its social contribution was that it shifted the positioning of the lens from which questions deemed worthy of engaging were posed. This repositioning rendered the intimate and immediate settings of home and neighbourhood as sites of valuable knowledges that could not be obtained from the outside view or without multiple views. Thus, in some contexts, such as its long-term study of Worktown (Bolton), it deployed a novel but intrusive strategy called functional penetration, described as 'the unobserved infiltration of investigators into given environments, combining the use of all indirect methods, actual participation in group activities, recording of overheard comments and conversations and the controlled description of events and circumstances'.[83] But, more crucially, Mass Observation sought to bring in the voices of people who inhabited those sites as knowledge producers. Hence, the active participation of volunteers who observed and wrote as mass observers or investigators, along with its orienting vision of a more inclusive and vibrant public sphere born out of their critique of centralized communications, lends support for the categorization of Mass Observation as a social movement.

Despite their acceptance of Mass Observation as a social movement, both Summerfield and Hubble have described its orienting vision as vague.[84] Identifying and articulating Mass Observation's goals is further fraught since organizers often disagreed on what those goals were,[85] and the goals of its participants were distributed and thus impossible to enumerate beyond brushstrokes.[86] In the present digital culture characterized by the intense interactivity of what is often called Web 2.0, however, decentralized social movements held together by loosely shared goals are ubiquitous, and so the definition of Mass Observation as a social movement would perhaps be met with less caution today.

Mass Observation's ongoing inquiries into the formation of opinion, combined with their critical observation of media communications, provided the groundwork for significant social interventions at critical moments during the war. For instance, when, in the crisis of spring 1940, the government and the press debated the merits of mass internment for aliens, Mass Observation was uniquely positioned to gauge the effects of this public discourse, using as a background their monitoring of feelings of racialized prejudice that they had been carrying out for several months. While Mass Observation had been cautious about presuming access to private opinion, their study of press coverage and the fluctuations of people's stated perceptions on the question of internment enabled Harrisson to argue that private opinions people may feel ashamed to share become public 'if their expression is made respectable or conventional, if people feel that a lot of other people are holding or stating the same opinion – for instance, if the Press starts proclaiming these views as socially desirable, or if a respected statesman or Royalty publicly advocates them'.[87]

While the organization rejected one-directional, causal relationships between media exposure and opinion, holding that people are not convinced by appeals to opinions and perspectives inconsistent with their own, according to Mass Observation, the implication of this inquiry was that official channels of communication had a crucial responsibility to inform audiences of the facts and should be careful not to conflate qualitatively different phenomena. The brief spike in public support for the internment of aliens in Britain was influenced not so much by the thread of the arguments made, but by the use of language in what Harrisson called a 'perfect storm of Press material' that, for instance, gave platform to politicians urging action to combat the fifth column (a supposed network of loosely connected internal enemies involved in war effort sabotage and morale breaking) and even saw newspapers activating their own sustained campaigns for the total internment of aliens. Tracking the press's word-usage from mid-April to early May 1940 (Home Intelligence reported a spike in public support for internment in the third week of April), Mass Observation noted the increasing conflation of the terms refugees, aliens and fifth column.[88] By the end of April, the name fifth column seemed to have been used as metonymy for refugees and aliens, producing a sense of urgency that would make the ground favourable to such an extreme measure – what amounted to partial suspensions of law and liberty in the name of sovereignty and its security. The general climate of support for the implemented internment policy, however, was soon to give way, as Harrisson bluntly put it, to 'our better selves'.[89]

Hubble characterized Mass Observation as a social movement and situated it within the broader cultural, historical and theoretical contexts of its emergence, but he also elaborated the double characterization that Dorothy Sheridan and Angus Calder gave to the orientation of Mass Observation as part social transformation, part social therapy. This is a productive way of conceiving Mass Observation's anthropology of ordinary life, which was normative in its aim to foster conditions for a vibrant public sphere founded upon dynamics of decentralized communication rather than the flattened one-directional transfer of information that routinely positioned ordinary people as receivers of elite messages. The methods that Mass Observation used made the intimate routines and knowledges of everyday life significant to emergent public discourse; this is most striking in Mass Observation's influence on government in the tense months of 1940, when their work on morale and rumour gave the kitchen, the workplace, the pub and the corner shop new political significance. While Mass Observation's investigations into opinion, feeling and morale served a reporting function that could inform policy and social action, the results of these inquiries were also conceived as the necessary means for making cultural interventions into the landscape of public feeling insofar as they threaded relational attachments between publics within the horizons of social-historical events. These aspects of Mass Observation's normative programme weaved its double impulse towards social therapy and social transformation, the complementary dimensions of Mass Observation as a participatory social movement. As we shall see, this complex programme was significant during the war.

Mass Observation plays two parts in this book. On the one hand, materials from the MOA provide much of the crucial empirical support for its arguments. The complex ways in which Mass Observation approached investigations into evacuation and the keeping of pets during the war, as well as the ways that people responded to observer prompts regarding evacuees and animals, instrumentally incited and shaped the questions that guided the research for this book. On the other hand, Mass Observation's methods, social interventions and collaborations, especially with Home Intelligence, will at times become an explicit object of study as an agent of social transformation and social therapy during the war crisis, for which Madge had once argued Mass Observation had enabled a productive 'emergency psychology'.[90]

An objection to my approach might follow similar lines to a critique that a contemporary, Marie Jahoda, levelled at Mass Observation, while animating the problematic distinction between subjective and objective inquiry. Of the panellists, Jahoda had argued: 'As, however, they are all casual and untrained observers, they must show bias in the observations. They cannot be … quite representative of the mass of people for they are themselves a selected group of people whose types require examination.'[91] Sheridan, Street and Bloome pointed to the contradiction inherent to this critique by noting that

> as Jahoda and other critics of Mass-Observation argued, if the observers as the subjects of the study are not 'trained' as professional social investigators, then they and their writings must be seen as the *objects* of study, *in which case, they must somehow be representative*. This anxiety to define observers as either one thing or the other, as either 'objective' or 'subjective', continues to preoccupy some of the users of the Archive today as well as some of the current correspondents themselves, as does the anxiety about 'representativeness'.[92]

While I agree with Jahoda that the writings of Mass Observers warrant examination as objects of study, her justification arises from positivistic assumptions that are furnished by the hierarchies of knowledge that Mass Observation had critiqued from the outset. Donna Haraway has intervened into the subjectivity-objectivity dichotomy with her proposal for partial and situated knowledges that 'require that the object of knowledge be pictured as an actor and agent, not as a screen or a ground or a resource, never finally as slave to the master that closes off the dialectic in his unique agency and his authorship of "objective" knowledge'.[93] Mass Observation materials can and should be treated as objects of study insofar as they were disseminated at the time through a variety of media targeting different audiences and had effects on public discourse and policy. In this sense, they can be agents. Simultaneously, however, even the rich empirical materials from which I draw that were not disseminated during the war transform how the relationships between things and processes are perceived, and the critical use of them in a diverse range of inquiries demonstrate that 'the world encountered in knowledge projects is an active entity',[94] not a container of still objects waiting to be discovered and counted. Indeed, for different reasons, the participants in Mass Observation can too be objects of study that provide uniquely textured access to the past.

Further, Jahoda's accusation of the panellists' bias is tied to the belief in a position that an individual (whether trained, and therefore institutionally legitimated to make knowledge claims, or not) can occupy from which they remain unmarked by experience and power and from which they can make claim to a dispassionate stance. Again, I turn to Haraway, who argued for the 'mobile positioning' and the 'passionate detachment'[95] of situated knowledges that forward 'the view from a body, always a complex, contradictory, structuring and structured body, versus the view from above, from nowhere, from simplicity'.[96] Mass Observation's relationship with the academy was initially antagonistic,[97] but it is now recognized as invaluable to historical scholarship. In many ways, this is suggestive of its innovative anticipation of, and participation in, the changing conditions of knowledge production and the productive *a-disciplinarity* that its initial separation from formal academia afforded.

One of the contentions of this book is that Mass Observation both urged and enacted forms of public caregiving during the war. Mass Observation's delivery of care, however, was fraught with contradictions. Such contradictions are inherent to the concept of care itself and to the disconnect between Mass Observation's involvement in the motivating contours of its participatory project and its surveillance of public feeling. The tensions are perhaps most animated in Mass Observation's contract work for Home Intelligence through which the nation's population was observed, measured and acted upon for its protection in the collaborative enactment of a watchful form of care focused upon civilian feeling.

In the absence of consistent funding, Mass Observation often struggled to keep going. Like many mass observers, Julian Trevelyan remembered that the organization's finances were an ongoing concern. While he stressed that observers' work was often done for love, full-timers still had to find ways to scrape by, and Harrisson had to deliver at least token amounts to them from time to time. Trevelyan recalled that Harrisson obtained funds, sometimes by writing for popular presses pieces with sensational titles such as 'I Married a Cannibal', or 'Tom would go hat in hand to his richer friends, and M.O. was often the recipient of generous cheques from such benefactors as Victor Gollancz, Sir Thomas Barlow, and Lord Simon of Wythenshaw. These, he impressed upon us, were free gifts to M.O. without any strings.'[98] Even if these were without strings, it was more difficult to make the same case about contracts Mass Observation engaged, such as those with the government and the Advertising Service Guild; endeavours that produced source material crucial for responding to the questions raised in this book concerning evacuees, pets and shifting norms of care.

It is well-known that the work for the Ministry of Information's (MoI) Home Intelligence division exacerbated existing tensions between Harrisson and Madge. Before Madge left the organization, he had objected to the government work as spying and argued that Mass Observation's labours in the absence of stable financial subsidy, and the fact that it was kept afloat in large part by the direction of 'penniless but enthusiastic' fieldworkers, had the benefit of keeping their 'ideas and methods independent'.[99] His correspondence with John Maynard Keynes in the spring of 1940, which brought some work for Mass Observation from the National Institute of Economic and Social Research, illustrates Madge's vigilance in distancing himself from the Ministry contracts, notwithstanding the MoI and Mass Observation's mutual need to keep their collaboration discreet.[100] In the 1980s, Madge suggested that his criticism of the work for the MoI may have been misdirected, conceding that it 'has an enduring human and historical interest', though he felt at the time that their independence was threatened by doing work for a ministry that prevented publication until after the war.[101] The two founders had struggled over the question previously. In 1939, when they studied public reaction to the morale posters for the MoI, Harrisson had entreated Madge by arguing, 'what we want is to do enough useful work to be allowed to keep going, so that after the war we may tell the truth for the first time'.[102] There were compromises. What would have been the truth that Mass Observation would have given in different material circumstances? In what forms would it have been presented? While these questions cannot be answered, what can be addressed is what Mass Observation did within the constraints it worked.

Although it was perhaps necessary, there is reason for caution as well as criticism of apparent co-opting of Mass Observation into state and commercial activity. Although not solely targeting the work done for Home Intelligence, Hubble's characterization of the Mass Observation's engagements with popular culture in their publication *Britain* as indicative of a possible distortion of their transformative goals into 'a strictly limited exercise in social therapy: one which might even be pejoratively labelled social engineering'[103] resonates with the contradictions at the heart of the biopolitics of care to which this book attends. That Hubble finds aspects of their book *War Begins at Home*, a study of the first four months of the war, to be 'nakedly authoritarian'[104] relates to the contract work for the state even though much of it was independently produced,[105] since the book addressed leaders in policy making, as well as the press, in anticipation of securing wartime government contracts. After all, *War Begins at Home* opened with: 'We believe, basing our belief on much evidence ... that one of the vital needs now in this war is that the Government should be fully aware of all the trends in civilian morale. They need an accurate machine for measuring such trends; a war barometer.'[106] The implication that Mass Observation was that accurate machine that the government needed was not subtle, and the rest of the book substantiated that Mass Observation had achieved more than what it promised in the announcement of its formation in *New Statesman and Nation* in January 1937; namely, that it would 'provide the points from which can be plotted weather-maps of public feeling in a crisis'.[107] Indeed, this work, as well as the earlier and widely read publication *Britain*, which had demonstrated that 'MO had provided exactly the sort of [home intelligence] that the MoI had as yet been unable to organise for itself',[108] positioned them well for the contracts they received in the spring of 1940 and afterwards to make reports to Home Intelligence throughout the blitz.[109] Hubble's critical caution about the nature of Mass Observation's social therapeutic impulse combined with state war work brings attention to what is at stake in the contradictions of Mass Observation's social project. He suggested that, while Mass Observation's influence with governing organizations during the war may have instrumentally supported the shift to the post-war social welfare state, it may have simultaneously given the ruling class the tools to maintain their hegemony.[110] Hinton situated the question concerning 'whether MO was doing more to empower the masses or to facilitate their manipulation by existing elites' within the context of the popular front strategy to confront fascism, 'MO's political aims were sufficiently vague and open-ended to elide the difference between giving existing elites the knowledge of the masses necessary to rule them effectively, and empowering the masses to overthrow those elites.'[111]

As a final orienting note on the role of Mass Observation in this book, I provisionally position this endeavour with respect to the Harrisson-Madge falling out, which can be traced though their reflexive reports on the organization's work and then their personal correspondence with each other in 1940. It is unfortunate that this charged communication has sometimes served to crystallize a binary and oppositional characterization of their respective approaches and visions that obscures the extent to which these tensions are strengths and furnish some of Mass Observation's rare texture, without which it might never have been.

In January 1940, Harrisson described the two organizers (he and Madge) as lacking cohesion and he formulated a dichotomy between his own vision of an 'anthropology of ourselves' and the Madge-Jennings avowedly surrealist approach as attending to 'a documentary and literary record of mass-life'.[112] These are tensions that the scholarship concerned with mapping the contours of the Mass Observation initiative has inherited; tensions that sometimes call upon Mass Observation scholars to position their projects in relation to this polarized depiction of the differences between Madge, who left Mass Observation in June 1940 to collaborate with Keynes, and Harrisson, who distanced himself from the movement's poetics informed by avant-gardist intervention into the methods and framing of social study.[113] The aesthetic and methodological textures of Mass Observation's cultural interventions are layered and multiple. In this, Sayer has found similarity with Émile Durkheim, who 'inspired not only positivist American sociology but also the Collège de sociologie' and the surrealism of Michel Leiris and Georges Bataille. It is not just that though. Sayer pointed out, '"The first and most basic rule is to consider social facts as things," said Durkheim. By this he meant "to treat them as *data*," about whose *essential* nature we cannot presume to know anything a priori. The corollary is that sociologists must "*systematically discard all preconceptions*" – which is exactly what Mass-Observation's rudely unscientific methodology does.'[114]

On the one hand, this book will draw upon the Mass Observation collection as historical source material responding to the repeated appeal, usually forwarded by Harrisson, that Mass Observation offer material for the future historian. While Harrisson had envisioned Mass Observation as making an offering to historians of the future, the Mass Observation project since 1981 was framed for participants explicitly in these terms, prompting Highmore to highlight the unique temporality of those documents, which concern the past, present and future, while addressing future readers for whom the present being worked out on the page will be the past. Of this, Highmore observed: 'and this accounts for something of the temporal atmosphere that often pervades these documents: all this, the correspondents seem to be telling the reader, will have happened a long time ago'.[115] The early Mass Observation promised to 'record history in the making; a new sort of history',[116] but also imagined a historian of the future, who through its investigations would gain a window into the everyday lives not captured in, perhaps obscured, or left out of, official sources.[117] This appeal, however, appears to be motivated in part by political ideals – a particular democratic imaginary, a potential, defined against the fascist threat – taking aim at what they called the invention of unanimous feelings for a 'country', which in fact can only have such apparent unanimity under Fascism. In the absence of machinery for finding out what people do think, it is a natural and even unconscious tendency for leader-writers and leaders of all sorts to turn all the individuals into such a unity, and thus constantly to balance the scales a little more against democracy.[118]

On the other hand, drawing upon this source material will bring productive and exciting encounters with characterizations of Mass Observation that capture what Laura Marcus calls 'an interface between documentary realism and surrealism',[119] what Sheridan, Street and Bloome referred to as 'acts of serendipity',[120] and Highmore has stressed as the defamiliarization of everyday life.[121] These are partially indexed in Madge's characterization of the panellists, who were to be neither disciplinarily trained, nor united in a particular view, but to share a democratically informed commitment to 'social fact as a touchstone to social theory'.[122]

## Humanitarian reason on the home front

Forwarding the concepts of humanitarian reason and humanitarian governance, Didier Fassin has observed the central force of moral sentiments in politics today. Fassin's emphasis on 'emotions that direct our attention to the suffering of others'[123] in government, defined broadly 'as the set of procedures established and actions conducted in order to manage, regulate, and support the existence of human beings',[124] highlights the tie between affect and reason that adjudicates legitimacy in contemporary politics. Fassin insisted that, while humanitarian reason is effective for mobilizing consensus, the language that characterizes this form of reason prefers to animate words such as suffering and compassion over interests and justice;[125] exclusion, misfortune and trauma over inequality, domination and violence.[126]

According to Fassin, this novel political discourse has been accompanied by a new moral economy that took a more defined shape in the closing decades of the twentieth century. In this emergent economy of moral sentiment, humanitarianism has unseated politics, while suffering, rather than violence, makes a more efficacious appeal for remedial action.[127] Though now, as Fassin described it forming explicitly in French social policy from the 1990s, everyone is perceived vulnerable to suffering towards which compassion may be mobilized, this is because the legitimizing force of the words suffering and exclusion had lent to 'a broad consensus in ascribing exclusion to a new social order that was no longer "vertical" but "horizontal," and a growing proportion of the French population lacking *lien social* (social links) – an expression that soon became a cliché'.[128]

While Fassin found consistency with the French context in his ethnographic studies of humanitarian work in other parts of the world, such as Palestine, Venezuela and South Africa, relatively recent events in Britain also speak to this shift towards the perception of a horizontal form of social differentiation in which everyone is equally exposed to exclusion and suffering. For instance, proposed explanations for the 2016 vote in favour of Brexit suggest that feelings of exclusion may have played a large part. But, then, whose feelings of exclusion did so? Drawing from Lord Ashcroft's referendum exit poll, Sayer observed, 'The fact that 81% of Leave voters viewed multiculturalism, 80% immigration, and 69% globalization as "forces of evil" strongly suggests that these are simply codes for xenophobia.'[129] Sayer compared the 'politics of resentment' that contributed to the Brexit vote to the election of Trump in the United States later that year as showing 'much the same cocktail of nativism, xenophobia, misogyny, "traditional values," and mixed messages on capitalism that animates Donald Trump's base in the United States, minus the evangelical Christianity, which is a genuine American peculiarity'.[130]

With respect to the concern noted above that French social policy has placed emphasis on lack of social links in connection with horizontal exclusion, it is significant to note that, in the American case, the feelings that were attributed to Trump supporters in 2016 became popularly coded in euphemistic terms of 'fears of cultural displacement', following wide press coverage of a research report from the Public Religion Research Institute (PRRI) and *The Atlantic* that found this to be a crucial motivation. The PRRI report, which also cited 'fears about immigrants' as a factor in the 2016 U.S. election results, elaborates what it described as fears about cultural displacement in the following way: 'White working-class voters who say they often feel like a stranger in their own land and who believe that the U.S. needs protecting against foreign influence were 3.5 times more likely to favor Trump than those who did not share these concerns.'[131] Selected appeals to cultural vulnerability, it would seem, are more effective for motivating change than appeals to social and material inequality.

Returning to Britain to consider another development, at the start of 2018, Prime Minister Theresa May responded to the Jo Cox Commission on Loneliness by announcing the new portfolio of Minister for Loneliness and the appointment of Tracey Crouch. The report from the Cox Commission described loneliness as a social epidemic impacting over nine million people with its reach stretching beyond the disabled and the elderly, to carers, new parents and people who have experienced a life event. Even being young is cited as a risk factor for loneliness, a scourge now described as more dangerous to health than a smoking habit. According to the government press release, loneliness 'can kill', and it can impact anyone – it 'doesn't discriminate'.[132] Rachel Reeves, MP and commission co-chair, commented, 'When the culture and the communities that once connected us to one another disappear, we can be left feeling abandoned and cut off from society.' In bringing the urgency of loneliness to the forefront, Reeves made direct appeal to Beveridge's 1942 report that was key to shaping British post-war social welfare policy, speculating that, if Beveridge were alive to assess the present, he would add loneliness to 'want, disease, squalor, ignorance and idleness',[133] which the wartime report cited as obstacles to post-war reconstruction.

I raise the appointment of a Minister for Loneliness and the justifications for it not with intent to belittle loneliness as a significant social problem worthy of the attention and resources that the government promised to give to it. Rather, the point I wish to underline is that the discourse that justifies social policy mobilization on the problem of loneliness seems to illustrate the humanitarian governance and reason that Fassin found very explicitly expressed in French social policy and activated in global humanitarian efforts. The compassion that this rationale calls upon is unquestionably laudable, but the rationale itself rests upon the effacement of social questions that become invisible, or even unspeakable, when the social structure is rendered as horizontal in shape. Thus, when Fassin illustrated how a politics of compassion is an asymmetrical politics, involving an objective domination, offering that: 'a critique of compassion is necessary not because of the attitude of superiority it implies but because it always presupposes a relation of inequality', he showed how the new force of the language of compassion has assigned the concepts of inequality, domination and violence to a symbolic void.[134]

As mentioned, this book analyses imperatives of care in Second World War Britain to determine how they supported the encroachment of humanitarian reason by indirectly making the home a discretionary site in which informal asylum for vulnerable social subjects could be deliberated. I consider the wartime decentralization of governance into regional systems, which was a response to anticipated social disorganization following air war on civilians, as setting conditions favourable to the encroachment of this type of reason. Titmuss characterized the rationale for decentralization in the following way: 'If disorder was to be prevented the chain of civil command on the home front would have to be kept intact';[135] therefore, this process was understood as pragmatic, given projections based upon the experience of civilian attacks during the First World War and the casualty figures from aerial attacks on Spain, with which the British government was working. Each region was furnished with small home departments able to govern independently if major disruptions of communication made it necessary, while preparing the ground for the government to relocate in the worst case that may render the central state unable to govern.

A possible objection to the use of the concept of humanitarian reason in the framing of this subject matter might be that Fassin located many of the crystallizations of humanitarian government roughly in the latter third of the twentieth century, while this book, addressing the Second World War, as well as interwar anticipatory policy deliberations, concerns the 1930s and 40s. I offer two initial responses to this objection. First, the book does not argue that humanitarian government and its logics, in the senses that Fassin's ethnographies have elaborated, were developed and fully operational in Britain during the Second World War. Instead, it proposes that crucial characteristics took shape then, especially sparked in home front civil defence imperatives and the Mass Observation movement's interventions – a connection that will be fleshed out in a subsequent section. The home front predicament offers glimpses into moments of its fragmentary emergence. Second, insofar as Fassin presented humanitarian reason as possessing a 'duel temporality', with its long-term anchored in eighteenth-century thought, I believe that there is no temporal inconsistency between my identification of flashes of this reason during the war and Fassin's formulation centred on the short-term temporality when, with more frequency, conflicts, measures and initiatives are cast as humanitarian in character. As Fassin remarked, 'This politics, which brings into play states and nongovernmental organizations, international bodies and local communities, has a history.'[136] In concrete terms, the chronology he presented begins in the 1940s; thus, he references, for instance, the Battle of Normandy and the establishment of the International Committee of the Red Cross Nobel Peace Prize, both in 1944.[137]

Connected with the encroachment of humanitarian reason is a historical process to which Hilton et al. have attended. It has two defining dimensions. First, the privatization of politics that citizens mobilized as they increasingly pursued their political concerns through participation in voluntary, charitable and advocacy groups rather than through formal political parties. Second, the professionalization of politics that emerged from those groups and positioned 'professionally minded experts ... to tackle the issues at the frontier of social and political reform'.[138] Thus, from the voluntary spirit that Beveridge found laudable and necessary in the 1940s grew 'an ethos of professionalism', technocratic logics and cadres of experts that would eventually furnish NGOs, which are so influential today. Paradoxically, however, Hilton et al. stressed that the distinction between state and non-governmental forms of governing has historically become less defined, as they have a shared 'mission': to reform behaviour and influence 'the moulding of modern citizenship'.[139] An example of the early deepening of cooperation between the two spheres that Hilton et al. offered was the Home Office's creation of the Women's Voluntary Service during the Second World War.

## Biopolitics, post-humanism and animacies

With some glossing, we have already brushed with aspects of biopolitics above. For instance, the concept of biopolitics sits closely with the concept of humanitarian reason, which Fassin argued is supported by 'the politics of life'. These politics activate the 'differentiated meanings and values of human life'[140] that have human lives categorized in terms of their assumed value and capacity. The shadow of biopolitics is cast over Stevenson's definition of anonymous care, as that which indifferently manages life, sometimes even as 'serialized bodies',[141] as opposed to everyday forms of care attuned to personalized bonds, particular circumstances and meanings. According to Michel Foucault, biopolitics describes technologies of governance concerned with preserving and enhancing life, but life here is conceived first in terms of population rather than individuals, and generally take as a point of departure a conception of the population as a living organism or body. In this respect, biopolitical governance is concerned with individuals only insofar as they function as parts that optimize the functioning and enhance the capacities of the population as an organic whole. Biopolitical governance is not wholly restricted to formal state operations. At different times, biopolitical objectives oriented towards the good of the whole have animated administrative and charitable organizations, the delivery of social services, medical and public health care, academic disciplines, counselling and pastoral services, education and child rearing and much of what is accepted as common sense as they respond to the articulated and contested concerns of their present time. In other words, it is the performance of a modern form of rationality that informs its regulation of people and things. Its shape and focus are subject to historical shifts.

To the extent that biopolitical regulation enacts a form of rationality applied to the enhancement of life, particularly directed at the population, its operation requires techniques designed to produce knowledge of the population to which it invests interest. Thus, it demands observations and measurements of the population; the kinds that a national census provides, for instance, although there are many other arenas in which this knowledge is produced. The statistical norms that some of these endeavours reveal are used to inform the apparatus of policy and techniques for the regulation of the life of a population conceived as an organism whose equilibrium is a biopolitical objective. Thus, Foucault argued that biopolitical regulation operates with a focus on the administration of, and imperative towards, the amplification of life through attention to biological processes such as life, death, fertility and illness, as well as conditions of security, communications, economic markets, hygiene, safety, happiness, natural and built environments and so forth.

There is another part to this too, which involves the cooperation of individuals. It requires that people assent to these measurements and regulations, as well as to mechanisms put in place for the protection of the population. In the twenty first century, we have seen biopolitical rationality exercised overtly in relation to the concerns of global and national security against an apparent ubiquity of terrorist threats, which, in the equation render individual sovereignties and privacy as presumably worth sacrifice under emergency, anti-terrorist legislations. In the present, this cooperation takes form in the ambivalent acceptance of surveillance and the more contested fact of facilities in which some people can be detained without being charged with a crime. Or, to take what was not long ago a more mundane example, the message that handwashing saves lives was ubiquitous in many Western countries. In 2011, Nicole Shukin observed that 'hand sanitation comes to epitomize the responsibilization of the biocitizen, whose social duty now revolves around the personal priority of *not contracting or transmitting* disease'.[142] Thus, even though the wartime Ministry of Health instructed home front citizens to 'HELP TO KEEP THE NATION FIGHTING FIT', by trapping germs in their handkerchiefs because, as it warned: 'COUGHS AND SNEEZES SPREAD DISEASES',[143] the techniques and relationships that governed the British home front are historically distinct and specific and so are the kinds of cooperation that were negotiated. It could be said that this cooperation in everyday terms also takes the form of individual or subjective alignment with characteristics, such as independence and rationality, that, as mentioned earlier, Rose noted are assumed to be possessed by, or developed in, individuals recognized as 'good citizens'. So, the relationships between concerns, practices and techniques of regulation and cooperation that were specific to the home front will be examined in this book.

**Figure 0.1** Coughs and sneezes spread diseases, Poster issued by the Central Office of Information.

But if, as noted above, the preservation and enhancement of life, and the equilibrium of the population's norms, are objectives of biopolitical regulation, this form of reason that guides it also calls for calculations to be made regarding that which threatens the strength of the whole. The modern state's aim to enhance, preserve, and prolong life also involves exercising power over death by, as Foucault put it, making live and letting die. A key assumption of biopolitical logic is that, to protect the life of the nation, distinctions of relative value must be made between groups within its population between those who function to enhance the population and those who may threaten it. From this point of view, the vitality of the population can be maximized by producing divisions (actively identifying, labelling them) within it to remove or neglect perceived internal threats or weaknesses with an aim to strengthen the whole. Foucault called this 'state racism',[144] a process of dividing or imposing breaks within the population as the state's target object of knowledge and regulation. This imposition, or fragmentation, produces sub-populations that are then ranked.

Racism, Foucault argued, has two functions for this kind of regulatory calculation. First, it enables 'power to treat that population as a mixture of races, or to be more accurate, to treat the species, to subdivide the species it controls, into the subspecies known, precisely as races'.[145] In other words, it makes race by ascribing meanings to otherwise arbitrary differences. Second, it appeals to a positive relationship between living and letting die. This relationship, he insisted, is 'modeled on war',[146] but it operates differently than war does in that it concerns a power that, rather than wielding the sword to exact life from its subjects, it 'wishes to work with the instruments, mechanisms, and technology of normalization'.[147] It therefore operates indirectly, through 'the fact of exposing someone to death, increasing the risk of death for some people, or, quite simply, political death, expulsion, rejection, and so on'.[148] It operates fundamentally as a biological relationship, draws its support from nineteenth-century biological theory and its application of evolutionary thinking to the population and the species 'dressing up a political discourse in scientific clothing', and makes appeal 'to the principle that the death of others makes one biologically stronger insofar as one is a member of a race or a population, insofar as one is an element in a unitary living plurality'.[149] The concept of state racism then illustrates how elements of a population come to be 'known' according to statistical and other measurements, divided up and regulated with concern for the functioning of the population. It also explains how a form of governance dedicated to the protection of life can assign death – social or physical – to the sub-populations it identifies as a threat to the life of the population.

One of the ramifications of this is that social categories whose functioning in relation to the population become a site of concern are produced by this logic. This implies, for instance, that gender is intertwined with the biopolitical discourses of sex.[150] Given that the feminist appropriation and re-accentuation in the 1960s of the medicalized concept of gender has combatted the kinds of claims that the concept of sex had bolstered and presented 'a more sophisticated understanding of the world beyond crude biological sex'[151] and its controls, this may seem to be a strange proposition. Bringing attention to the psychiatric introduction of gender in the 1950s as a mechanism for ordering sex, Jemima Repo argued, 'The postwar invention of gender in the clinic to manage sexual socialization and its present governmental deployment to control demographic and economic processes are not unrelated. Both represent different disciplinary and tactical events' and 'provide an impetus to re-examine gender as a biopolitical apparatus'.[152]

Like gender and all concepts, biopolitics has histories and, while they will not all be attended to here, these threads have ramifications for the context of civil defence on Britain's home front, primarily the discourses that both policed the boundaries of categorization between displaced persons, usually working-class children and non-working animals. To return briefly to the elaboration of how the familiar concept of gender fits into biopolitical governance and racism, since this book concerns the 1930s and 1940s, prior to the invention of gender, I draw from Kyla Schuller to link back to Foucault's more abstract description of racism. Schuller argued,

> the rhetoric of distinct sexes of male and female consolidated as a *function* of race. Yet my formulation does not relegate sex difference to the role of secondary or analogical effect of racial formation. Rather, I name sex, sexuality, and, in the post-World War II era, gender as key ways that race fragments the domain of the biological ... In other words, not only gender but also the physiological category of sex are variegations of race and effects of racial biopower.[153]

As this book examines how the wartime household in Britain was endowed with 'forms of governmental reason'[154] and became an arena in which biopolitical concerns could be addressed through routine acts of caregiving oriented towards identifying and minimizing threats to the food supply, to the war effort and to the population, anxieties about race, class and reproduction articulated in the elite interwar panic over depopulation and the presumed decline of civilization[155] are relevant to the deliberation of which social subjects were worthy of protection. This problem requires interrogation into how social subjects, human and non-human, were categorized and ordered with respect to the affordances of informal care in times of crisis. The question is not necessarily what kinds of life were given care, but how care could make distinctions between lives by identifying different kinds and assigning them different worth.

To this point, discussion of biopolitics as technologies of care has been focused on the governance of human life, but animal social subjects, and their relationships with people, are governed too. As mentioned earlier, Mass Observation found that keeping dogs who do not work during the war could elicit social disapproval under certain circumstances. Some people expected that they might be forced to give up their dogs, and dogs were not allowed in public air raid shelters. But what do official planning documents suggest about government attitudes towards non-working dogs or even cats? While ARP documents identified lost, hungry and traumatized dogs as a security threat in the aftermath of an air raid, officials considered some types of cats in similar terms to that of essential workers. As the government drafted emergency schemes, planners came to imagine some types of cats as essential. Therefore, these essential worker-cats were to stay behind, with essential human-worker counterparts, if an area was at immediate risk of invasion or if most of its infrastructure was destroyed.

In part, the sometimes unusual and contradictory positioning of cats on the home front was possible due to official acknowledgement of their independent ability 'to fend for themselves'.[156] Yet the presumed independence and essential status of some cats did not necessarily afford them protection, as one MP was briefed: 'The cats which would be left behind [in an emergency] would be of the warehouse type which, I am told, require little or no looking after. Consequently, no avoidable suffering to any of the animals in these areas will result from the decision not to retain any representatives of the animal welfare societies.'[157] Instead, the cat was acknowledged for its capacity to enact wartime duty for the good of the whole. In official discourse, certain types of cats were indeed imagined to have their part to play in preserving abandoned areas from insects and other animals classified as vermin. Thus, such cats could, and should, stay behind in bombed out areas that would otherwise provide ripe conditions for the vitality and teeming growth of rat and maggot populations, which posed threats to food security in war time. Notes from a meeting between the Home Office and the National Air Raid Precautions for Animals Committee (NARPAC) state: 'In order to ensure that a certain number of cats should remain in the town [in the case of compulsory evacuation], propaganda should concentrate mainly on dogs, though cats should be accepted for evacuation if resources permit, or destruction if necessary.'[158]

What we have here is a number of breaks in the continuum of biological life consistent with the regulation of life and the protection of the population as a whole that Foucault described, as conceived in plans for emergency compulsory evacuations. There are cats who can fend for themselves, therefore, humans engaged in animal welfare work are not essential and should be evacuated. These independent cats who are said to be endowed with a capacity called independence will stay behind to control and curb populations of a different kind, say rats. This is another break, as rats are designated as a threat to the food supply, as well as the health and hygiene of the population that government targets for protection. Dogs, often thought of as man's [sic] best friend, as one of the family and who often occupy a place of intimacy in the home, come to be viewed through a different lens in the context of security planning (insofar as the dogs in question were not employed in agricultural, war or other kinds of work). Here, the unemployed dog's animality is primary since the domestication of dogs that enables their humanization also renders them dependent, and therefore dangerous when they become homeless. Indeed, as the NARPAC reported during wartime,

> in the early days of the raids on London, vast numbers of dogs and cats were rendered homeless in the Silvertown Area, which in a few days became dangerous to human beings because of starving packs of dogs taking possession of evacuated houses. The situation was only got in hand after various Animal Welfare Societies co-operating with NARPAC drafted skilled personnel to the Area.[159]

The report did not offer details about how the concrete dangers manifested or the skills the personnel who ascended upon the Silvertown homeless dog squatting community exercised. Nevertheless, in the production of ARPs, it was assumed that dogs who did not have the capacity to care for themselves and who became separated from companions in an emergency would revert to some kind of prior animality and thus they were, in this scenario, deemed a threat that must be removed in advance through either private evacuation arrangements (which were simply not available on a scale that would provide for most dogs), or death.

There is much going on here, but I'd like to underline two main points about these ranked breaks imposed between dogs, rats and types of cats. First, these sub-populations are all part of the order of life that is governed through biopolitics, and their management and use are understood as necessary precisely because these forms of life, as well as that which is marked as human life, are all relationally intertwined. Their longevity and their death stand in relation to each other. Second, even this brief tracing of such breaks reveals the operation of the politics of life or what could be called an animacy hierarchy. Animacy hierarchies, according to Mel Chen, 'conceptually [arrange] human life, disabled life, animal life, plant life, and forms of nonliving material in orders of value and priority'.[160] How such hierarchies organize and order material 'might possibly come out of understandings of lifeliness, sentience, agency, ability, and mobility'.[161] But as this surface-level glimpse of what justifications come into play in the animacy hierarchy that informs these emergency planning discussions also shows that slippages differentially occur on that hierarchy, it is possible to recognize why Chen insisted that multiple animacy hierarchies can be at once in operation. They are culturally and historically specific, and hence, they are themselves subject to ordering, as well as to change.[162]

Emergency planning, in this case, makes the lives of some cats more useful (indeed, even essential to civil defence protocols) than those of non-working dogs or rats (although outside of emergencies, cats might slide back down at least to a notch below dogs and they certainly won't be imagined as necessary personnel). Simultaneously, the dog now unleashed from domesticity is refunctioned from best friend and family member to a dangerous threat that might need to be annihilated for the good of the rest. Lastly, while the rat is rarely greeted by humans as a friend, the perceived capacities that rats possess have been routinely harnessed and put to work in medical and other laboratories in service of knowledge production, health, longevity and so forth. One of these capacities that the rat is granted is its ability, through various similarities, to stand in for humans in experiments and procedures that produce knowledge about a category of animal called human. The ways that these differences, or similarities, come about are contradictory and shifting. The labour of rats that is put to the service of human health and knowledge contrasts with the emotions of disgust and fear that they can elicit in intimate domains. Labouring dogs also trouble their characterization as fully dependent. Chris Pearson's work has shown that dogs have been 'increasingly enmeshed in social and national defense' in Western states since the late nineteenth century.[163] Their sensorial capacities were also harnessed for civil defence and rescue in the ruins of the blitz.[164] As animal subjects are perceived and valued in ways that are contradictory, animacy hierarchies are shown to be neither stable, nor coherent. One of the things I will consider in this book is how multiple animacy hierarchies operated during the war and created or underlined breaks in the population and the re-ordering of categories. Through examination of evacuation stories that depict ungrateful, infested and unruly evacuees, as well as the fierce public contestations over the worth of animals who do not work, this book will track the blurring within and between the categories of human and animal to identify emergent and shifting home front animacy hierarchies that imperfectly mapped onto each other.

Post-humanist scholarship informs critique of biopolitical thought by interrogating the distinction between human and non-human subjects and highlighting the conceptually troubled ways in which the line that distinguishes human from non-human animals has been underpinned. To the extent that the line between human and non-human is subject to revision, particularly in times of crisis, and implicates the perceived value of a form of life, post-humanist theory posits the warning that 'the humanist discourse of species [is] available for use by some humans against other humans as well, to countenance violence against the social other of whatever species – or gender, or race, or class, or sexual difference'.[165] Cary Wolfe's observation has political implications, as it complements Hannah Arendt's distinction between human rights that only preserve bodily existence, and civil rights that support the political existence of subjects.[166] The lines that demarcate human from non-human, useful non-human from useless or threatening non-human, and human being from citizen are re-drawn and activated in the increased emphasis on care on the home front, where, in September 1939 evacuees were frequently compared to or described as animals, and, simultaneously, tens of thousands of pets were put to death by their caregivers, which, as Hilda Kean has noted of the latter, challenges 'the popular memory of the "Good War," the unified "People's War"'.[167]

Consideration of multiple and shifting animacy hierarchies enables a nuanced and critical post-humanist critique of biopolitical governance and its racializing functions because it destabilizes the ways in which kinds of matter become tied to properties, 'equated with propensities',[168] as well as the ways they are defined and demarcated from each other, and the mechanisms of difference that justify their relegation to higher or lower orders that represent their capacity for animacy, in terms of presumed agency, mobility, sentience, moral capacity, language and so on. Although language, as 'meaningful and credible speech', has long been mobilized as the capacity that marks the 'sacrosanct dividing line between human and non-human'[169] animal, for many reasons this mark of distinction does not hold. For Kalpana Rahita Seshadri, one of the central reasons why this fails is that language also refers to silence, which has no place in the law: 'In fact, the *locus* of power's decision on life is the conflation of language and law, while the *exercise* of power is the withholding of access to the law-speech nexus in order to consign the other to silence'.[170] This deprivation of speech, according to Seshadri, has been central to the practices of racism, divisions that deny personhood: 'the task is to ask how power emerges from the recognition of the instability and indeterminacy of all identity as endlessly divisible'.[171]

Chen's preference for the concept of animacies, over life and death and other binaries, addresses 'anxieties over the production of humanness',[172] and places emphasis on other assumptions that play into the divisions. Chen showed how, for instance, in the 2007 United States lead toy panic concerning products manufactured in China, 'dead' lead could become mobile and racialized as Chinese, and addressed 'the vulnerability of [white, presumably heterosexual and middle class] human subjects in the face of ostensibly inanimate particles. These particles are critically mobile and their status as toxins derives from their potential threat to valued human integrities. They further threaten to overrun what an animacy hierarchy would wish to lock in place'.[173] In this way, Chen underlined that matter, which in some circumstances would be seen as dead, can be endowed with racialized, as well as racializing, capacities that the consideration of animacy hierarchies makes palpable. It brings mobility and other sensorial capacities to bear alongside language as making and drawing breaks between kinds. Evacuation invented and brought the so-called 'problem family' into power's grasp in particular ways so that work could be done upon the working classes to free them from the supposed 'slum mind' and the contaminating dangers it posed by its 'gravitational pull'. The 1943 report *Our Towns: A Close Up* suggested targeting efforts on what it called 'grey rather than black families' since, while the 'grey' families were unwholesome, they were considered capable of improvement, the 'black' ones were not.[174] The presumed lines between animal reaction (or instinct) and human responsiveness, responsibility and care[175] were activated in, for instance, deliberations concerning post-war housing, which granted to dwelling and neighbourhood architectures more agency and more morality than those who would inhabit them. These themes will be worked out in further context in the chapters that follow, however, the next section will suggest how the pressures that Mass Observation exerted on public discourse during wartime relate to the concerns raised in the concepts of biopolitics and humanitarian reason.

## Mass Observation and the biopolitics of care

The Mass Observation movement was implicated in the complementary logics of humanitarian reason and biopolitics. Although it contributed to the official work done to socialize civilian commitments to the nation's war effort through new provisions for caregiving under ARPs, one of its main targets was government. While the state engaged in the shaping of public feeling to entreat citizens to perform their duties to protect the life of the nation, Mass Observation actively turned these same logics back onto the state, attempting to arouse in decision-makers virtues and actions informed by compassionate feeling or care. By embedding observers in evacuation reception areas, blitzed towns, rest centres, tube shelters and on nightly treks East Londoners embarked upon to find accommodation during the blitz, mass observers witnessed first-hand the struggles of those most impacted by the vicissitudes of war from the air. Back at the Mass Observation offices, investigators' notes were reviewed, analysed and synthesized into reports. Where the conditions described in field notes exhibited patterns that required urgent remedy, a list of recommendations would be drafted for dissemination. Some of these recommendations proposed bureaucratic technologies to manage the population, but they also pushed back upon this kind of abstraction, advocating efforts attuned more intimately to the social side of things. Mass Observation routinely drew from a logic of care that mediated between anonymous and everyday forms of care. Mass Observation dramatized the individual's devastation experienced after an air attack as material but also emotional and cognitive, highlighting feelings of grief, shock and bewilderment, to mobilize local and central authorities via appeals to what roughly engaged in the sentiments that animate humanitarian reason.

Mass Observation's appeals to agents of governance were not only formally procedural, demonstrating competent understandings of what they criticized as the sometimes poorly integrated workings of formal government and civic institutions, but delivered emotional instruction to these bodies. Harrisson's article 'Blitz Information – The Lifeline of Civil Defence' arose out of Mass Observation's investigations into blitzed towns and was submitted to *Local Government Service*. This article was addressed to government personnel and decision-makers. It reported a pattern of inadequate awareness and circulation of emergency information following the blitzes, for instance, in Coventry, Plymouth, Stepney and Greenock. Although it is procedural and concludes with fourteen organizational recommendations, it expends considerable effort to regulate its readers' compassion, while also granting public feelings a critical place in the war effort. The tactic used here was to ask the reader to imagine herself as the wife of an absent serviceman, managing a small shop and caring for three children. After the building that houses both your dwelling and your shop is hit, imagine that one of your children has been killed, a second is injured, and your family is rendered homeless. In the intimacy that his second-person prose invited, Harrisson provoked the reader to consider, 'You are living in a badly hit working-class area. You find yourself homeless, moneyless, without a thing except your spirit, your morale, your commonsense and your two legs. When the dawn comes and the loudspeaker van hands you a leaflet, what do you have to do?'[176] Among other crucial moves, this article painstakingly traced the bureaucratic knots and impasses that the homeless and grieving citizen would have to negotiate in the immediate term, it underscored the emotional and cognitive strains under which this enigmatic maze of emergency social services would need to be navigated.

A critical point here is that Harrisson was not advocating for better services or for a more paternal state relationship with the people. Rather, he was advocating that 'information should be recognized as a primary social service'[177] for individuals to be better equipped to locate these services to help themselves. 'But what a good citizen this would have to be!' to know what to do in an emergency, Harrisson remarked regarding the lack of organization of services and poor dissemination of information. This call to equip ordinary and even traumatized people with the material and subjective resources to self-regulate in accordance with the desires of the state – in this case, with the smooth operation of the war effort – is consistent with biopolitical governance, which relies upon assent and individual responsibility rather than direct forms of social control. Moreover, these internal states must be fostered actively. Listen again as Harrisson makes appeal to the readers of *Local Government Service*: 'Courageous, calm, solid, and uncomplaining, are these blitzed citizens of Britain. But those virtues come from within themselves, and could be much added to, rendered more dynamic, by a little more leadership. Information is the essence of leadership. Propaganda is the message of leadership.'[178]

Biopolitical governance works, or perhaps one could say, the good biopolitical subject endowed with the internal virtues requisite to the social-historical conditions in which it is situated, works on its own when its desires are in alignment with a form of governance centrally concerned with the enhancement of life. Further, biopolitical governance, as Foucault argued, is structured not by a power of limitation, not by saying no or demanding obedience in the strict sense,[179] but by amplifying choices that fall around the norm, as equilibrium is its aim. Returning to the matters of caring, in this article, Harrisson also calls for the introduction of a new post, the 'Helpful Warden', a figure who would be solely dedicated to attending to 'the worries and doubts of blitzed people'.[180] But, crucially, the Helpful Warden does not assume the tasks of distressed citizens, instead such a warden assists them in gathering their internal resources to be better able to locate and access existing external ones. In other words, this warden helps them to help themselves.

Thus, this offers one illustration of how Mass Observation's instruction targeted to agents of government fostered an expectation that decision-makers and their policies demonstrate not only effective governance in emergency, but compassionate citizenship. As Harrisson urged,

> the whole atmosphere of the town after a blitz is directly relevant to its war effort. It is more important to get cinemas open quickly again than to dynamite a wall which may fall on a cat in a derelict area. Music to gladden the heart is as necessary as music to sadden the heart – the only bands I ever heard in blitz-towns were the ones leading the impressively depressing mass funerals.[181]

There is much to unpack in this short passage, not least of which are the contradictions raised by the possibility that it motivates the external regulation of mass emotion as a way of assuring cooperation with the desired scripts of behaviour from traumatized and homeless citizens. Approaching this call for compassion with consideration of how biopolitical governance works, it is necessary to acknowledge how care for suffering individuals and assistance in their prompt and successful re-orientation to the rhythms of everyday life in the crisis of war is a strategy for ameliorating the risk that the suffering and the bewildered will pose internal threats to the population's security in an emergency. It is in pragmatic predicaments, such as the ones to which Mass Observation brought detailed attention, that we are given access to the fine meshing that intertwines the concepts of care and security in the context of Britain's experience of the Second World War – notwithstanding the etymological relationship that Latin establishes between these two terms.[182]

These contradictions of compassion and care will be examined more closely in the chapters that follow. The brief collaboration between Mass Observation and British Home Intelligence provides the point of departure in chapter one by examining the ways in which Mass Observation performed an ambivalent form of care on the home front through the surveillance of public action, belief and feeling as well as its efforts to influence the MoI and the forms of care it exercised over the population. Chapter two examines evacuation rumours that were populated with recurring character types and tropes. Considering the ways that Mass Observation addressed the respective images of evacuees and hosts as they related to the shifting and tension-filled construction of good citizenship during the war, the chapter shows how Mass Observation's critiques attempted to mobilize forms of care and governance that were attuned to specific circumstances and the unique social bonds that characterized them. Mass Observation's indirect interventions into the debate over the worthiness of pets' lives to emphasize the ways in which non-working dogs enhanced morale and provided an outlet for the indirect communication of fears and difficult feelings is the subject of chapter three. There, I argue that Mass Observation's work furnished arguments that supported the keeping of non-working animals by making appeal to everyday forms of care enacted in cross-species social bonds. Chapter four operates as a conceptual hinge by weaving together threads from chapters two and three. Specifically, chapter four gives attention to how the language used to describe evacuees as animals at the same time that the worthiness of some animal lives was debated to examine the shifting and contradictory ways that social subjects were categorized and ordered with respect to the affordances of informal care. It argues that discourses surrounding animals and displaced persons strengthened, countered and stretched dominant assumptions about animacy during the war and, thus, anticipates the closing chapter's observations about the perceived agency of 'slum' housing. Chapter five takes as its point of departure the perception of the home as having its own socializing agency, or even the power to make imprints upon its inhabitants and degrade genetic inheritance. The chapter examines Mass Observation's more participatory approach to framing the problems of housing, which stood in contrast with such assumptions, and facilitates the drawing of conclusions for the book.

While Mass Observation's interventions may have helped administrators, politicians and social service providers to maintain public consent by governing with more compassion, this book will emphasize how Mass Observation performed a socially therapeutic advocacy for the mobilization of modes of care and humanitarian reason in governance and social provisions made for ordinary citizens. But it will also elaborate how Mass Observation denoted the care it gave as manifested in physical objects (in the work it did then, the archive it left us, the alternative futures it imagined and worked to bring into being and so forth) and activates one of the multiple senses of Latin *cura* (or, care) that John Hamilton examined: 'positive *cura* is the work itself, an object of study, a work of art, or simply the beloved person for whom one cares'.[183] Mass Observation itself operated from a position of caregiving, in concern for the nation conceived as a field of meaningful social bonds and the democratic enrichment of its public culture through participation.

1

# Keeping Watch Over the Population

The gathering of state intelligence is not usually considered a form of care. In this chapter, however, I will consider the brief collaboration between Mass Observation and the British Ministry of Information (MoI) to elaborate ways in which Mass Observation attempted to influence the Ministry and performed an ambivalent form of care on the home front under contract with Home Intelligence beginning in April 1940. At that time, the German occupation of Denmark and Norway punctuated a period of anticipation on the home front and marked the beginning of a heightened crisis. In response to the rumour and apprehension that flourished in a 'fast-moving sequence of military disasters'[1] initiated that spring, including the taking of Paris, the evacuation from Dunkirk and the passage of the Emergency Powers Act at home, the MoI Home Intelligence division increased the frequency of its reports that tracked the indistinct object of home front morale to predict and to shape it. The tasks of Home Intelligence were initially imagined and brought into being by its director, Mary Adams, formerly a producer for BBC television. Acknowledging two forms of public resistance, both material and mental, it was the role of Home Intelligence to deal with the latter's emotional and rational resistances.[2] Adams determined that Home Intelligence must locate the sources of these resistances and keep its hand on the pulse of public opinion and feeling, monitoring their flux in response to events as they occurred to ensure that official publicity campaigns would resonate and intervene in ways favourable to the war effort.[3]

Home Intelligence's constant assessment of the public's morale was supported by a vast and partially covert network that extended beyond their own Regional Information Officers (RIOs), who reported on casual conversations and behaviour in public spaces. The Wartime Social Survey (WSS), conducted by the National Institute for Economic and Social Research, also furnished critical information collected in door-to-door interviews that were analysed using social scientific methods. Postal censors made reports to RIOs based upon their perusals of letters, and the BBC passed on information derived from its listener research surveys. Political parties, the London Passenger Transport Board, the

Citizen's Advice Bureau and even the Brewers' Society were called upon to provide responses to Home Intelligence prompts.[4] As noted, Mass Observation began a series of contracts to furnish Home Intelligence with reports on various subjects from the spring of 1940. This monitoring machinery was dispersed into minute spaces of everyday interactions. For instance, a small discouraged comment made during a visit to a local shop might be incorporated into these reports, as individuals whose employment brought them into concentrated daily interactions with others had been recruited to respond to inquiries about 'the feelings of those with whom they came into contact'.[5]

Adams's proposal to contract Mass Observation for Home Intelligence met with initial hesitation within the Ministry, since some considered the organization to be subversive. Indeed, several of Mass Observation's key investigators and organizers had involvements with the Communist Party (Brian Allwood, Kathleen Box, Jack Fagan, Celia Fremlin, Charles Madge, Nina Masel, Henry Novy and John Sommerfield), trade union and other leftist groups. In response, Adams offered that it was crucial to distinguish between subversion and criticism, the latter of which could be valuable. In any case, she wrote,

> I myself am satisfied that the machinery provided by Mass Observation will supply us with the facts we need, and that as a fact-finding organisation Mass Observation is 'neutral'. But no man of Harrisson's temperament and drive can be without ideas and even convictions. It is for us to use his *findings* and not his opinions. I believe, with supervision, we can do this.

In attempting to assuage the Ministry's concerns about Mass Observation's perceived politics, Adams nevertheless resorted to saying that contracting the organization would enable the Ministry to control them: 'It would be useful if their resources were mobilised for our purposes rather than for their own,' she argued.[6] Mass Observation was contracted and, by September, the Ministry reported, 'In emergency, Mass Observation is the most valuable piece of machinery Home Intelligence possesses.'[7]

Thus, Mass Observation was for a time an integral part of the network Home Intelligence managed, a network that it referred to internally as a 'morale barometer'. Its reports were concerned with what people did, said and presumably thought, and yet they were often structured by apprehension about how civilians felt. The MoI considered the information that Home Intelligence provided to be integral to the department's work and management of the 'five menaces to public calm': fear, confusion, suspicion, class-feeling and defeatism.[8] According to a Ministry review of Home Intelligence, Mass Observation reports directed attention to matters of particular topical importance and have supplied information as to the way in which the public is reacting to the news of the day, to public statements, and to the Ministry's publicity measures. These reports have been used at the Ministry's daily Press conferences; they have afforded evidence of need of information on many current problems, and have led the Ministry to promote broadcasts, to improve leaflets, to correct defects in distribution etc.[9]

Morale barometer was an animating metaphor for Home Intelligence's vast observational machinery. Both Adams and Mass Observation used this atmospheric term,[10] but Mass Observation likely borrowed from BBC Listener Research nomenclature of the 'listening barometer'[11] when calling for such a mechanism in the preface to their book-length study of the first four months of the war. *War Begins at Home* opened with: 'We believe, basing our belief on much evidence ... that one of the vital needs now in this war is that the Government should be fully aware of all the trends in civilian morale. They need an accurate machine for measuring such trends; a war barometer.'[12] Due to her friendship with Harrisson, Adams was familiar with Mass Observation, which had previously done intermittent work for the MoI, including a request for the analysis of the red morale posters in 1939 that Mass Observation fulfilled despite the arrangement's sudden cancellation. Thus, Mass Observation was contracted to provide reports to the MoI throughout the blitz[13] on a vast array of subjects, from civilian sleep troubles, to reactions to events, to civilians' use of leisure time. Such reports informed those that Home Intelligence in turn produced and disseminated as part of the Ministry's communications tasks of 'systematically making recommendation to government, producing unique, lengthy, detailed and generally accurate weekly reports on public opinion and public spirits'.[14] According to a MoI document, Mass Observation's study of morale in London's East End during the blitz 'provided much of the basis for action taken in evacuating women and children from Thames-side boroughs. Had Home Intelligence relied on its random contacts, the picture would have been overdrawn and a false impression produced.'[15]

The story that documents in the Mass Observation Archive suggestively tell about the organization's tenure as an intelligence-gathering limb for the MoI has personal dimensions. As noted in the introduction, Mass Observation was a movement involving numerous participants across the country, who would have unevenly shared the goals that its early work articulated through its internal reports, publications and correspondence. Much of this was directed by its organizers and full-time investigators, and participants were not aware that the material was being reported to Home Intelligence. In many ways, the watchful caregiving that this chapter describes with respect to Mass Observation's intelligence activity can be attributed to Harrisson's belief that the war was necessary (many full-time observers were anti-war), and it was he who negotiated and managed Mass Observation's formal relationship with the MoI. The contract with Home Intelligence was certainly not the sole reason for the dissolution of Harrisson and Charles Madge's dynamic collaboration, but their disagreement about what it would mean for Mass Observation was a decisive breaking point. For Madge, reporting to the Ministry skirted too close to spying on the public and risked Mass Observation's principle of independence. While Harrisson's tendency towards self-publicity that his biographer says was often ascribed to him[16] may have played part in his stubborn insistence to tie Mass Observation with government, the contents of the archive do not rule out self-promotion but nevertheless suggest there was more animating Harrisson and give insight into motivations that remained faithful to the movement's interest in the making of a vibrant public sphere in Britain. These contracts presented Harrisson with a new route through which he could further Mass Observation's objectives, critique leadership that was out of step with the lives of ordinary people, and inform policy that was responsive to broad lived experience rather than to paper plans. In doing so, Harrisson attempted to influence a more caring and participatory form of governance. To the extent that these efforts involved such close surveillance which hoped to penetrate the most intimate feelings of individuals, the implications of these activities remain politically ambivalent and furnish Nick Hubble's concern that Mass Observation's social therapeutic approach may have at times blurred into a form of social engineering.[17]

    Due in part to Home Intelligence's provisional adoption of Mass Observation's concerns and theories of morale, opinion and rumour, much routine intelligence gathering and interventions into conduct that concerned morale was performed within a caregiving modality that was pastoral in character, exhibiting commitment to a secularized form of the relation between the shepherd and flock. Michel Foucault elaborated the pastoral themes of keeping watch and 'final kindness' to account for the individualizing pole of modern power, which complements its regulatory techniques that preserve and strengthen the social body.[18] In other words, even though biopolitical logics aim to protect and enhance the social body (the imagined organism of the population or nation), mechanisms of power must be available to gather knowledge about individuals so that, if necessary, wayward behaviour, health, productivity, aspiration and so forth may be gently nudged towards the population norm. For a home front example, we might look to exhortations for the wives of servicemen to observe marital fidelity (or at least to observe strict silence if she did have an affair so that she did not trouble her husband), while overlooking any of their husbands' affairs. The preservation of the social bonds at the core of the marriage was a matter of personal concern, but, as Jennifer Purcell has pointed out, the reasoning extended beyond the individual relationships concerned: 'Fears were widespread that women's home front affairs might distract servicemen on the battlefront from their soldierly duties. This, of course, put not only the soldier at danger, but also his comrades, and ultimately, his nation.' Therefore, the government reserved the right to withdraw the allowance that a wife received while her husband was away in service if it was believed that she had committed adultery.[19] Here, we see an example of how the intimate matters of the heart and body were constructed as a problem of government that fundamentally concerned the very life of the nation, and thus seemingly justified disciplinary measures to be taken upon individual conduct.

As a vital part of the living organism to which biopolitical mechanisms are directed, the individual is subject to exacting forms of observation and guidance that Foucault traced through the historically shifting themes of pastorship, deriving from the Egyptian Pharaoh shepherd, through the theme's development in Hebrew theology, to its adoption by Christianity and gradual secularization in modern institutions, which wield a form of power that Foucault called biopower.[20] Aimed towards the preservation and enhancement of life, biopower is more permissive, distributed and ambivalent than top-down sovereign power that was primarily concerned with preserving the principality, the relation between ruler and territory. Biopower does not simply tell subjects what they cannot do, it also works to expand individual capacities and limited freedoms to the extent that they may contribute to the vitality of the population as a living entity. Thus, Foucault argued that biopower (modern power) operates via two poles: disciplinary mechanisms (drawing from pastoral influences) that target the individual to act 'as entrepreneur of himself' even though biopower considers the individual to be a machine with a lifespan,[21] on the one hand, and biopolitical regulation of the population through interventions concerning fertility, mortality, public health, mobility, happiness, environmental and urban problems, security and so forth, on the other hand. Foucault considered the promises the Beveridge plan forwarded as exemplary of the tensions between these two poles. He remarked,

> if I am not mistaken, this is the first time that entire nations waged war on the basis of a system of pacts which were not just international alliances between

powers, but social pacts of a kind that promised – to those who were asked to go to war and get themselves killed – a certain type of economic and social organization which assured security (of employment, with regard to illness and other kinds of risk, and at the level of retirement): they were pacts of security at the moment of a demand for war.[22]

Foucault articulated how pastoral themes, including responsibility, obedience and individualizing knowledge, are enacted through techniques of examination and secular confession that are consistent with the motivations and needs of the welfare state. Individuals do not submit, they tacitly agree – sometimes actively elect themselves – to a myriad of these techniques, from the census to the counsellor's office, to the playful personality assessments we find on social media platforms today. Foucault insisted that the historical themes of pastoral power, including those of responsibility, obedience and individualizing knowledge, 'are still quite important for contemporary society. They deal with the relations between political power at work within the state as a legal framework of unity, and power we can call "pastoral," whose role is to constantly ensure, sustain, and improve the lives of each and every one',[23] even while risking them (a fundamental paradox), for the sake of the population. This relation was animated in efforts to manage wartime morale through exhaustive monitoring and the submission of civilian speech, actions and feelings to exacting analysis, synthesis and diagnostic reformulation.

While the memorable wartime publicity campaign targeting *careless* talk warned that careless speech could cost lives, intelligence machinery was designed to support governance that was care*ful* or, indeed, full of care. But the relation of care that it initiated requires closer consideration. To the extent that public feeling was bound to the concept of morale and the survival of the nation, Lisa Stevenson's distinction between anonymous forms of care, which manage life with indifference to individuals, and everyday forms of care, which arise from social bonds situated in circumstances and the shared negotiations of their meanings, can inform the kind of care[24] that Mass Observation mobilized from within Home Intelligence's morale barometer machinery. In critiquing the biopolitical motives of wartime government for looking 'on the population as so many mathematical units, to be blacked out, registered, detained without trial, evacuated on a certain train, conscripted at a certain age',[25] Mass Observation, and Harrisson particularly, sought to personalize the care that was given to civilians under strain from air war fear and wartime suffering. The positive pastoral techniques that watched over and gently guided feelings and their expression for the sake of shaping and maintaining a strong and unified home front morale offer routes through which this chapter can approach the complexities of the care that this form of intelligence performed at once both outside of the civilian home and penetrating within it to exercise biopolitical governance that would exceed the bounds of strictly state actions and permeate civilian activities that were presumed to be private in the routines of their everyday lives.

## What people say on a windy night in March

In London, the climate was described for its 'Cheerfulness with an undercurrent of anxiety' on 8 June 1940,[26] which was a positive advance from the previous day, when the people of Britain were described as 'anxious with an undercurrent of cheerfulness'.[27] Home Intelligence reports often drew upon weather motifs to describe sudden shifts in morale. When Mass Observation announced its formation in a letter to *New Statesman and Nation* in January 1937, it promised that its 'observers will also provide the points from which can be plotted weather-maps of public feeling in a crisis'.[28] Indeed, it attempted to fulfil this task directly. To map public feeling, something that was so impervious to observation, Mass Observation designed an experiment that intimately tracked fluctuations in subjective feelings. Subjects were asked to map their feelings between noon and two o'clock daily, and these findings informed reports to Home Intelligence on morale.[29]

Morale was a rhetorically forceful concept in wartime, despite a lack of stability in the ways in which it was operationalized in official discourse and by observers of social practices. In his study of the MoI, Ian McLaine asserted that there was not a clear referent for morale until the latter part of 1941. At that time, morale was finally defined as a 'state of conduct and behaviour of an individual or a group' and good morale as 'conduct and behaviour indicating that they are prepared to go through with the war to final victory, whatever the cost to the individual or the group'.[30] Prior to that, the Ministry 'persisted in confusing morale itself with certain of its isolated components. Starting from a bland confidence in the resilience of the public, they swung sharply in the other direction in 1940 and seized upon the slightest grumble.'[31] McLaine describes internal negotiations concerning the tension between behaviour and attitude – action and spirit – in the Ministry's belated efforts to define the very phenomenon 'they were charged with sustaining'.[32] Therefore, much monitoring and shaping of morale preceded its definition that came into shape through the reciprocal sense-making of officials, its intelligence machinery and citizens.[33]

Harrisson described public mood as one of the key objects of Mass Observation analysis,[34] and its handling of morale indirectly anticipated what contemporary scholarship in affect theory proposes; affect is pre-conscious, while emotion can be articulated. While Mass Observation sometimes conflated words like feeling, opinion, attitude and thought, they attempted to systematize and inquire further into these phenomena. Their inquiries into opinion formation distinguished between the things people will say and what they think. What people will say while communicating with a stranger 'as opposed to a conversation with the wife in bed',[35] constituted the difference between public and private opinion. Harrisson argued that the former is constituted by what people are comfortable enough to say to a stranger, which the interviewer most surely is, while the latter can be expressed in intimate contexts. Thus, private opinion is of the greater significance because it is 'the public opinion of tomorrow, more strongly held, more liable to stir up into an explosion and often more closely related to real behaviour and morale than public opinion'.[36] Therefore, the study of private opinion requires more innovative methods, those that Mass Observation provided through watching, indirect interviewing and embedding themselves in unfolding situations.

Acknowledging that the shift from pre-conscious affect to conscious feelings that can be defined and named occurred over time, Mass Observation considered it crucial to pay attention to minute changes or undercurrents of feeling, since 'Today's words are last week's thoughts, and today's thoughts are next month's words.'[37] Likewise, Madge described the concept of morale as a 'floating abstraction' that needed to be approached by identifying shared practices and forms of social organization in the making. Much like how Mass Observation theorized opinion formation, for them, morale could not be fully apprehended through direct questioning. Rather, to understand morale, one was required to locate and define tendencies that are emergent but not yet institutionalized.[38]

Harrisson also remarked upon the confusions inherent in the wartime use of the term morale and was critical of Whitehall's tendency to equate morale with cheerfulness, as the 1939 morale posters proposed,[39] so that a good citizen would 'make the V-sign when he saw a cabinet minister ... A lot of them didn't do much cheering even at the best of times. But they could cry and carry on all the same.'[40] Though Mass Observation warned that direct experience with bombing tended to turn people inwards towards their personal problems and dislocate them from the broader landscape of circumstances,[41] Harrisson also noted that apparent morale was often counter to expectations when tracked in relation to events. In a report on morale at the end of April 1940, he asserted, 'What people will do in a really big bad crisis or in an extended period of intensive physical suffering is hardly indicated by their behavior on the sunny morning of May 2nd, 1940. It is better reflected in the nightmare of a windy night in night in March.'[42] According to him, '"Morale" proved such a mishmash of fantasy and fact that it could vary almost in direct contrast to outside events, so that a real bomb could be "better" for morale than the dread of one in dreams.'[43]

While both Mass Observation and Home Intelligence sometimes acknowledged that morale seemed disjointed from the actual circumstances, they understood this disconnect in different terms. Home Intelligence at times judged public morale as wrong or, as the reports frequently put it, out of step with the facts. Particularly in the early days of June 1940, when the morale of some regions was judged to be 'too high' given recent events, high morale was taken to signal that the public was in denial of the facts.[44] Mass Observation had argued that denial was one of the three public responses to anxiety, and 'war is above all a process of anxiety' for civilians, for which the three usual forms of reaction are to rationalize it, deny it or drug it.[45] Preferring stability of emotion, Home Intelligence tended to support the control of information for the sake of morale, particularly when events became turbulent.

> Reports show a certain steadiness of morale over the weekend. This is partly due to acceptance of what is believed to be a deliberate policy of restricting the news. One gets the impression that opinions are being withheld and emotions held in suspense deliberately. It must be remembered, however, that this suspension of feeling (which gives an appearance of steadiness and calm) is arrived at partly at the expense of identification with the events in France ... There is a distinct advantage, however, in preventing by these means the violent day-to-day swings of opinion and feeling.[46]

For Mass Observation, however, morale could be out of step with the facts, either due to lack of information or by unconscious retreat. Positive morale, characterized by cheerfulness, courage and certainty of victory without 'study of the facts' or through 'retreating *from* the facts, putting the unpleasant out of mind' was not of the same value to the war effort as that which was informed by the realities of the situation.[47] Borrowing from psychoanalysis, Mass Observation often characterized unfounded optimism as 'wishful thinking', and a symptom of a lack of effective leadership.[48] Thus, Harrisson insisted that 'the problems, and particularly the repression of real problems down in the secret places of the heart' came from political leadership.⁴⁹ Noting Freud's use of the term in his studies of hysteria and dreams, the organization pointed out that 'psychologists and psychoanalysts have not traced out wishful motives socially, but have rather emphasized the individual context of "wish fulfillment"', by which Mass Observation framed such social tracing within their own emergent project. For them, while wishful thinking could lead to dangerous optimism, it could also aid people in the acceptance of catastrophe and 'satisfy more obscure emotional needs'.⁵⁰

The problem of public feeling was one that weighed heavily on Harrisson personally, and he believed that the conflict at the heart of the war between democracy and totalitarianism would not be remedied even when the war ended, regardless of who would be its victor. Harrisson depicted fascist propaganda as a virus that had 'infected, both from above and below, the structure of our own democracy'.⁵¹ He wrote this in the immediate fallout from Germany's invasion of Norway in April 1940, a moment when Harrisson's writing provides immediate access to the sense of urgency that struck him regarding morale – the public's, as well as his own. If at times he could be opportunistic in the way he framed Mass Observation's findings to meet broader audiences, this report takes the reader to a place that is raw and vulnerable, where Harrisson at times steps outside of his characteristic expert assurance on the feelings of others and stumbles into his own sinking feelings:

> In this war we are violating the whole ethic of our own civilisation . . . violating the ethic of youth, especially of young men, who have been brought up, perhaps for the first time in the history of industrial civilisation, on an ideal of peace and world fellowship. I could make a great many other suggestions. But frankly, when I reach this stage and think about what is happening to the generation of which I am a member, I am so sickened that I cannot think about it.⁵²

At that time, reports coming from investigators to Mass Observation headquarters showed that interviewing was increasingly becoming a challenge. People were suddenly more reticent, unwilling or unable to express their thoughts. Harrisson considered that interpretation now needed to be more intuitive than ever, and perhaps required the aid of psychoanalysis, though he lamented that he could not afford to pay a psychoanalyst to do this work. He wrote that 'the war gnaws on in Norway, and there are little straws in the wind of a disquieting sort, which people however push aside, accepting gladly the headline of a transport sunk'.⁵³ Had recent crises finally shifted the scales 'from belief in swift victory' to 'clear-cut doubt'?[54] Further, what was being done about it? Not enough, he thought, or certainly not the correct thing. Harrisson saw the MoI *Grab, Grab, Grab* poster depicting and predicting Germany's encroachment across a map of Europe to be altogether the wrong image. Mass Observation's own study showed that viewers commonly reacted to it with something that resembled admiration for 'Hitler's foresight and extra-ordinary judgement, his super-astrology'.

Harrisson believed that Mass Observation was capturing the process of a large-scale shift in morale that had not quite taken the shape of despondency but was becoming something different, an attitude that was notable primarily for its absence of content. He poetically described this public mood as a 'negative horizon of grey',[55] but assigned the term 'defendism' to the emergent attitude he thought was taking shape. Defendism, he argued, held mere survival as the objective of a war in which people seem to be 'fighting for 1935, not 1945'. Although Harrisson admitted to thinking that offering a utopian promise was an unpleasant proposition, this was indeed what he urged leaders to do to confront a mass problem: the inability for people to envision their own futures.

Building upon his concept of defendism, Harrisson critiqued the logical terms in which leaders were casting the problems of war. With this, he directly referenced political tensions between parties and states, but he underlined leaders' emphasis on instrumentality, while stressing that war is not a logical exercise and that logic alone could not sustain a situation in which individuals must fight, kill and 'organise themselves for death'. For this, he insisted, an 'illogical dynamic' is needed. War requires a utopic promise, people need to feel that 'Tied on to the Peace at the other end of the war is a dim Utopia, a Second Coming, and a heavenly calm, where the good are together in green fields and the bad are cast way (or corpsed).'[56] Reporting frequently to Home Intelligence that antisemitism was 'a major feature of the mental landscape',[57] Harrisson believed it had a direct connection to the absence of a symbolic framework that could help people deal with the violence of war. Hence, Harrisson consistently advised that official publicity should give people something to imagine, and this often meant seizing concrete things to make into mass situations with the personal touches that Mass Observation's work could inform. In a clear instance of Harrisson's influence, one of the Ministry's planning committee documents note, 'Too much stress has been laid on abstractions like Liberty and Democracy, not enough on things that people can see and hear – flags, brass bands, marching soldiers; the countryside, the homes and garden[s].'[58]

## Careful propaganda

At the start of the war Harrisson had argued that 'The present position of devalued or relatively idle channels of publicity automatically leads to waves of rumour, bewilderment, increasing criticism of the status quo; talk and personal opinion develop as an opposition to inadequate information and instructions not publicized in popular form. The results are deplorable for civilian morale.'[59] Official planning for a new war characterized by the threat of air attacks had determined that the BBC would be crucial to home front security as the key communicator of public instructions and in the management of morale.[60] In the 1930s, the radio played an integral part in many people's daily lives. The BBC developed programming that aimed to engage a variety of demographics, particularly youth, to enhance public discourse, while drawing from their listener research to broaden their appeal.[61] Furthermore, BBC news broadcasts enjoyed a solid reputation for their 'objectivity and veracity'. But from the start of the war until the end of 1941, the BBC was under the control of the MoI and served as the public voice for the Ministry's communications.[62] While BBC bulletins were considered accurate, press censorship frustrated the public and was believed to drive listeners 'to any available source, including enemy stations'.[63] Reporters and editors from other news providers shared this frustration. Although the submission of news copy to the censor was voluntary, critics suggested that the vague contours that defined content in violation of Defence Regulation 3 as 'anything whatsoever which would or might be of use to the enemy', amounted to compulsion.[64] In November 1939, the *Picture Post* published a feature called 'Black-out: A Symbol of the War Which Mustn't be Photographed'. Since the photography published in the *Picture Post* was known for what Stuart Hall called its innovative 'way of seeing' and likewise ascribed to the British documentary style that seized ordinary experience and understood it to be worthy of attention (a commendation Hall gave to Mass Observation as well),[65] this feature's layout of blacked-out photographs delivered stark criticism of the information landscape. The only photograph that had visual content was of a darkened exterior where a sign read: 'KEEP OUT! This is a private war. The War Office, the Admiralty, the Air Ministry and the Ministry of Information are engaged in a war against the Nazis. They are on no account to be disturbed. Nothing is to be photographed. No one is to come near.'[66]

By the spring of 1940, Mass Observation was reporting what it had from the start of the war: public trust in news was waning.[67] People were increasingly turning to newsletters – a medium that Mass Observation itself used for dissemination in their publication of *Us*, which Julian Trevelyan remembered as an influential instrument that more firmly situated morale within the consciousness of politicians and ensured the recognition of Harrisson 'as an authority on the fluctuating desires and anxieties of the Common Man, Tom [Harrisson] was now commissioned to advise the war cabinet, and was often closeted with Churchill for this purpose'.[68] While wartime censorship of the news was a significant factor in the public's turn from official sources, Mass Observation reasoned that the news was often 'dull, lacking in action, and repetitive, mere boredom may be the motive for the creation of newshunger in other people who might obtain some gregarious satisfaction from "exciting" news even if they did not entirely believe it'.[69] Even more significant, according to Mass Observation, was the lack of common bonds between readers of the dailies. In contrast, newsletters were tactical in responding to this lack of solidarity and shared purpose because of their critical feature, their promise to provide private news, doing so (if not by suggesting that it offered secret, insider information) through personalized conversational modes, sometimes marked by careless grammar and vernacular expressions not present in news reporting. Mass Observation warned that, if the people's newshunger was not properly fed and if leaders would not take civilians into their confidence, then morale would stand at risk of crumbling. Further, Mass Observation advocated that official communications be more compelling and more like the *Picture Post*.[70]

Likewise, in unsolicited suggestions that Harrisson gave to the Ministry of Supply, he advocated the use of picture postcards, celebrities and economy dance hall events. He urged the Ministry to draw upon the best popular lyric writers and produce gramophone records, advising that the most effective at unconscious impact are dance and jazz music – just be sure to avoid making 'one of those painfully propaganda songs,' like 'God Bless you, Mr Chamberlain'.[71] But Harrisson advised more specifically that, in his 'understanding and investigation of the public mind, you have to plug the same idea over and over again'. If the Ministry wanted to convey that there is waste in shipping bread, Harrisson advised that they focus on economy (but coin a new, more widely relatable word), using bread as the crystallizing symbol. As Harrisson pointed out, bread already operated as a significant symbol, 'mixed up as it is in people's minds with mythology and religion, and the basic facts of life'.[72] Further, Harrisson stressed that food habits and cooking represented more than mere preference over which people could be expected to exercise discipline governed by good morale. Effective plans and publicity must account for habits which derive from communities' food superstitions and the differential social prestige attached to certain foods for different groups, margarine being the most transparent example. Harrisson offered more subtle examples:

> The onion has difficult inter-sex complications. Spaghetti is feared by the socially insecure. Some groups believe that anything except the whitest white bread is beneath their dignity . . . a special male attitude to meat exists, tied up with ideas about virility, and fears of sterility. And there is a common resentment to the fat on meat, especially I think in the middle classes.[73]

Given the prevalence and power of food superstitions and prejudices that circulated differentially within social groups, Harrisson advised the Ministry to offer people both mental and dietary substitutes whenever the war effort required sudden changes to the civilian diet.

It was partially due to Mass Observation's inquiries into British superstitions that Bronislaw Malinowski, who titled his essay on Mass Observation's earlier work 'A Nation-wide Intelligence Service', contrasted the kind of intelligence that the movement provided with formal intelligence systems that supported the rise of police and the machines of war.[74]

## Mass Observation, rumours and morale on the home front

While the announcement of war did not immediately bring raids from the skies, it did release a flood of rumours from the ground. Within the first week alone, Pam Ashford, a Mass Observation diarist in Glasgow, recorded with scepticism numerous tales. On 4 September 1939, she noted several rumours that spread through the office where she worked, including that an air raid attack on London had taken the lives of 1,400 people. Her boss seemed to enjoy social and political connections that provided a store of information to share with his employees. Ashford wrote on 5 September: 'Mr. Mitchell came back with a story "straight from the lips" of the Editor of the Glasgow Herald, i.e. that the black out has given rise to a big increase in crime – brawling, attacks on women, burglaries, etc. The newspapers are keeping it out or there would be a "riot" in the country.'[75] She also documented rumours encountered in the neighbourhood, including those surrounding an ice cream shop that had been vandalized. Some rumours explained that the shop had been fronting a ring of spies, others that it was targeted because the vendor had fascist tendencies.[76] But this diarist's observations offer only one window into the plethora of stories that spread during the war.

In December 1939, a rumour that inspectors would soon be checking private larders for hoarding led one family to go on a pre-Christmas binge to avoid trouble. As the woman explained in a letter to the *Picture Post*, to put her husband's mind at ease, they called in their friends and ate all their Christmas cake and pudding more than a week before the holiday as a precautionary measure. 'Of course, there was no search of larders, nor was there any food in the larder for Christmas. But that didn't matter – my husband was in bed with a bilious attack for a week after the party.'[77] In the following year, there were variations of several tales of intrigue: dance band pianist Charlie Kunz had supposedly been caught transmitting secret messages while performing on the radio and had been interned for doing so;[78] service men were being routinely served food laced with bromide to induce temporary impotence and keep them out of trouble with the WAAF;[79] an experiment was underway that involved retrieving sound waves from the past so that history could be experienced again. In a side note to this one, Mass Observation advised Home Intelligence that it exhibited the present 'tendency to retreat from the future'.[80] The infamous nun rumour warned its recipients that fifth columnists were travelling about disguised as nuns. In one iteration of the rumour, a nun was spotted reading a religious text on a train departing from Derby. The nun accidentally dropped her book and, as she reached out to collect it, her movement revealed a man's wrist marked with a tattoo of Hitler. This rumour gained its authority with a decisive element of interpersonal indeterminacy: the nun was ostensibly witnessed by the speaker's brother-in-law. Harold Nicolson reportedly responded to this rumour with the retort, 'chatterbugs always have innumerable brothers-in-law'.[81]

While rumours changed shape over the course of the war, their initial prevalence and spread in September 1939 provoked the interest of Mass Observation, prompting Madge to write to Geoffrey Thomas at their headquarters in Bolton not even two weeks after the start of the war, 'Could you organise with as many of our contacts as possible a survey of rumour? Even if rumours occur again and again they should be noted each time with date, time and details of rumour-monger. Could you get Bill Naughton doing this whole-time and making reports at least daily – suggest that he dictates to you.'[82]

Rumours are statements of uncertain, though plausible, veracity that convey information of public, often political, significance to communities.[83] Although gossip tends to focus on immediate persons and events (the person next door, rather than a public figure like Churchill), Melanie Tebbutt stressed its significance as a mode for the expression of 'the politics of everyday living, and as such was an important vehicle for the informal power' of working classes.[84]

Although both rumour and gossip have developed negative connotations, Tebbutt's historical unpacking of the concept of gossip, which once referred to the god-parents at Christian baptisms, uncovered the strands of caring, concern and protection that gossip retained in its secularization and performance within close friendships and neighbourly communications.

Much research into these forms of informal communication followed the war; therefore, rumour was relatively under theorized at the time. Mass Observation nevertheless tracked rumours closely and, by October 1939, it reported that it had identified three hundred in circulation in London alone. By analysing the details and circumstances of these tales, Mass Observation posited three distinct rumour formations: impressive, informative and inhibitive.[85] While not fleshing out definitions of the impressive and inhibitive, Mass Observation focused attention on that which it identified as the informative rumour, claiming it to be most salient. Informative rumours inhere, according to Mass Observation, because they contain their source of authority within their content by suggesting that the story was originally conveyed by someone directly involved, a first-hand witness, or an actor in the scenario being relayed. Although a rumour travels across space and (to a historically restricted extent) across time and is subject to revision along the way, it usually retains a connection to an authoritative source. Mass Observation argued that, by forging a link between the immediate place-time of its communication and an authoritative but unidentifiable source, the informative rumour capitalizes on the interpersonal informative formulation: I know someone who knows someone for whom this information is first-hand knowledge or experience.

Rumours were considered both the reflections and ingredients of home front morale, therefore, the governance of morale could scarcely be imagined without the study and tracking of rumours. As part of the machinery by which the MoI attempted to monitor and shape home front morale, Mass Observation made considerable interventions into the working theorization of rumour within Ministry divisions that handled rumours. While Mass Observation was concerned that rumour gained salience in part due to the inadequacies of other 'channels of publicity', such as the news, pointing to 'a direct inverse relationship between the amount of official information allowed and the amount of rumour developed',[86] their ongoing provisional analyses of rumour formation and spread produced more textured understandings and propositions about rumours than the primarily negative evaluation that prevailed within social psychological scholarship that constructed rumour as a dangerous social problem without much internal debate until late in the twentieth century.[87] Mass Observation insisted, for instance, that not all rumours posed a threat to public morale. Many rumours 'provide a very valuable index of people's hidden wishes and hopes for the war'.[88] Mass Observation's analysis offered a window into people's hopes and fears and was a critical gauge for the success of wartime leadership which required government to be attuned to the real lives of civilians.

Thus, Mass Observation objected to the state's unwillingness to bring the people into their confidence and saw a connection between a lack of information, wartime censorship and general distrust of the news and the tendency to spread rumours.[89] Mass Observation argued that, in this war, conducted under 'scientific' means and involving the recruitment of virtually every civilian, it no longer made sense for war and diplomacy to be matters controlled from above; in this war, the 'decisions by statesmen and diplomats have to be translated in terms of mass action and reaction'.[90] During its formal relationship with Home Intelligence, Mass Observation carried out the studies required of it while consistently advising the Ministry on its relations with the people, advocating for relations of mutual confidence, cooperation and care for the hopes and fears of citizens. According to Mass Observation, these were the crucial components of morale, the object that the MoI was tasked with fostering.

While Mass Observation consistently advocated for change to the ways that leaders communicated with the public, leaders were concerned that unchecked private communications would inadvertently impede the war effect. The Careless Talk publicity campaign aimed to guide the informal communications of civilians. For the MoI, careless talk, which referred to any communication of a fact that could be helpful to the enemy, was distinguished from rumours and defeatist talk,[91] but these three forms of communication were all thought to undermine the war effort and the nation's safety. Rumours were very closely tracked, and it was assumed that some members of the public engaged in their exchange due to ignorance and even neurosis, as a Home Intelligence report notes, 'rumour originates mainly in a minority group of neurotic individuals'.[92] Yet in Ministry settings, rumour served as a key source for the state's ongoing production of knowledge about the public mood to predict the strength of civil defence during a period that has been referred to perhaps most memorably as Britain's 'finest hour' in Churchill's famous speech. It was at that time, however, when a psychologist had advised the MoI on the need for 'palliative publicity'.[93] To target this publicity according to the concerns of various sub-populations, rumour – its frequency, spread and variation – was treated as a sign and index for the morale barometer.

In response to the prevalence and persistence of Lord Haw Haw rumours, Churchill directed the MoI to produce a morale publicity campaign to bring

**Figure 1.1** Careless Talk campaign, Poster issued by the Central Office of Information, artist Feibush, c. 1939.

attention to the dangers of rumours. The Silent Column campaign, headed by Kenneth Clark and introduced on 11 July 1940,[94] invited individuals to counter the effects of fifth column activities by joining the Silent Column. This campaign stretched the definition of fifth column activity by drawing a distinction between professional and amateur fifth columnists, for this reason, the Silent Column campaign departed from the careless talk initiatives that preceded and followed. On Clark's account, fifth column amateurs could be anyone, and individual intent was irrelevant. This campaign cast any utterance or action that may be favourable to the enemy as fifth column activity.[95] Preparation notes for a brochure on fifth column activity assert that 'Naturally, there is not a British man or woman who would not immediately report to the authorities any case of sabotage, parachute landing or other obvious enemy activity. But there is, unfortunately, a great mass of people always prepared to give credulity to rumours no matter how unlikely they may seem.' The press insisted that the Silent Column campaign fostered an atmosphere of distrust oriented inwards towards each other with the suggestion, 'Therefore it is the duty of every one of us to trust no-one, not even our next door neighbours, and to ignore completely every sort of talk or news that is not official.'[96] Mass Observation argued that public disapproval of the Silent Column campaign was exaggerated.[97] Nevertheless, the campaign entreated members of the public to report not only suspicious activity but also the utterances of their neighbours and friends. Jo Fox has argued that this stood in contradiction with other official discourse and undermined the unifying notion of the 'People's War'.[98]

Although the campaign complemented new mechanisms that enabled the prosecution of a range of speech acts, the invitation to join the Silent Column was delivered in a comical way through the introduction of fictional characters and given in second-person prose, which included imperative instructions for dealing with them. Mr Secrecy Hush-Hush seems always to have some very confidential news that he would not want to get out, but he will share it with you, while Miss Leaky Mouth talks incessantly about the war. Mr Pride in Prophecy insists that he knows what will happen before it does, while the danger that Mr Glompot presents resides in his negative feelings about everything, as he 'is convinced everything is going wrong and nothing can go right. He is so worried about the enemy's strength that he never thinks of ours.'[99] These figures dramatized the forms of communication that the MoI aimed to curb through example or social disapproval and, failing these, legal prosecution, which would, as Jean Freedman remarked, show 'that if careless talk did not cost lives, it could at least cost fifteen guineas – no mean sum in 1940'.[100] Fox observed that, while some of the tensions introduced by campaigns, such as the Silent Column, 'threatened to destabilize wartime propaganda tropes',[101] collective public opposition to these may have indirectly contributed to positive morale.

McLaine recounted the precarious status of the MoI's legitimacy with the public, the press and even within Parliament. According to him, the Ministry had the confidence of neither Chamberlain nor Churchill.[102] Further, in the popular entertainment provided by *It's That Man Again*, the MoI was fictionalized as the Ministry of Aggravation and Mysteries.[103] A freelance writer noted in her Mass Observation diary that the organization was 'known as the Ministry of Little or No Information, the Ministry of Misinformation, and later, the Ministry of Malformation. "We are under a polite dictatorship," said someone'.[104] The MoI was a major target of Evelyn Waugh's novel, *Put Out More Flags*. When, in the midst of one of the Ministry's fictional restructurings and reforms, the character Ambrose is appointed to the MoI, Waugh poked fun at the burgeoning staff and extensive range of MoI activities by listing its reforms to include the shuffling of personnel in the departments of Folk-dancing, Woodcuts and Weaving and Arctic Circle, while 'Thirty or forty officials retired thankfully into competitive commercial life, and forty or fifty new men and women appeared to take their places'.[105] Even the *Picture Post*, which cooperated with the Ministry at times,[106] published several attacks, including an article featuring Minister Alfred Duff Cooper that described the Ministry as 'a mausoleum which for so young a cemetery has already provided graves for a respectable number of aspiring politicians'.[107] McLaine remarked, 'It is ironic, and not a little poignant, that the body charged with sustaining public morale and with maintaining confidence in the government should itself have suffered from chronically low morale and been the object of general ridicule'.[108]

In the summer of 1940, the newspapers and the House admonished the MoI, questioning the legitimacy of Home Intelligence's tactics in the public controversy popularly referred to as the 'Cooper's Snoopers' scandal. For weeks, the daily newspapers made accusations of state spying in response to the door-to-door interviews conducted by the WSS. In a letter to a distant colleague, Adams shared, 'We have been having a horrid time'. She conveyed, 'Only ten days ago I begged the Minister, in answering Acland's question in the House, to say that our methods were not secret and to give a brief résumé of our machinery'.[109] The information gathered and methods used in the academic WSS were not nearly as invasive and encompassing as Mass Observation's. Mass Observation was by then well-known, and its findings widely reported, but it evoked a range of reactions. On the playful side, Denis Dunn of the *Sunday Graphic* reported on his staff's attempt at the 'new science' of Mass Observation, 'Observing 1,000 tea drinkers in a café, 256 poured it into the saucer, 27 fanned it with their hats, one drew it through his moustache like a dredger, one blew bubbles in his, and the other 715 threw him out.'[110] But in the context of fifth column fear, Mass Observation's activities drew suspicion; perhaps it is somewhat surprising that there is only one account documented in the archive of an observer being arrested under such suspicions.[111] Given the more covert approaches to Mass Observation's anthropology of ordinary people, such as the use of active eavesdropping, following people, engaging unsuspecting subjects in casual conversations that were treated as interviews, the Cooper's Snoopers ordeal would have been heightened. Most explosive would have been the revelation that Mass Observation reports on dreams documented by their national panel participants had been passed on to the MoI, for whom they were examined by a psychologist for glimpses into public anxiety and morale.[112] For these reasons, Paul Addison and Jeremy Crang noted, 'From the point of view of Adams and Home Intelligence the attack on the Social Survey had one redeeming feature. It served as a lightening conductor diverting the attack away from the eavesdropping activities of her department (and those of M-O) that could well have got it into serious trouble if they had been exposed.'[113] Anticipating the possibility of this kind of scandal, Adams had previously advised the Ministry that Mass Observation's employment with Home Intelligence should be disclosed to the political parties; this had not been done.[114]

Survey research was still a relatively recent development in Britain then, as was recognition that ordinary people had valuable information to give. Mass Observation contended that people do not mind being interviewed. During the scandal, Mass Observation conducted door-to-door interviews asking what people thought of Cooper and the surveys: one respondent called back into the house, '"Mum! Here! They've come to Cooper-Snoop us!" And the whole family trooped out on to the doorstep, answering and talking and asking questions.'[115] When applied outside of strictly market research contexts to understand the people of Britain to inform policy, surveys apparently threatened members of the press and politicians. According to MP Sir Percy Hurd, the methods of the WSS were nothing other than 'new-fandangled nonsense' and quite unnecessary, as 'you can find out all you want to know by asking M.P.s or Local Authorities'.[116] But respondents to Mass Observation's inquiries repeatedly expressed that they thought that the government should be asking the people what they thought. Several people asserted that they would like an opportunity to give their opinions: 'One of the few opportunities they give you to talk these days'; 'If anyone came to my door, I'd jolly well answer their questions – only too glad to.' Some even suggested topics for interviews, such as evacuation. Others expressed concerns about privacy and spying, though they seemed to distinguish between the interview in which they were participating and the so-called snooping that the press was reporting. Regarding press criticism of Cooper, one person insisted, 'I think it's right to show him up. Coming round and sneaking on us like that.'[117]

## Careful intelligence saves lives

Biopolitical governance is concerned with individuals only insofar as they function as parts that optimize the functions and capacities of the life of the totality, conceived as abstractions, such as the population, the nation and so forth. Yet forms of government organized around the aim to enhance the strength of the population or the national body must contend with individuals to ensure the good of the whole. Foucault drew attention to the ways that modern institutional forms of examination, such as secularized forms of confession that offer access to private thoughts, feelings and motivations, are put to work to produce knowledge about individuals and inform techniques of correction that are applied to individuals for the supposed greater good. Thus, the well-disciplined individual has been measured and shaped to play its part as a healthy organ. During the crisis of spring 1940, the Morale Emergency Committee considered this problem in characteristic terms,

> The best antidote to fear is to provide each citizen with a definite function under such slogans as 'Each citizen [is] his own warden' or 'It all depends on me'. The difficulty is however that, whereas it is the incompetent who may first sow the seeds of panic, it is almost impossible to devise employment for such people.[118]

The individualizing power to which Foucault drew attention seeks to know and correct individuals whose assent to the ostensible common sense of biopolitical logic will ensure that they indeed recognize themselves as their own wardens dedicated to the population, the People's War, or whatever unifying concept strikes the right chord. On the underside of this resides the so-called 'incompetent', who apparently sows panic and for whom it is even dangerous to design artificial functions. These individuals come to be seen as threats to the longevity and life of the population, and, as Foucault warned, may be politically abandoned or neglected to the point of death. So, the watchful caregiving that modern governmentality (which is built upon the traditions of the pastorate[119]) exercises over individuals is always conditioned insofar as the individual can be guided to enhance biopolitical aims.

As a part of the official machinery that managed the war effort, Mass Observation reported to Home Intelligence on subjects such as morale and rumour, as well as reactions to news and war experiences. In doing so, it participated in the gauging and governing of public feelings in 1940 – a particularly tumultuous year during which a pastoral mixture of anxious urgency and caregiving informed intelligence gathering and interpretative procedures to save the population by 'scanning' localized or individualized feelings and expressions. Thus, to nudge the grumbling British civilian towards good morale was to bring 'back the stray and bleating sheep'.[120] In this respect, Mass Observation's performance of care supported the biopolitical logic that governed wartime Britain to the extent that its observations operated tactically to measure and provide governing institutions 'a continuous guide for action' that allowed for public opinion to 'be adjusted by appropriate propaganda'.[121]

Mass Observation frequently stepped outside of the topics Home Intelligence requested. Its reports included observations that are pragmatic, poignant and sometimes eccentric, such as when a report to Home Intelligence described how the conditions of air war negatively impacted séances, 'mediums are having technical difficulties in dealing with the new situation of bombed and exploded spirits, and of requests for information about suddenly lost relatives'.[122] It also took its contracted tasks a few steps beyond what Home Intelligence asked, empathetically raising concerns about the use of leisure time, for instance, reporting that during the blitz people were spending more time at home, but that a considerable amount of that time was spent 'negatively', by listening for, and talking about, noises.[123] Or noting that women have fewer opportunities for leisure, but reporting to Home Intelligence that, since the housewife's 'whole pattern of life is broken up', leisurely distractions will become more necessary for her as the war continues.[124] In these ways, Mass Observation expressed and tried to foster in the institutions it served more intimate and less bureaucratic forms of care towards the specific and differential realities that civilians faced in their everyday lives, with no concern or discomfort considered too small to matter.

2

# Verminous House Guests and Good Hosts: Evacuation Stories

Acknowledging that the Second World War would be fought not only on the front lines but in the intimate spaces of kitchens, homes and neighbourhoods, government publicity hailed national subjects the 'frontline troops' of the conflict, implicitly promising to bring citizens into the government's confidence.[1] Nearly every aspect of daily routines would be changed – from what could be taken on toast to how the evenings could be spent. Yet the expected attacks on towns for which these measures were planned did not occur until spring 1940, several months after Chamberlain's declaration of war on Germany on the Sunday morning of 3 September 1939. Although the period constituting the first eight months of the conflict has been referred to as the Phoney War,[2] the precautionary measures themselves and the first wave of evacuation under the government scheme, officially named 'Operation Pied Piper', mobilized the most entrenching of impacts of ARP provisions on everyday life in Britain in the early months of the war by migrating residents from hot zones, separating families, importing strangers into quiet communities and into the intimate settings of other families' private lives.

The influx of working class urban dwellers, primarily unaccompanied children, but also expectant mothers and those with infants, as well as the elderly and infirm, into country villages during the first official evacuation was accompanied by a wide circulation of alarmist stories that described incoming evacuees as verminous, unruly and destructive house guests, whose existence was ostensibly unmarked by civilizing forces. Evacuation stories confronted their preferred audiences, to whom they appealed on the grounds of what constitutes a good home, with the spectre of radical otherness in ways that often resonated with imperialist concerns, dramatizing and racializing social class differences by producing a cultural image of the undomesticated, lousy evacuee who soiled carpets and ate from the floor. Indeed, the cultural image of the evacuee these initial stories constructed described a figure whose existence was ostensibly animal and presented children deterritorialized by the war as barbaric and unhomely, even while the act of billeting was often described in patriotic terms. In an additional paradox, these stories drew the contours of absolute difference in the proximal contexts of the family home in communion with other British citizens proper.

Mass Observation meticulously tracked these stories that dramatized and racialized social class differences through the production of the image of the undomesticated evacuee, who soils carpets, eats from the floor and threatens to contaminate the bedding with lice and the culture with norms unfit for the good British home. Conceiving these as part of 'a war of "atrocity" stories'[3] that arose from the social consequences of treating evacuation 'as a technical problem of train time-tables and reception units',[4] the Mass Observation movement made active critiques of official schemes that ostensibly worked on paper but had no basis in 'psychological and social planning'.[5]

The Mass Observation movement embedded observers in public shelters, reception areas, blitzed towns and routes away from heavy bombing to gain understanding of people's heterogeneous experiences and characterized the problems of evacuation with attention to social gaps and social processes. By drawing upon its situated participants and tactically embedding other observers, Mass Observation witnessed (and some experienced) the struggles of those most impacted by the vicissitudes of war from the air. Back at the Mass Observation offices, investigators' notes, panellists' responses and diarists' daily entries were reviewed, analysed and synthesized into reports and recommendations that would be used to arouse in decision-makers virtues, actions and compassionate feeling or care informed by realities not easily observed through administrative distance and impersonal policy management. Thus, Mass Observation was well-poised to critique different modes of caregiving, implicitly drawing a distinction, similar to what Lisa Stevenson has made between the *anonymous care* that the government scheme enacted by indifferently treating 'citizens as mathematical units, all alike',[6] an orientation that is consistent with biopolitical governance of populations, and an *everyday form of care* that is attuned to personalized social bonds.[7]

In this chapter, I draw from mass observers' field notes, reports and other source materials to consider evacuation storytelling or rumours, as well as evacuation jokes, as informal communication that helped to work through rapidly shifting demands on civilians during the war. Since Mass Observation activity at the start of the war aimed to 'present facts about mass-mentality and mass-reactions' that could 'enable other students, in other countries and other times, to get from our work a fair objective picture of what was happening, and to use these data to fit in to their own ideas and re-interpretations',[8] it offers an unusual window into the stories people shared about evacuation. Its archive makes it possible to go well beyond what was published in newspapers, suggested in advertising and noted in ministry archives. By providing such a high volume of accounts derived from multiple methods, Mass Observation invited readers of its archive to consider these for more than what they seem to say about individuals or the people from a certain 'slum'.

About the qualitative material arising from its national panel, Mass Observation noted, 'when the same attitudes, and often even exactly the same words appear in observer reports from all over the country, and from every age, sex and class ... we know that we are on to something really important in terms of mass behaviour'.[9] While evidence of such similarities and repetitions might seem to suggest that there was mass agreement on the successes and failures of evacuation, neither Mass Observation nor its documents suggest this. In fact, documents illustrate that people occupied multiple and dynamic positions concerning evacuation, its necessity, its relative successes and its role in civil defence. Among these differing and changing perspectives, however, resemblances in the misunderstandings between evacuees and hosts, of phrasing and tone to describe events, the tropes animated through food, gardens, forks and fine china, broken chairs, burnt blankets and re-used water indeed make their presence felt in evacuation stories. Thus, we might consider the possibility that stories concerning the war's internal displacement of targeted urban populations were not always strictly *about* their ostensible subjects. Instead, such stories and rumours had the capacity to operate on multiple fronts to negotiate social expectations with respect to caregiving and to reinforce or question moral regulation that made and engaged shifting notions of citizenship and its virtues as realized in intimate routines of everyday life. For instance, rumours that explicitly repudiated the improper socialization of evacuees, and later air war refugees from towns, also produced a salient image of the host as a good citizen, who was presented as impervious to the threat of contagion presented by the cultural invasion of the ostensibly ill-mannered, dirty and destructive house guest. Since, however, Mass Observation stressed that these communications constituted a kind of 'war' of clashing representations by which the repetitively negative construction of reception areas and hosts was also one of its products, it must be acknowledged that the image of the dutiful and caring host was never truly a secure one, even if stories of animalistic evacuees foisted upon bewildered host families enjoyed wider circulation, at least during the war's first year.

Yet, regardless of which characters were presented as hero-protagonists or their foils, evacuation stories played their part as conduits for moral, emotional and cultural negotiation in rapidly changing circumstances. A joke shared in a Windsor pub in October 1939 went as follows:

> Hostess to evacuee child: 'If you'll go and wash your hands I'll give you a penny, and if you wash your face as well I'll give you twopence.'
> 'Gor blimey, I might as well have a bath and make my fortune.'[10]

Such informal communications could be open to multiple and polyvocal interpretations. On a quick reading, it may seem that this pub joke merely reinforced the figure of the always dirty evacuee who seemingly remained impervious to the expectations of hosts and required bribing to be houseable. But could it not have been read otherwise, as a commentary on the preoccupation with town children's hygiene? Perhaps many of these informal communications were not strictly prohibitive in their effects, as they may have amplified new possibilities for social action and cultural identity.

Nevertheless, one of the central considerations in this chapter concerns the paradox of the care mobilized towards the earliest evacuees as a biopolitical problem of government of populations and selves that – although managed by a network assemblage that included policy, planning, teachers, billeting officers, voluntary organizations and sometimes welfare officers – was in large part left to the discretion and goodwill of private households and villages. Indeed, the sentiments activated to support this care for displaced evacuees were humanitarian and – to the extent that they placed emphasis on billeting homes – individualized. Thus, in the first weeks of evacuation, Queen Mary's message of gratitude addressed not only those who opened their homes to evacuees, but implicitly and negatively those who did not volunteer: 'I wish to express my admiration at the way my countrywomen have come forward in their thousands to give their help.'[11] It subtly signalled that those who did not participate would perhaps not have been included among the Queen's countrywomen.

Situating these stories of cultural clash within Mass Observation's ongoing 'live survey of major social changes which Germany's march into Poland precipitated'[12] in Britain and their critique of impersonal forms of care, this chapter asks: How did these stories of displacement, so often populated with recurring character types and tropes, inform modes of care that are consistent with biopolitical concerns that placed the life and longevity of abstractions –

civilization, the population, the nation, or the national effort – above that of real, breathing, feeling social subjects and their bonds? In what ways did Mass Observation address the respective images of evacuees and hosts as they related to the shifting and tension-filled construction of good citizenship during the war? To begin, I will provide a brief discussion of the evacuation process as a preface to a closer examination of stories about displaced persons and their chief characteristics.

## Implementation

Although criticized for being delayed, evacuation planning came together in time to carry out rehearsals with the children beforehand, as schoolteachers, whose lives would be completely usurped by the intricacies of the scheme for several years to come, were being actively prepared for the first official evacuation for several months in advance.[13] Thus, when the Ministry of Health gave the first evacuation order on 31 August 1939, the scheme was ready to commence on the very next day. The first day of evacuation was briefly covered in the 16 September issue of the *Picture Post*. A photograph overlooks a crowd of parents, mostly mothers, as their children were assembled to disembark. Parents had been separated from their children and had to stand back, content merely to look on while the children were organized into groups for their journey to undisclosed destinations in safe zones. The photograph's caption underlined the paradoxical emotions of 'thankfulness' and 'sorrow' sparked by the event of separation.[14] Another image in the *Picture Post* layout shows the children assembled into organized lines. The caption read: 'They meet at the schools. They file out of the playground. There is no fuss. Everything has been rehearsed. Everyone knows what to do.'[15]

The image is consistent with how Mass Observation described the scene at Victoria station, but in its field notes we find more texture and more emotion. While observers characterized the parents as generally stoic in their presentation of outward emotion, since the children did not understand the 'gravity of the situation', a quarter of the mothers were reportedly crying or held handkerchiefs ready. When one mother in the back sobbed, another tried to sooth her, and a policewoman approached to do the same. The mother stifled her cries into a handkerchief, 'They don't realise.' The policewoman responded, smiling, 'They'll be alright.' 'Oh, yes, I know they'll be alright. (sob) They've got lovely teachers (sob).' The observer concluded:

Atmosphere is one of very strong emotion trying to be kept down. There is a strong contrast between the happiness and unworriedness of the children, their loud singing and whistling, and fear of the parents. It is the children and not the parents that keep the semi-normality of the atmosphere afloat, and absence of panic and scenes seems to be effortlessly produced by the children themselves. The lead comes from them and not from either police or teacher and certainly not parents. That is obs's subjective impression.

Another note from the observer stated, 'Obs's personal *physical* reaction is to stream tears for the first 20 minutes and afterwards not.'[16]

Meanwhile, another observer, who served as an escort for a group of evacuated mothers and children under the age of five from Euston on 6 September, wrote at length about the wait and the goodbyes to fathers and husbands just before departure. The observer describes how Mrs M, who had been so collected, standing there clutching her child's hand and chatting confidently,

suddenly gave a gasp as though someone has given a vulnerable part a stab with a dagger & burst into quick hot tears, a wave of tears like a warm shower, crying 'God help us all' & calling on her husband endearingly. She soon recovered herself & became motherly & admonishing, turning to Mrs D… [who had already been crying], exhorting her to 'keep up.' 'Ah we must all keep up, me dear, in these terrible times, God help us all, we must keep up for the others' sake.'

The observer's field notes go on to reflect,

You felt petty & useless in the face of this. Efforts at brightness, 'you'll see them again soon,' cheerful wavings & and reminders of sending post-cards when they got there might just as well have been left unsaid. You felt an object of shame because of it, something artificial that of necessity became ignored in the face of a reality you couldn't touch.[17]

Yet, despite the well-laid plans that ostensibly left everyone knowing exactly what to do, evacuation had impacts that stretched far beyond what could have been anticipated in official plans, although the weight of some of those impacts may have been felt by those saying their goodbyes in train stations. It is not surprising that there were unanticipated consequences given that the evacuation was an enormous administrative and practical endeavour that concerned approximately one and a half million people, consumed the majority of the nation's transportation resources during its execution and took at least three days to implement.[18] When some children returned home almost as quickly as they left, either at the behest of their parents or of their own accord and by foot, when expectant mothers returned to areas deemed high risk, and when some householders in reception areas reportedly refused their charges at the doorstep, vocal critics judged the evacuation scheme a failure.

Evacuation reversed at high-speed the historical movement of people from country to town and brought an uneven flooding of urban dwellers into parts of the countryside. The arrival of evacuees into rural communities underlined, and possibly exacerbated, vast social, cultural and economic class divides in the nation rather than fostering social ties and bolstering wartime morale, as was hoped. A Mass Observation investigator interviewed a bartender and the proprietor at the Imperial Hotel in Henley-on-Thames who complained that evacuation had 'given London a bad name for uncleanliness', while evacuees had transformed the lawns at Greenlands into something more like Hampstead Heath. One criticized the scheme for not taking social class into consideration, remarking that 'Quite "nice" children are sent to cottages and those from the East End bathe in the swimming pool, and are driven round in the car.'[19] A domestic worker said of the evacuated children for whom she cared at their billet that she had not enjoyed having them, 'you wouldn't get fond of cockney children like children of your own class'.[20] But this sort of expression of the gulf of class difference could run in the other direction as well, though, when expressed by evacuees, it was usually less direct, as one evacuated teacher focused remarks on the backwardness of the reception area, located '"somewhere" in England' where the school is a '25 minute walk across a barren and exposed countryside picturesquely dotted with sand-pits. The smell of cess-pits and sewers is tremendous, on a dark night one smells one's way home. Life seems to be one long struggle along this road garbed generally in gum-boots – 2 raincoats and surmounted by an umbrella.'[21] It had been assumed that the meeting of town and country would encourage stronger social integration within Britain during war time, however, many evacuation stories suggested that it had evoked greater separation.[22] At the start of 1940, Mass Observation made a scathing evaluation when it reported, 'evacuation has not only been the biggest shift of population in our national history, but has also had the biggest single effect on class-attitude, understanding and misunderstanding, town and country's attitude to each other too. Or, again evacuation puts back the clock not only on human but on all animal progress, reverses the pre-historic role of the family.'[23]

Yet social science researchers during the war observed that evacuation had been widely promoted as posing a rare social opportunity in which the middle classes would see first-hand the bitterness of poverty experienced in the 'slums', while poor children would benefit from the higher living standards of being placed in middle-class homes.²⁴ The discourse that presented these positive outcomes was often laden with moralizing class judgement. It was not just that the children from the urban working classes would benefit from clean countryside air, fresh milk and chicken. Rather, it was assumed that some of the children would be positively disciplined by their placement in 'better-class homes'.²⁵ It was not anticipated that 'the utter destitution of some children' would, as one mass observer noted, '[evoke] horror among the middle class' so that '[i]n one case a woman was driven mad by the vile filth and disease of two children. It is doubtful whether she will recover.'²⁶ The first official evacuation was widely interpreted as a failure, so that social sciences researchers from Liverpool, who were sceptical about the veracity of evacuation rumour contents and representativeness, at the time asked:

> [I]s it not unlikely that the horror felt by so many of the middle classes who were confronted by what they considered to be the dirty habits of the slum people in their own homes, and the disgust felt by slum people who suffered from what they felt was cold and inhuman treatment from their hosts, will lead to a weakening of the social ties which bind the community together, rather than the reverse?²⁷

Numerous factors contributed to the marking of social divisions during evacuation, and conflicting interpretations came from social research studies done during the war to evaluate evacuation experience and perception. Significant cultural differences across Britain, marked by social class and social geography, became palpable in incisive ways in the intimacy of the households in reception areas. Even a nine-year-old boy apparently received the message, remarking, 'Missus always looks at us sideways, as if we was muck.'²⁸ Furthermore, these cultural differences, as circulated evacuation stories illustrate, were frequently interpreted in moral terms that were cut free of the economic, regional and class contexts from which daily living practices were situated and normative.

Such differences were apparently noted from the outset on train platforms and in public dispersal centres when children, expectant mothers or those with infants and other evacuees arrived in reception areas. Despite billeting officers' plans to keep school groups close together and siblings in the same household, and teachers' plans to break up groups of more demanding children, some of the householders in reception areas acted upon their own preferences. Turner has noted that 'Foster-parents descended on the marshalling centres and took possession of those children who most appealed to them – the brightest, the cleanest, the best-clothed and the best-spoken, leaving the ill-favoured to be distributed through official channels.'[29] This scene reportedly occurred in several reception areas. A teacher described the distribution centre that her students arrived at as 'akin to a cattle or slave market' with foster parents very selectively scanning for the children they would take, leaving the picked-over children in tears.[30] Another compared it to scenes observed in 'Selfridge's bargain basement'.[31] The distribution process was a harrowing experience for the adults subjected to it. For instance, one mother evacuated with her two young children described their reception in this way:

> When we got down there it was quite dark, and we had to stand in the road for ages while two women looked us over. We were just like cattle at a fair. None of them had room for us three as there were only two double beds to spare in each house. I was parted from both my children, and each had to sleep in with a strange child.[32]

But such experiences were also disconcerting for children old enough to understand them. An evacuee who had taken a tumble during an on-route picnic with her school group, arrived in the reception area with her clothes dirtied, bandages all over her legs and her face swollen from nettle stings, later described her experience of being one of the last four children to be chosen: 'I remember the deep humiliation of sitting there as others were selected ... On that day I likened myself to a bruised apple at the Co-op, being passed over by fussy shoppers.'[33] In some cases, evacuees were not chosen at all, and other measures had to be taken to house them. There were even reports of some districts 'poaching' groups of evacuees destined for other locations.[34]

While some observers from the evacuated areas looked on with affection as the children assembled for transport – noting as a colleague of one Mass Observation diarist did, that '[t]hey were such dear little mites. No one could object to taking them in'[35] – the horror stories presumably of those who received them circulated so rapidly and widely that the complaints were heard even as the first round of children were still embarking. The University of Liverpool social scientists whose evacuation study was published as *Our Wartime Guests* argued,

> Much harm was done by the carping attitude of those who spread alarmist stories, especially before the last batch of children had even arrived, and who uttered pontifical advice which served to excuse those who found their duty difficult and were glad of any means of saving their faces. 'If only this had been done, if only that had been done, if only camps had been built'.[36]

A mass observer doing investigations in Romford, still zoned as a neutral area in October 1939, would write, 'the majority of people have no direct connexion with evacuation... however, evacuation plays a fairly important part in Romford life. Nearly everyone knows some evacuation anecdote or "misfit" story, which was heard from a friend or read in the paper, and which he can be relied upon to recruit, whenever the subject is introduced into conversation.'[37] Evacuation stories appeared to have lives of their own that were cut off from the direct contexts of evacuation. One needed not to have experienced evacuation for the story to have social significance, and most of the tales were not relayed first-hand.

## Evacuation stories

Mass Observation referred to evacuation stories or rumours as 'atrocity stories'. They were exchanged like coins imprinted with striking similarities, as though they had all been stamped with the same anxieties about physical and cultural contagion expressed through concerns about cleanliness, manners and financial burden. Turner has given a sharply illustrative description of the negative sentiments with which people in reception areas were thought to have responded to the arrival of evacuees in the early days of the war:

> From the outraged cries of gentility, it appeared that evacuation was a cunning conspiracy by the cities to unload their human refuse into the innocence of Arcadia. People began to say that they would go to jail rather than let evacuated children in their houses. In the Highlands, according to *The Tattler*, the scenes when the children from Glasgow first descended would be remembered when the massacre of Glencoe was forgotten.[38]

Even advertisers saw opportunity in these rumours of evacuation terror to promote commodities that could be branded to mitigate the harrowed householder's struggle. For instance, an advertisement for Scrubb's Ammonia drew the reader's attention with the heading: 'Strange Children in Your Home'. The text elaborated, 'If you have the care of "Evacuation Children" one famous household product will be of the greatest help to you – Scrubb's Ammonia. A dash of it in every bath will ensure that your charges are in thorough health, and a weekly headwash with diluted Scrubbs will keep their heads clean.'[39]

Richard Titmuss's review of effects upon reception areas brought by the scheme's asymmetrical planning, which had placed priority on removing target populations rather than preparations for receiving them, led him to remark that the mutual expectations of evacuees and hosts were out of step with the reality of the plans and that many reception areas were immediately faced with unexpected and urgent requirements, including the improvisational requisitioning of buildings to provide maternity homes and so forth. The scope of this ill-preparation, he insists, contributed to disillusionment and hostility, feelings that materialized in articles and letters to MPs describing evacuees as dirty, verminous and immoral.[40] Yet evacuees also made negative evaluations about their experiences. For instance, a Mass Observation diarist recorded the following from an evacuee in her village, who remarked: 'I'd rather be bombed on me own door step than stay here and die of depression.'[41] A boy claimed that the elderly lady with whom he was billeted routinely served him the water in which she soaked her false teeth at night.[42]

The *Picture Post* gave measured treatment of presumed tensions and soon became known for its support of the evacuation scheme and scepticism towards evacuation rumours. The 30 September 1939 issue put it in the following way:

> The problem of evacuated mothers and young children is becoming pressing. From both sides come many bitter outbursts. Recipients complain of the inadequacy of the billeting allowances, overcrowding, and the neglected condition and dirty habits of the evacuated children. Evacuees complain of insufficient food, lack of accommodation, incivility and boredom. Thousands of mothers with small children return to London and other danger areas, despite official appeals. But the motorist in a country lane can still see groups of city children who would otherwise be in the slums going out happily in the autumn sunshine to pick blackberries.[43]

Although implicitly judging a country childhood as inherently superior to an urban one, the above press description is far more balanced and less sensational than what was being actively conveyed through popular stories of displacement. In the same issue of *Picture Post*, letters from readers were pointed in their negative portrayal of evacuees and were consistent with the content of circulating evacuation rumours. For instance, a lengthy letter submitted by a resident of Colwyn Bay described his community as bitter from their experiences with evacuees originating from a 'slum' in Liverpool. While noting that not all the children are 'this bad', the letter listed several horrific descriptions of things suffered from evacuee behaviour, including: 'Rather than use the lavatory, children stand against walls and filthy floors and bedclothes'; and, 'After the first night, dozens of beds had to be burnt.' The letter concluded with the request that the editor only sign it with the author's initials, 'In case I am judged to be unpatriotic – which I certainly am not.'[44]

Some evacuees had lice. Some of them were improperly clothed for rural life. Bed-wetting was one of the most vexing problems of evacuation and, although this was likely associated with the heightened anxiety of being separated from family and community and the stresses of resocialization within a strange place, it was widely interpreted as a sign of the evacuee's 'slum' behaviours and lack of socialization.

As Mass Observation could not help but note, negative evacuation stories were almost always conveyed second-hand and only very rarely came from hosts who were representing their own direct experiences of billeting. This can be seen, for instance, in the wording and punctuation of one of Tom Harrisson's notes regarding information given to him from someone who claimed to have a 'first-hand, she says, evacuation story of her cousin who expected to have three children in her house, and instead received 47 slum grandfathers who fight constantly, wet their beds, and can only be punished effectively by having their false teeth taken away!'[45] Despite the lack of first-hand accounts of these supposedly epidemic assaults upon countryside homes, evacuation rumours enjoyed wide dissemination and they dovetailed with existing class-based hostility, as expressed by this railway man who responded to a Mass Observer's inquiry about the effectiveness of the scheme: 'Damn silly scheme: government should have had more sense. Let the scum get wiped out. Only the scum came out of the towns. Decent folks wouldn't let their kids come. I know that. Talk about slum clearance: their evacuation has been the best there's ever been.'[46]

Notwithstanding hosts' reasonable reports of their direct experiences, University of Liverpool researchers noted that public reaction to the evacuation plan was at times so hostile, likely informed by the passage of evacuation rumours, that there were even calls for more camps to be built to house displaced people,[47] and Mass Observation reported intimidation of evacuees that wore them out until they had to take refuge in public halls.[48] A teacher evacuated with her students to Brighton observed the gap between the image evacuation stories circulating in their reception area constructed and her direct experience:

> The first week of evacuation was unbearable. The rumours of lousy, dirty, ill-behaved children bandied about Brighton were exasperating. We knew that 90% of the children were well behaved and happy. But the only stories regaled to me were of the horrors of the wild London children. We check up in every case. Each teacher visited sixteen children, 'her beat', twice a week for the first month of reports.[49]

Insofar as displacement stories were given life through wide circulation, they presented a picture that is socially significant quite apart from their veracity or their capacity to define normatively the evacuation experience. In what follows, my goal is not to find the truth of evacuation but to examine communication about evacuation. That popular stories of displacement were rarely relayed firsthand is critical to their study. The most vivid of these stories almost always presented someone else's experience and they were exchanged by speakers who were often distanced both socially or geographically from their subjects. One woman interviewed by a mass observer suggested this distance by prefacing her report of what she has heard by remarking: 'All stories have passed through many hands before they have reached me.'[50] She noted that, while reports of verminous children seemed to be increasing, she did not know of anyone who was concerned with these cases.

Many of these stories amused and entertained tellers and audiences, but is amusement alone enough to explain their vitality, especially when many of the kinds of tales collected by Mass Observation and in other sources did not enjoy the same level of popular dissemination? It is possible to sketch the contours of the social anxieties that are given shape in stories of evacuation by looking at several of them to identify the recurring elements and figures. The identification of key themes and figures helps to challenge the assumption that these stories were engaged for their reflection of the social reality of evacuation. The shared characteristics of these tales instead reveal shared themes that prompt consideration about how displacement stories engaged their senders' and recipients' beliefs about acceptable and expected conduct and social norms during the upheavals of wartime. In the following section, I will elaborate on contamination as a key theme of evacuation stories.

## Contamination threats

Many of the stories that emerged quickly after the first wave of evacuation was implemented were vivid and alarmist and gained immediate salience. Some were widely circulated, while others such as those that Mass Observation documented through indirect and direct interviews, their panellists and participation at key sites of investigation, were perhaps more localized. While these tales took various forms and arose from different positions, including host, evacuee, billeting officer, parents who remained at home and evacuation town residents, key elements were present across many stories and are thus structural. These structural elements include descriptions of evacuees as dirty, verminous and without manners consistent to the rituals of a proper British household. Although some of these complaints were made of hosts as well, frequent charges of ill-mannered behaviour that became descriptive of evacuees in general concern coarse language, lack of table manners, or lack of socialization appropriate to the way of life in the reception villages. At times, these depictions drew upon language usually designated for the description of non-human animals, describing evacuees as not 'house trained'.[51] Displacement stories also consistently suggested that evacuees contaminated or destroyed property that symbolized a proper domestic field. In countless stories, homes and possessions were all threatened by the presence of alien guests who were sources of hardship for the hosts who received them. A partial list of household item casualties and uncivilized behaviours derived from evacuation rumours Mass Observation tracked include: linens that had to be burned, furniture with carved initials, walls with writing on them, broken china and beds, trampled gardens and food being eaten from the floor.[52] These added to common complaints that evacuated children were verminous and wet the bed. Follow up wartime research, as well as the primary source materials, furnishes some evidence of such occurrences and provides explanations for them.

An article published in the *Daily Herald* in November 1939 told of one resilient Brighton woman who stoically cared for a house full of unmanageable, destructive boys, despite undergoing the physical and emotional hardship of the stillborn birth of her own twin infants. The story came to be known when the woman was summoned for violating the blackout order. She explained to the magistrate that she had fifteen evacuated boys in her Beaconsfield Villas home and that she could not manage them. One of them, she said, brought a lit candle into a room intended to be empty during the blackout. She later told the *Daily Herald* how the expenses of keeping fifteen evacuees were beyond her means: 'To give them plenty of good food and comfortable beds I've practically sold my home up. Last week I sold £20 worth of furniture to buy bed linen.'[53] While describing some of her evacuees as 'fine kids', their play, including dancing and jumping on furniture, had destroyed the beds and several chairs. The reporter concluded the story by noting that the children broke a chair while he was visiting the household.

Yet, as sad as this story is, examination of source materials and studies shows that the evacuation stories that enjoyed wide circulation are disproportionate to, and unrepresentative of, the overall evacuation experience. Indeed, they were not representative of the experiences that reception hosts themselves relayed to researchers. Teachers' reflections in the Cambridge survey also challenge popular characterizations of evacuation. One teacher, for instance, offered: 'I recall with pride the good impression created by our youngsters, and I have been privileged to make many friends through them. Wherever I have been I have been received with kindness in the foster homes, and many have sought me out to say pleasant things about our children.'[54]

The cultural image of the verminous evacuee contained in evacuation rumours suggests the presence of a social concern associated with the image of respectable families being socially threatened by their infiltration with members of the lower-classes, or from what was called the problem family, the loss of property associated with the image of a good home, and a lack of control over physical integrity symbolized most starkly by the preoccupation with lice and skin diseases, as well as by general descriptions of bodily filth and fluids. Significantly, these latter characteristics all carry with them the potential for contagion.

Many rumours that spread widely told of householders who had to burn blankets and of villages in which remedies for lice became unavailable due to the heavy demand. In Stirling, the children evacuated from the supposed slums of Glasgow were said to have been sent straight to the billeting homes without any inspection by authorities, and people circulated a story about a little girl who supposedly arrived in such an extreme state that the hostess had to burn all the child's clothes, shave the girl's head and bathe her in disinfectant before she could be incorporated into the household. All of this was carried out only to have the child's family arrive and remove the girl a few days later, as her hair was shorn and she was dressed in clothing provided by the host.[55] It is unclear if the delousing of evacuees became a general practice as an effect of these kinds of stories, regardless of whether the presence of lice was confirmed. Apparently in Wigtown, '[w]ith the aid of many helpers (including three detachments of V.A.D.s) all heads were shorn. The thing was done without formality and without permission.'[56] But if the spread of lice was not enough to fear, a published letter to the editor of *The Spectator*, ostensibly penned by a billeting officer, reports that one of the evacuated children had both scabies and 'venereal disease'.[57] That child evacuees were supposed to have been carrying sexually transmitted infections that were assumed to pose a direct threat to reception families is curious. Associations of evacuees with lice, scabies and venereal disease present evacuees as the vectors of physical and social contagions that they brought to an otherwise presumably unaffected community. This anxiety figures into other alarmist evacuation stories that spread in the early months of the war. Stories concerning sexually transmitted infections articulate how the contamination that speakers feared was simultaneously physical and cultural.

Popular displacement stories painted a distorted picture of the encounters evacuation afforded, since perceptions of strangeness, dirtiness, impropriety and recklessness in these meetings between town and country moved in both directions. Not all evacuees accepted the image of the countryside as a paradise. The food came as an unpleasant surprise to some guests and contributed to misunderstandings between evacuees and hosts. While what appeared dirty or disgusting to hosts might not have appeared so for many of the evacuees, in an intriguing reversal, the evacuee looked upon many of the ways of the countryside residents with a cool response or even disgust. The many stories describing evacuated children and mothers who looked suspiciously upon fresh milk illustrate this well. Milk from a cow seemed dirty to town dwellers used to getting their milk from a bottle or a tin.[58] Hosts complained that 'Londoners don't appreciate Eggs and Butter. All they like is Fish & Chips and things out of tins. They don't like vegetables with the meat. One woman expected Beer with her supper.'[59] When women from Liverpool were evacuated to a Cheshire village, they were uncomfortable with the fresh milk and the food, and later tried to purchase cooked meat, which they could not acquire. Town dwellers largely remained distanced from aspects of food production, and so this new proximity was defamiliarizing and unsettling. When such stories were relayed, however, the reactions to fresh milk or fresh chicken were not coded in terms of the mutual differences arising out of social and infrastructural geographies from which these strange encounters derived. Rather, the mother who worried about her child's consumption of fresh milk was understood at best to be intellectually simple or at worst to be ungrateful. Likewise, a child might interpret a home cooked meal as a sign of an austere family budget. A child evacuated to Blackpool who was served hot meals every day for a week finally asked the host if they could not afford chips and thus appeared to be intentionally rude and hurtful. 'You could give them the moon,' the host insisted, 'and they wouldn't so much as thank you.'[60]

Mass Observation stressed that the mutual strangeness of town and country contributed to misunderstandings between guests and hosts. Even the social coding of clothing, Mass Observation noted, was influenced by social positioning such that '[t]he worker wears his old suit at work, his best suit at home; the clerk wears his best suit at the office, his old suit at home'. Therefore, the lack of appreciation for the ways in which 'habits and behaviour have formed themselves around a definite set of social conditions and economic needs'[61] could lead to mutual misinterpretation.

Even the landscapes of reception areas could seem alien or threatening. Mass Observation collected numerous comments that show signs of disorientation arising from the defamiliarizing re-locations brought about through evacuation. For instance, an evacuated teacher saw in the landscape only 'a few old farm houses, a number of bungalows, a spicing of council maisonettes dropped casually into a sea of mud'.[62] Some evacuated mothers expressed fears that their children would fall into rivers, be harmed by country animals or have trees fall upon them.[63] Observations about evacuated mothers bewildered by their new surroundings were common, as in this note: 'The Liverpool women had never seen fields before, and did not know what to do. They looked, as one of the village women described it, fish out water.'[64] These reactions also made their way into the newspapers. The 'Country Life' feature in *The Spectator* told of two expectant London mothers who mysteriously disappeared from their billeting home; it turned out that they had left and issued a complaint that ARP authorities had 'sent them to a place "where there were no streets"!'[65] But, again, as Mass Observation underlined, these experiences of estrangement were neither fully appreciated as *mutually* experienced, or as situated within respective social and material ecologies and 'the whole living pattern' of the communities concerned.[66]

The Cambridge Evacuation Survey asked children to write essays about what they missed while evacuated. The responses show that many felt that the reception area held its own threats of filth, traffic and nuisance. A boy, aged thirteen, complained, 'I miss the safety of London in leaving your bike about without having a post-mortem on it by Cambridge boys who fool about with your brakes and my dynamo has been mucked about with lots of times already.'[67] Another boy, fourteen years old, wrote, 'I miss the careful driving of the buses and cars in London, they are reckless and dangerous here. I have had accidents already in Cambridge which I didn't have in London.'[68] Several children characterized Cambridge traffic as more dangerous than London traffic, while they also reported missing the sounds of buses and lorries in the London streets. One child missed 'the thunder of the tube in the underground railway'.[69]

Responses also indicate that activities in Cambridge brought situations that some of the children defined as dirty, such as this fourteen-year-old boy who missed the enclosed swimming facilities of London, remarking, 'I do *not* like the dirty slimy rivers in which the people in Cambridge have to swim.'[70] In the essays, there are repeated references to the cold interior of the school building and the lack of parks designed for recreational activities. A teacher observed that while the children's overall health had improved, 'there has been more skin trouble than usual'.[71] Some parents also considered the conditions in which their children were staying to be dirty, as the survey report notes, 'When Margaret (girl, 14) came home at Christmas time, the mother found that she had not had a bath for three weeks. She found her clothing very dirty'.[72] Parents of another fourteen-year-old girl removed their daughter and brought her back home to the evacuated area because they deemed the household bathing routine and the social conditions at the foster home to be 'indecent', as their daughter was expected 'to wash in the kitchen with grown-up sons about, and share meals with garage hands'.[73]

Beyond the Cambridge context, we see further examples of evacuees' complaints about lack of cleanliness and propriety in reception homes. One woman described being placed in a household in which the hosts drank heavily and gave beatings to their own children. She reported that the room in which she, her children, another woman and her infant were set to sleep was in poor repair with a broken window and a loose door, where the baby got sick with whooping cough and the other child 'caught some kind of vermin in her hair and had to have it cut off'.[74] An evacuated mother, who had resolved to return to London, described her child as more dirty in the billet than at home and further expressed anxiety about her own state of cleanliness: 'I haven't really felt clean since I've been here [three weeks]. It's not like your own place, where you can wash any time you like.'[75] Another parent remarked, 'My boy is sharing a bed, single, with an improperly washed coalman.'[76] Mass Observation reported that a woman had visited the home in which her son was billeted because he had begged to be brought home. She found that there was no sugar or soap and it seemed that no washing had been done for her son, who reportedly had to steal apples, as the bread and tea he was given for both dinner and tea time forced him 'to struggle for existence'.[77] In a relatively superficial case, a lower middle class couple expressed concern that that their son was placed in a very large home that employed servants. They regretted that the boy will be under the supervision of servants, and not parents. Their complaint specifies that such a home lacks in family life and possibly a concern about the influence of servants upon the child.[78]

While there were many negative evacuation stories detailing dirty homes and practices told by evacuees and their families, these stories were also often coded in terms of class difference. A seventeen-year-old, middle-class evacuee, who was sent to an unnamed industrial town, was very conscious of the class situation. She noted, 'A good deal of publicity has been given to the hosts burdened with dirty, verminous evacuees, but none, or very little, to cases where well-brought up, middle-class girls and boys have been billeted in poor, dirty homes, where they have little to eat and none of the facilities they are used to.' She remarked further on the difficulties of adjustment for both evacuees and hosts due to their differences, but also complained that many evacuated girls were treated as unpaid housemaids rather than as part of the family. Most significantly, she expressed concern about the longer-term social effects of the meeting between these different worlds: 'Being billeted in such houses has a very bad effect on the younger girls of an impressionable age, and they grow slack in their care of their personal cleanliness and manners.' Hence, she suggested that evacuation posed a threat to 'well-brought up' children, in whom the habits of the hosts would be inculcated.[79]

Yet it would be incorrect to assume that only guests of higher-class standing were anxious about the possible transmission of habits and manners. Working-class families expressed concerns about the class differences and their potential impact on the formation of children. For instance, many shared anecdotes concern routine table manners and suggest that the table was an important site of social struggle in reception homes. In one reception home, the evacuated children were taught to sit up at the table through a game by which they were to avoid being called out for having their elbows on the table. In it, the children were said to have 'found a great subject of amusement as the house-holders were often "caught out" themselves'.[80] Interactions around table expectations were not always received so playfully. What seemed to be an obvious practice at one table would seem showy and arbitrary for another, as expressed in the following report to a mass observer: 'Two children from a very poor home were taken care of by very nice people who were teaching them to use table napkins and suchlike things that the children had never seen before ... The mother came to see them and complained that they were being brought up "narky" and that she wasn't going to have it.'[81]

Margaret Visser has argued that the standards of table etiquette by which people have been trained from childhood to observe 'are invisible to us most of the time, but which become more obvious when we hear how people behave who have different ideas, and expectations other than our own'. But she also noted that, while reaction to 'unmannerly' behaviour at the table may include 'disgust and revulsion, shock or laughter', people are amused and enjoy stories about others who appear not to know how to behave.[82] For her, this gulf between rules that are rarely considered or evaluated and the hapless breaches of them opens the potential to be reminded that these practices are contingent and could be different. Yet, in the context of evacuation, it seems that if these sometimes amusing and other times disgusting stories of guests who did not use utensils and tales of hosts who served meat derived from a freshly slaughtered animal had introduced the possibility that our manners and behaviours might have been altered in different conditions, this produced only a dampened sense of wonder, if it produced wonder at all. In the context of war's upheaval, under the spectre of air war, the fluidity of conduct posed a potential threat. As one woman from Eastbourne conveyed in a letter to her sister, many people in the reception area were worried that evacuees would soil their furniture and their carpets and teach their children bad language.[83] Acknowledging that if manners are not natural, then they must be subject to influence and thus there stands a risk of being contaminated by difference.

Perhaps the imagined threat runs deeper still. As Visser pointed out, at the table that host and guest share, there is danger:

> For this is the theme that underlies all table manners: we may be slicing and chewing; we may have killed or sacrificed to supply our feast; we may be attending to the most 'animal' of our needs; but we do so with control, order, and regularity, and with a clear understanding of who is who and what is what. We are neither beasts nor monsters with no manners, but men and women of culture. We do not treat people as though they were the swine or the oxen slaughtered for the feast: *we do not get the guests mixed up with the dishes*. For the point is that we so easily could. At table we are both armed and vulnerable; we are at such very close quarters. The laws of hospitality deal firstly with strangers—how to manage their entry into our inner sanctum, how to protect them from our own automatic reaction, which is to fear and exclude the unknown, how to prevent them from attacking and desecrating what we hold dear, or from otherwise behaving in a strange and unpredictably dangerous manner.[84]

Therefore, table manners navigate borders of identity, those that demarcate the eaters and the eaten, but they also distinguish between those who eat and those who do not, between those who are familiar and those who are not. In this realm of hospitality that the meal constitutes, the lines between care and security – the two stand as each other's limits – are always under negotiation and surveillance.

If the table was a complicated site that had to be shared, the lavatory could likewise bring anxiety about the eliding of borders. This is illustrated well by a story relayed to a mass observer about evacuees from Liverpool who were said to have had 'primitive' understandings of hygiene: 'The hosts have to share their bathrooms and lavatories with the evacuees, and my own doctor has told me that in seven houses in this district the hosts have contracted gonorrhea as a result of this'.[85] There are several things that are notable about the above rumour conveyed by a West Kirby resident. First, the story was not first-hand, and the speaker was not a host. Second, the tale ostensibly originated with an 'authority', but in this case, the authority was special because it was the speaker's own doctor. In most cases, evacuation stories made their appeal to the authority of 'I know someone who knows...'. In this case, perhaps because the claim that the families of seven reception homes had contracted gonorrhoea from their evacuee-contaminated lavatories is such a fantastic one, it demands a special kind of rhetorical reinforcement. Third, to the extent that this rumour claimed that there had been an actual physical manifestation of a presumed social ill that was thought to be derived from sexual promiscuity within the proper folks of the district by means of proximity and contact with a surface, it generates further concerns about physical contagion. Even more significantly, this rumour linked up with, and amplified, the anxieties about cultural contagion that were expressed in charges of ill-manners and destructiveness regularly attributed to evacuees, since it described the rampant emergence of presumed urban ills manifested in the very bodies of the community members for whom such ills were presumed to be previously absent and alien.

Stories such as these might have had some force in maintaining firm boundaries, both social and physical, between community members and guests. Only in some cases, however, is there is evidence of a concerted effort to abide by boundaries and avoid social communion between residents and guests. For instance, a resident from a Sussex village noted that there had been very little social interaction between evacuees and village people, describing the park as divided almost as though by an invisible line that kept local people on one side and the evacuees from Sydenham on the other.[86] In the case of refugees from abroad, many respondents to mass observer inquiries reported having very little to no interaction with them, even when there were a number of refugees present in their communities. For instance, as one Cricklewood resident shared with a mass observer regarding Belgian refugees living in the community in June 1940: 'I don't know what to think about them. There are plenty about. I've not really come into contact with them at all' and 'They keep to themselves, out of the way a lot.'[87]

As these stories and anecdotes show, concerns about boundaries and the potential for social contagion were held by hosts and guests alike, however, the concerns expressed by guests tended not to be reflected in circulated stories of evacuation. While evacuees did give account of their negative experiences of evacuation, these were not represented in the evacuation stories that were widely disseminated in letters to newspapers and so forth. John Welshman has observed that voluntary organizations tended to accept the stereotype of the evacuee, and 'the feckless mother and dirty child became stock characters in the popular novels of the time'.[88] Yet some of the criticisms that evacuees made of reception areas and homes were relayed in tales that reinforced the dominant narrative of evacuation and the interdependent cultural figures that it produced, those of the good citizen host and the dirty, ill-mannered and unruly evacuee. In these stories, criticisms that evacuees made, which seemed to undermine the significance of their hosts' routine gestures of care, only rendered proof of their ungratefulness. Insofar as this was the case, a key tension in evacuation stories is exemplified in the tension between the dutiful host and the ungrateful evacuee.

## The good citizen and the ingrate

A frequently used adjective to describe evacuees and their families was 'ungrateful'. While it was not used with the same frequency as dirty, verminous or ill-mannered, it was among the linguistic staples of popular evacuation stories. On an individual level, it makes sense that hosts felt the painful sting of what appeared to be signs of ungratefulness whenever a guest winched at the sight of a hot meal, broke or stained a beloved object, unleashed hurtful or foul language, or rejected outright an offering of hospitality by running away or being removed from the billet. Assessing evacuation with consideration of what it meant to the individual lives of those involved, the magnitude and generosity of the gifts of hospitality and care that were given with social sacrifice and, for some, economic hardship can hardly be denied. When, however, evacuation is studied as the policy initiative that it was, designed for the protection of the population (the response to a necessity I do not wish to reproach wholesale), the significance of the trope of the ungrateful evacuee presented in the dominant collective narrative of evacuation circulating in the autumn of 1939 takes a different intonation that I wish to explore in this section.

To begin, I'd like to provide some examples of the discursive construction of the ungrateful evacuee. Concerning adult evacuees, often second-hand tales were conveyed about lazy mothers evacuated with their infants. These mothers reportedly rested all day and went out at night while the host toiled around the clock, doing the cooking, cleaning and caregiving. For instance, a Mass Observation diarist recounted gossip concerning an evacuated mother who reassured her host, 'You needn't bother about me, I'm here for a week or two. I want a holiday.' The diarist also recorded a rumour concerning the difficulties of a host who owned an old lodging house to which five women with babies were assigned. When all five women were on their way out for the evening, the host asked them who would respond if the babies stirred, they told her that she ought to, as the government was paying her to do so.[89] In another case, the mother of an evacuated child was said to have sent a postcard from Brighton addressing her child, 'Am here on holiday, hope that you are alright'.[90] Such stories relied upon the implicit understanding between speaker and listener of the work and expense required of the reception host and seemed to weigh that against the presumed to be easy existence, or the inherent laziness, of the evacuee who took advantage of the host's hospitality, either by refusing to contribute to household tasks, caregiving and expenses or by complaining about the village.

Indeed, many adult evacuees had a difficult time adjusting to the change of pace and lack of amenities. A Mass Observation report noted that the lack of entertainments in some reception areas was a source of disgruntlement for adult evacuees. An investigator tasked with tracking evacuation rumours in September noted resentful comments from residents of Cirencester about evacuated schoolteachers who have hardly any students to manage, but 'seem to be living on the fat of the land' and 'only complaining of ennui'.[91] Unfavourable comments about unfamiliar features in the area perhaps contributed to the perception that guests were ungrateful. A bartender told a mass observer that one woman complained, 'What a hole this Henley is – the kids fall into the river,' although she also admitted that many kids had done just that.[92]

Hosts widely perceived their guests to have been sent improperly clothed and inadequately packed for their stay, and this perception provided another crucial source for the charge of ungratefulness towards hosts. Despite reports of ill-prepared evacuees, a schoolteacher from an economically depressed evacuated area reported that parents went to great lengths to pack for their children's departure, noting that, upon inspection of the luggage, only one family out of twenty did not have all the required items. Most of the families had spent considerable amounts to furnish their children with new and extra items, sometimes going beyond their means to do so.[93] The discrepancy in presumed preparedness underlined the vast differences in social standards of hosts and guests and the lack of awareness of these differences and their causes, which were often assumed to be moral in character.

The appearance of equitable distribution was often reached at considerable hardship for hosts, especially where clothing was concerned. It was commonly the case that the children were re-clothed in the reception area at the expense of the host family or by means of local voluntary organizations. Mass Observation researchers note that hosts' comments frequently conveyed the sentiment that the evacuees should not feel out of place, which implicitly expressed a desire to reduce the visible gaps between the respective social classes of hosts and guests.

Mass Observation researchers insisted that one of the major flaws in the evacuation plan was that it 'assumed social equality where none existed. Someone has to pay to help cover up the inequality.'[94] 'The result,' Titmuss noted, 'was an outburst of scrubbing, washing, mending and reclothing in the reception areas.'[95]

This work was carried out by many of Queen Mary's 'countrywomen', those for whom she expressed admiration for opening their homes to evacuees. The good citizen that evacuation stories – tales of household invasion and disorder that were most suited for wide circulation or mimicry – seemed to construct and, more rarely at the time critique, was indeed gendered. One of the posters issued to recruit host volunteers depicted a kindly, aproned woman emerging from a line of uniformed service personnel with her arms outstretched to receive an infant from the arms of its mother. It read, 'She's in the ranks too! Caring for evacuees is a national service.'[96] Viewers were thus promised that the duty performed by evacuation hosts would be viewed and valued alongside uniformed services in its critical contribution to the defence of the nation at a time when the home was granted a unique significance in the war effort.

Sonya Rose has shown that representations of the nation's unity in terms of a national family placed conflict at the core of wartime citizenship for women who were simultaneously called upon to shore up the home as a key site of civil defence and expected to extend into factory work, various forms of national service, agricultural work, voluntary work and so on. While working in factories, women were instructed to maintain feminine appearance by keeping their hair styled and their nails done, but their conduct or sexual morality was suspect when their war work brought them into spaces and contexts previously reserved for men. Of these tensions, Rose argued, 'By fulfilling their wartime obligations women put themselves in the position of being accused of bad citizenship. In World War II Britain women and men could enact good citizenship in numerous ways, but for women, sexuality and motherhood were fundamental.'[97] According to Rose, one occupation that seemed to mediate these tensions well was that of the nurse, who 'symbolically epitomized the qualities that all women should emulate in performing their patriotic duty – they were quintessentially both caring and heroic.'[98] While the evacuation host cared for evacuees emotionally and materially, and therefore simultaneously played a key role in implementing a central ARP and military strategy, she embodied femininity while doing so. Unlike the nurse who might do field service and be sent into dangerous and far places, however, her movements were in many cases impeded by her service. In some cases, depending upon the assignment of evacuees, her location and the supports she had around her and at home, the host's engagement with public

**Figure 2.1** She's in the ranks too, Poster issued by the Central Office of Information.

spaces and other activities could be far more restricted than it was for many other women, whose opportunities to move into new spheres grew significantly during the war.

Evacuation stories did not give their audiences a filled-out character sketch of the host. By virtue of the criticisms that they made of evacuees, such tales painted only the contours of what the host as good citizen who gave her service potentially day and night indefinitely might be, but this was a negative image defined against what a feckless woman did or did not do. The host was presented as stoic. She was not usually the one who told her story and made her complaints, others shared her tales second-hand. In representations, she generally did what needed to be done and that was all, but perhaps in frustration she may have been cold at times; who could blame her? The feckless woman, however, was given more shading even in the stories that offered one-dimensional and reproachful images. At times, she was the mother who stayed back when her children were evacuated and she might have been accused of not socializing her children and not washing them enough, and not packing well for them. More frequently, she was the evacuated mother who did not fit in, who complained about the food and the village, whose sexuality was anticipated as a threat, or the one who returned home with or without her children. The host and the feckless mother, I suggest, represent in different ways successes and failures in mirroring the image of the good citizen for women in the wartime home. Therefore, evacuation stories and their dissemination engaged women's wartime citizenship in the home by negotiating two strands of the good feminine citizen that Rose identifies that emphasized a woman's capacities for motherhood as a civic virtue and the integrity of her sexual morality. At a time when, as Rose recounts, attention focused much apprehension on the social conduct of girls and young women, as well as on 'married women who "find time to go to public houses with other men"', the figure of the feckless mother could operate as an instructional representation of the woman in wartime whose welfare was dependent upon the care provided by proper women. Rose noted the long-standing concern and belief held by members of the middle classes who judged working-class women as inadequate mothers and further cast them as a threat to society.[99] Rather than assuming her duty to the nation and to her children, then, the figure of the feckless mother represented women who shirked their domestic, hence civic, duties and exemplified poor citizenship. In the following section, I will examine this figure more closely and in the context of the sub-theme of the fall from Eden that stories that concerned the return of evacuees mobilized.

## Feckless Eve

As noted, the September 1939 evacuation saw an immediate return of persons who had been moved under the government scheme, a problem that became so acute that, down the road, officials considered prosecuting parents who failed to return their children to reception areas.[100] The thirty-five miles that an eleven-year-old runaway travelled from his reception billet in Eastbourne towards his home in Deptford illustrate the intensity of desire that some evacuees had to return home. Police officers found the exhausted boy and sent him back aboard a train. Not to be deterred, the tenacious evacuee ran away again the following day and finally reached his home.[101] When *The Star* gave the title 'Odyssey' to the article reporting this child's trek, it captured more than the astonishing difficulty of the child's journey. By drawing reference to Homer's epic poem, it implicitly and aptly invoked one of its central themes – the relation between guest and host and the paradoxes of hospitality. But the spectre of the troubled, mutually parasitic relation of hospitality was not to be the main motif invoked in stories of the return of evacuees from reception areas. The most crystallized image was that of the fall from the garden of Eden, which was, as the narrative goes, precipitated by Eve's susceptibility to temptation and her cunning ability to persuade Adam to follow her and share in her banishment.

When seven London children ran away from their foster homes, it was reported that the children planned their escape together, although they dispersed along the way, with four boys breaking from the group to catch a ride with a lorry driver, who dropped them off near a friend's home in Hounslow. Two girls, however, walked all the way home from Burchetts Green while encouraging the one girl's eight-year-old sibling to walk along. They urged him with the promise that his name would make it into the papers if they reached their destination.[102] When necessary, the two girls reportedly took turns carrying the younger boy. The narrative offered in the *News Chronicle* describes the eldest girls as the 'advance guard', and one of the girls as having taunted and tempted the older boys when she announced her plans to run away, suggesting that they did not have enough 'pluck to do the same'. The boys ran away, the article suggested, only because they were 'stung by the feminine taunts'.[103] Shortly after their return, the seven children were sent back to the safe reception area, which promised a follow-up inquiry. 'I don't think it will happen again,' the mother of the two siblings told a reporter, 'because really they seemed quite happy in the country.'[104] If perhaps this narrative construction of an older girl's 'feminine' cunning that tempted six others to embark on a thirty-mile journey, thus leaving the safety

**Figure 2.2** Don't do it, Mother, Poster issued by the Central Office of Information.

and happiness of the countryside, too subtly resembles the story of the fall, the Ministry of Health drew a much more explicit narrative connection between countryside reception areas and the garden of Eden in its instructional poster 'Don't do it, Mother'.

Initially evacuated in anticipation of aerial bombings that did not occur until the spring of 1940, many returned to the cities. A significant number did so within days of their initial arrival. Although many children took matters into their own hands and ran away from foster homes, it was usually evacuated mothers, or parents who had remained behind at home, who precipitated the return. Forty-four per cent of children and eighty-seven per cent of mothers had returned home by February 1940.[105] For ministries concerned with evacuation and ARP generally, this flow of women and children back to high-risk zones presented new challenges. Though the expected air raids had not occurred, it remained imperative to be prepared for them, since 'the whole scheme would have to be put over again if air danger became serious'.[106] Further, with only a few exceptions, schools in evacuated areas were closed. Many of the school buildings had been requisitioned for military and civil operations and, since the students and teaching staff had been evacuated, the buildings not in use were without the necessary air raid shelters. For these reasons, education advocates were deeply concerned. Lady Simon, who at the start of 1940 brought attention to 'the collapse of compulsory education', noted that there were at best only patchy initiatives for children who never left or who returned to evacuation areas and were let to 'run wild' in evacuation zones.[107]

The Ministry of Health attempted to curb the premature return of evacuees by issuing the poster 'Don't do it, Mother', which depicted an Eden-like scene in the foreground and London with war ships flying overhead in the distant background. The image denotes a young mother evacuee with her two happy children in the countryside. The three are seated on lush grass in front of a mature tree. The two boys seated by their mother are well-dressed. One is contemplative as he examines a toy plane, perhaps scaling it up in his imagination. If he were inside the plane swooping over the countryside, would he go back? The other boy, playfully on all fours, leans in to look at the toy plane. A most serene setting it would be if not for a ghostly apparition behind the mother's shoulder. The spectre is indeed that of Hitler himself, as though he had come from around the tree to hover behind the woman. He is leaning in to tap her on the shoulder as he whispers into the young mother's ear: 'Take them back! Take them back! Take them back!...' He points to the city on the other side of the water, a dark cityscape marked with St Paul's Cathedral and Big Ben. Mother has dropped her knitting into her lap, her left hand, which dons a wedding band, is raised to the corner of her mouth. Although she has not turned her head towards the whispering figure, she looks to her left as she contemplates the tempting message. Connotatively, the scene depicted on the poster 'Don't do it, Mother' drew the direct connection between Hitler and the serpent of the book of Genesis, who whispered the instructions to Eve that led to her family's expulsion from Eden into the harsh world outside of paradise. By extension, London is the place to which all who fall from paradise are doomed in exile.

In discourses surrounding the welfare of working-class children, the countryside as a redemptive paradise was often set against the dangers of the industrial town, widely considered a source site of degeneracy. This polarization of redemptive countryside and degenerate city motivated many schemes to bring working-class children out to the countryside. David Pomfret explained that, in the interwar years, 'the real target' of such extrication schemes 'was not the city as a whole, but the "slum" areas and working-class homes within them'. In the decade before the war, 'the discursive construct of "the city" was used as shorthand for' the care that working-class families provided for their children, which was thought to be characterized by poor feeding and lack of hygiene.[108] Taking children away from the city also meant taking them away from the perceived dangers of their homes and even their families.

The image on the poster is frozen in the mother's contemplation. Will she engage the call to duty by embracing good citizenship and staying put with her children in the reception area? Or, will she be swayed by whispers that tempt her return to the town? In what follows, I take a contrasting figure from a story that Mass Observation collected, the kind-hearted warden's wife, as exemplifying the good citizenship that women were called upon to perform as civic duty in the wartime home, while emphasizing that this good citizenship was inherently racializing in its practice.

## The kind warden's wife

While evacuation stories shared striking similarities, I would like to distinguish momentarily between the stories that were animated by amusement, wonder, or even affection at the differences that they underlined between guests and hosts and those that were animated by explicit disgust and sharp disapproval. Drawing such a distinction does not suggest that the former was accepting and the latter was negatively judgemental. Both tones make negative judgements, produce the differences that they animate as socially meaningful and are mobilizations of relative dominance over their subjects. But I want to bring attention to the affection inherent to the former tone. Although those of the former type are more subtle than those that are explicitly motivated by disgust, they highlight some of the nuances of evacuation stories. The rumours of interest here are those that appear to be exchanged to evoke amusement, surprise or comedic appeal for their recipients.

One example of an ostensibly amusing evacuation rumour is the story of the evacuated woman who was said to have boiled an egg for half of an hour before complaining to the host that it would not go soft. Another amusing story relays that an evacuated boy taken on a walk looked up and remarked, 'Eh, Mister, what a lot of blue sky you have up here.'[109] Many anecdotes of this kind were published at the end of the first week of evacuation in the 8 September 1939 edition of the *Northampton Independent*. The feature was titled 'The Lighter Side of Evacuation: Scores of Amazing and Amusing Incidents' and included the tale of a young evacuee, described as an 'urchin' who was excited that he had seen a 'cah', by which the adults thought he meant 'car' when he meant 'cow'. The immense surprise and novelty for the boy in seeing a cow, an animal he had only heard about but had never seen, was not really the emphasis of the story; rather his inability to articulate what he meant through proper pronunciation was the first punchline of the story. Yet this impression was deepened, as the letter went on to describe the boy becoming enchanted with another creature, which he had to be told was a frog. The boy had then asked if the frog could be brought to bed with him.[110] Here, the amusement originated in the lack of knowledge that was implicitly attributed to the boy and in the absurdity of the boy's lack of proper sense of what could be brought into the house and what kind of creature served as an appropriate bedmate. It was amusing that the boy could not recognize local animals, had difficulty pronouncing words so that they would be understood in the local dialect and finally had no appreciation of what kinds of creatures consisted the proper field of the home. The story assumed an insider-only audience insofar as it could only evoke amusement and wonder for those listeners who shared the same norms.

Taking this public interest piece with all of its tales as a whole hints that 'The Lighter Side of Evacuation' aimed to regulate its readers' emotions and to motivate them as good citizens. For instance, a child's thirty-mile trek back to a high-risk area was attributed in the article to evacuees' feelings of homesickness. Homesickness was presented as an emotion that was, while understandable, ultimately detrimental to the war effort and an emotion that evacuated children and mothers needed to overcome. In describing the reception of 39,000 evacuees to Northamptonshire, the article observed the generosity of residents' sympathy for 'the inner feelings of these little children and others being ruthlessly torn from their homes through the unknown contingencies of war; torn from their cherished belongings, their parents and relatives', and yet it praised children who 'showed a brave exterior and declined to succumb to the emotional pang of homesickness'.[111]

Yet the same piece shaded into the opinion-editorial that underlined its playful storytelling. It noted in passing that the incidents of missing fruit from gardens coincided with the arrival of guests, it relayed an anecdote about children flooding a second-story bathtub as they played with toy ships and told of an evacuated mother who refused to help with the cleaning. These anecdotes prefaced its call for hosts and evacuees to aim for mutual cooperation. Just as it was the duty of the host to mind the comforts of the evacuee, it was 'the duty of the visitor to see that the general system of the household is not disturbed'. The majority of visitors were observed to be 'as grateful as they are considerate', and it was noted that they 'unconsciously have done their bit in keeping the town lighthearted and amused'.[112] This amusement, however, found its source in the humour provided by the townspeople's ignorance of the environment's unfamiliarity, relating, for instance, that some slum children had never before seen a vegetable garden and thus believed that potatoes grew on trees. Or, there was the child the who saw a lark and reportedly exclaimed, 'Oo! Look at that bird a-'ollerin' because it can't get back in its cage.'

Thus, affectionate evacuation stories implicitly supported the normative force of stories motivated by explicit disgust and repudiation. This is illustrated by the story of a kind warden's wife that a mass observer collected. It was recorded in a list of circulating stories in the following way:

> The little coloured child that no one wanted, and billet after billet refused. At last the kindhearted wife of the local warden, though her house was filled to overflowing said that they couldn't bear to see such stupidity and took in the child. When she undressed the little dark baby she found a piece of paper pinned to the child's underclothes. In the paper was a fifty pound note, and on it was written 'To the kind woman who undresses my child tonight'. The money was banked the next day in the child's name and the child stayed in this house.[113]

This story feels warm on the surface though it delivers a moral and presents the warden's wife as an exemplary model of the good British wartime subject. While it is about placing civic duty above all else, the racialization of the child underlines this by imposing an implicit comparison between this evacuee and that evacuee, assuming racialized prejudice as a baseline stance. While the story commends the host for accepting the child, it is most certainly not an anti-racist story. The goodness of the warden's wife is demonstrated not just in her willingness to take in yet another evacuee, despite the overcrowding in her home. The goodness and kind-heartedness of the woman (known only relationally via her husband's post) reside precisely in the information that 'no one wanted' the child, a presumed reality that the story reinforced by having the mother anticipate that only the most generous woman would accept the child; thus, she acknowledged this by bundling the money and note in the child's clothing.

In reception of this tale, the warden's wife's refusal to keep the fifty-pound note would operate as a further sign of the woman's goodness depending upon whether the listener interpreted the money as a payment or as a gift. If payment was refused for caring for the child, this could be read as the act of a good British citizen supporting the war effort without the expectation of compensation. Such a representation would have perhaps responded to widespread complaints from hosts that billeting allowances were inadequate. If, however, the money was interpreted as a gift, its refusal could be understood as an appropriate act that maintained boundaries between the residents who demonstrated their patriotism in their offer of dutiful care and the evacuee who ought to demonstrate enduring gratefulness that will never be equivalent. In any case, the most forceful expression of goodness within this story seems to be illustrated by the host's willingness to take in this particular evacuee, despite racialized difference. Indeed, the assumption of shared racism is what promised this tale as an effective evacuation story that approximated a fable insofar as it ostensibly aimed to correct behaviours and confront resistances to accepting evacuees.

Yet the story of the kind warden's wife may have responded to another circulating story that the same investigator collected in the same area. This story was of the explicitly negative type but it approximated the genre of cautionary tale. It described a family who had generously agreed to take in five girls. After they had agreed, they were told that it was in fact five boys. They were then reluctant (girls appear to have been preferred to boys, excepting those who might be sought as farmhands), but agreed nevertheless. When they arrived to pick up the children, five Black boys were waiting for them.[114] The racialized revelation is the final line of the tale. Although the latter story was overtly racist, the former one derived its instructive force from an implicitly assumed implicit racism shared between storyteller and listener.

A letter submitted to the *Picture Post* without a return address gave a very stark but characteristically second-hand story that was at least in part meant to scold the editors of the publication for their diplomatic treatment of evacuation. The letter was printed in the 28 October 1939 issue with the title 'Butcher Boys of Birmingham'. It read:

> I'm sick of you and your sweet little refugees. Perhaps this story will make you sit up. Some friends of ours had seven lousy little Birmingham brats parked on them. These friends were farmers and kept poultry. Going into a coup where turkeys were kept, they found the little brats had cut the heads off 13 turkeys for fun! This story is perfectly true. I'd rather have a savage from Fiji than a child from Birmingham.[115]

This sensational and racist anti-evacuee letter provoked a pithy editorial response that called into question the veracity of its content: 'It won't make us – or anyone else – sit up unless we believe it. Come forward with your own address and details. If true we'll print them, if not we'll forward you the savage from Fiji'. Unfortunately, the racist discourse of the savage other, the Fijian other, if not the Birmingham other, in the original letter was reinforced in the editorial response that attempted to suture the break that the discourse of different and dangerous evacuees sought to make within the unified national identity as it was imagined in exhortations to come together during wartime.

## Conclusion

Evacuation stories that arose amidst the initial evacuation process at the beginning of September 1939 described British children evacuated from industrial towns often in disparaging terms. This stood in sharp contrast to the stories and representations that depicted Basque children evacuated from the conflict in Spain to Southampton in the spring of 1937. Kevin Myers's study of media representations of these children showed that coverage aimed to encourage humanitarian funds to house and care for them by activating discourses of childhood and nationhood that could bolster fundraising campaigns, while simultaneously distancing the children from the politics of the Spanish civil conflict. Myers showed that, while representations of Basque child evacuees presumed them to be bereft of any personal political commitments and thus distanced them from the political conflict, despite their ranging up to fifteen years old, such representations routinely coupled the children with Catholicism.

In Britain, their presumed faith would be, according to Archbishop Hinsley, 'safeguarded'.[116] Myers found that children were both described and photographed as passive; they were but 'poor little waifs from a stricken land', depicted being washed and clothed.[117]

Myers argued that the early representations of the children's arrival were simplistic in their presentation of the children as homogenous and apolitical. While this oversimplified presentation, which delinked the refugees from association with revolutionary politics, may have been critical to the initial success of the humanitarian aid campaigns, it also may have been one of the contributing factors to the swift decline in what was at first an enthusiastic outpouring of financial support that had been 'widely seen as a civic duty' and tied to conceptions of the nation and Britishness.[118] In practice, the children could not fit into the static and shallow mould that media representations had cast for them. Myers noted, for instance, that parishioners who had committed themselves to the care of several refugees were dismayed to find that only a tiny minority of the children were indeed Catholic. Refugees' political expressions were also not well received in some cases, and they certainly clashed with the repetitive and popular image that portrayed them as bewildered and standing outside of the political landscape of the civil war from which they had been immersed prior to their evacuation. According to Myers, '[t]he politically informed and relatively independent children who were dispersed throughout Britain were a shock for many people who had previously seen and read about pitiful and innocent victims'.[119] For him, the palpable disconnect between representations of passive refugees and the presence of real, live politically conscious ones is just one indication of why the diversely and individually sourced funds to support humanitarian efforts for Spanish refugees dropped off and gave way to the more stable and consistent financial contributions made by a range of collective, politically conscious organizations, from Communists to Quakers, who supported the children's stay into 1939.

There are several plausible explanations for the tonal differences between initial representations of Basque refugees and internal British evacuees. One possibility may reside in the different experiences and meanings of voluntary service in the respective cases. Indeed, giving money and limited portions of time is not equivalent to housing indefinitely; although some certainly did billet Basque children, the scale and context are not comparable. While billeting was technically voluntary under the British evacuation scheme, for many reasons, it was not evenly experienced as such. For many, their participation was compelled.

Another plausible explanation for the unfavourable view of British evacuees resides in the discourse of civic responsibility on the home front. To what extent were British evacuees, many of whom were still viewed as the undeserving poor, seen as inherently dependent and lacking in their capacity to fulfil the wartime duty to the nation? Children were not necessarily exempt from this expectation. One of the arguments raised in opposition to evacuation addressed this point precisely: 'How can we with any consistency continue to speak of training in citizenship and in leadership while at the same time we arrange for them against their will to leave the post of danger? I believe it is our duty to encourage those for whom we are responsible to stand fast and carry on.'[120] Additionally, a public information leaflet issued by the Lord Privy Seal's Office anticipated the critique that evacuation meant shirking duty: 'Everyone will realise that there can be no question of wholesale clearance. We are not going to win a war by running away. Most of us will have work to do, and work that matters, because we must maintain the nation's life and the production of munitions and other material essential to our war effort.' Unfortunately, it simultaneously reinforced the false sense that evacuees would not have work to do that mattered. The stated purpose of evacuation was to remove those 'whose presence cannot be of any assistance.'[121]

Notwithstanding these possible explanations, the point I'd like to underline is that what both complicated situations shared was the tension between social and political identity on the one hand and merely fleshy, passive existence on the other. Like the Basque children, whose mainstream individual support faded and withdrew when they became known to have potentially disagreeable political allegiances or when they rejected the faith of their supporters, British children, who carried the markers of class difference or whose cultural preferences raised the spectre of existing fears of civilizational decline that ran through interwar preoccupations with the differential birth rate in Britain, could no longer be seen as malleable children unmarked by politics and culture. Thus, the children who needed to be housed brought with them preferences, habits, beliefs, affiliations and commitments whose proximity and touch could be in some circumstances perceived as internal threats against which mechanisms of categorization and separation could be utilized to inoculate the family and community, sometimes imagined as one and the same. In the closing chapter, I will touch upon, for instance, the significance of the so-called 'problem family' and what the well-known *Our Towns* report called the unredeemable 'black family' to this process and understanding of negative evacuation stories. Categorization and separation, the forging of definitional breaks in the biological population, constitute the first step in the state racialization process that Foucault defined as key to modern power's deliberation over life worthy of saving (merely, or with investment) in its efforts to enhance life at the abstract levels of the population, nation, species, or civilization. Foucault drew a distinction between modern racism and historical or 'ethnic racism'. Foucault underlined that modern racism involved the active scanning for those who could be perceived to be

> carriers of a condition, a stigmata, or any defect whatsoever, [who] may more or less randomly transmit to their heirs the unpredictable consequences of the evil, or rather of the non-normal, that they carry within them. It is a racism, therefore, whose function is not so much the prejudice or defense of one group against another as the detection of all those within a group who may be the carriers of a danger to it.[122]

There is a eugenic impulse in modern racism. The breaks that it imposes between kinds of life, whether between the strong and the weak or the normal and the abnormal, decide upon which lives will be fostered and which will be deprived for the sake of strengthening the whole.

If evacuation was premised upon a logic of care that was oriented towards the security of the population, the anxieties about physical and cultural contagion expressed in evacuation stories illustrate how care can be mobilized and weaponized through biopolitical logics for which the equilibrium of the population's norms of birth, death, health and happiness is paramount. But since biopolitical governance is concerned with individuals only insofar as they function as parts that optimize the functioning and enhance the capacities of the population as an organic whole, the care afforded to concrete lives may be at times indifferent to their specificities, their circumstances, all the many ways they escape the paper plans that Mass Observation critiqued for having 'little regard for social consequences'[123] and treating 'citizens as mathematical units, all alike'.[124] As noted in the introduction to this volume, biopolitical logic and humanitarian reason work together in activating 'differentiated meanings and values of human life'[125] that categorize lives in terms of their assumed value and capacity to strengthen the whole. Evacuation was a civil defence operation that assigned deliberations about the meaning and value of the lives it cared for to private homes, albeit with some mediation from schoolteachers, voluntary agencies and billeting officers. Civil defence indirectly made the home and civilian neighbourhoods discretionary sites in which informal asylum for vulnerable social subjects, whether human or not, would be deliberated, insofar as routines of caregiving became more explicitly tied with the abstract and contradictory duties of wartime citizenship.

Even if, as Rose remarked, the presumed 'unified national community' to be protected 'was imagined to be a family',[126] and even if the deliberation of informal asylum for vulnerable social subjects expelled from high-risk zones was indeed assigned more or less to the private domestic homes and their familial relations, this does not mean that evacuation rid itself of the biopolitical logics of governmentality and its mechanism of state racism once evacuees were housed. For Foucault insisted that governmentality is not simply the activity or aim of the state and its official institutions and bodies, rather it finds its outlet and its justification in a wide range of relations and activities that stretch well beyond the administration of institutional regulatory mechanisms via the domains of health, education, religion, social welfare, voluntary works, political organization and humanitarian efforts. Governmentality intrudes into, and is already embedded within, the intimacies of everyday lives, routines in the home, child rearing, the emotional and physical labours of all dear relationships, household management, friendship, romance and cooperation within the community. Caregiving and love go hand-in-hand with forms of correction, regulation and so forth. Sometimes, care and love choose their targets. But the ones selected for care might also be the ones who are in some cases deprived, as a care can be either an object of devotion or a troublesome burden. Thus, care can also deliver a kind of profound deprivation. Care can be a weapon. Foucault had defined state racism as the mechanism by which modern reason, focused on the amplification and expansion of life and vitality, could 'kill' indirectly, even if by slow neglect, separation or withholding. Many of these stories of displacement, particularly those populated by recurring character types and tropes, negotiated categories of good and bad citizenship and reinforced anxieties about the relationship between poor genetic inheritance, hygiene, morality and civility. Thus, via these boundaries, they informed modes of care that were consistent with biopolitical concerns that placed the life and longevity of abstractions – civilization, the population, the nation, the race or the national effort – above that of real, breathing, feeling social subjects and their bonds.

Consideration of these evacuation narratives has above all relied upon their documentation carried out by Mass Observation. I have argued that evacuation stories helped to sketch provisional images of the responsible wartime subject, even though these were contested within and beyond such communications. Even if some stories had greater purchase and enjoyed wider circulation than others, mass observers, who embedded themselves in reception areas, blitzed towns, routes away from bombing and public shelters, gave a much more textured picture of both the vast range of experiences of evacuation and the ways in which the stories communicated a range of concerns. I have been interested specifically in how those concerns implicitly surrounded questions of citizenship, population security and the evaluation of worthy life in the Second World War. The Mass Observation movement's tracking of evacuation stories in the first place fulfilled their promise to make a 'live survey' of the war, but it succeeded in more than this. As a directive issued to their national panellists in the autumn of 1939 insisted, 'The full story will have to wait till the war is over. But there is no need for our lips to remain completely sealed.' Mass Observation stressed a two-fold function that it aimed to fulfil under the changing conditions that the war brought: First, 'sorting out the fact which will help to find a human, non-bureaucratic solution for problems of civilian morale'. Second, Mass Observation would

> aim to bring through the war a full record of its impact on civilian life and mentality. The inadequacy of press-cutting from a censored Press to form such a record would hardly need stressing, if social scientists had not been already heard publicly affirming their faith in this method. M-O prefers to rely on the day-by-day record by its observers of their reactions, experiences and overheard comment.[127]

In attempting to realize these aims, the directive prompted participants to note and collect circulars, jokes, wartime stories, graffiti, slogans and rumours. In these and other ways, Mass Observation captured the fine textures of wartime communications, as well as their changes. The dedicated documentation that the movement provided demonstrates that evacuation stories were not static, and changing configurations accompanied changing circumstances.

The severe bombing of the East End on Saturday, 7 September 1940 prompted a spontaneous evacuation from London on 'an unprecedented scale'. In *The New Statesman and Nation*, Harrisson brought attention to the resulting confusions and shortcomings of provisions available to respond to the crisis, framing the problem in the following way:

> By Monday many had wisely left the dockland area, carrying what they could, often having no idea where they were going. Some, drifting vaguely 'West,' formed into bands which grew steadily as they trudged through the city, and ended up in whole train-loads bound for 'anywhere.' Many slept in Greenwich Park, on Hampstead Heath ... Thus a mass migration spread out, swamping the countryside, so that even by mid-September it was difficult indeed to get a bed for the night anywhere within sixty miles of London.[128]

By examining their internal notes, we can find observers spreading outward via several different routes out of London in the autumn of 1940, stopping in various locations along the way to track the routes of refugees fleeing bombing, their demographics, mutual feelings between residents and refugees and the effectiveness of official strategies to address these changing conditions.

As a result, we know that some tensions appear to have softened with the commencement of air raids and heavy bombing so that there grew more sympathy towards evacuees and stronger expressions of gratitude from them into autumn of 1940.[129] In Salisbury, residents expressed sympathy towards evacuees, 'when we're fighting for life and death, no sacrifice can be too great'. In Andover, 'These Londoners are thankful for anything, you know, and of course the people do what they can. It's the soldiers that create the trouble'; the man only winked when the observer tried to get him to elaborate upon the soldiers.[130] As one observer put it, 'The village reaction is far more accommodating now they really feel the evacuees 'have been through it', and there is a general wish to do what one can to help – in a practical way, this time, as opposed to the rather mock-heroic, running-in-circles manner of the early days of the war'.[131]

Mass Observation was well-situated to document intimate communications that provided access to expressions of anxiety about biological and cultural contagion that characterized early evacuation stories, prompting Harrisson to warn that, in some places, 'a history of trivial tension and gradual drift looks uncommonly like repeating itself'.[132] Mass Observation work showed that discussion about evacuees then placed more negative attention on the presumed cleanliness and dispositions of air raid refugees and particularly targeted adult British Jewish evacuees. To elaborate, I follow briefly Celia Fremlin's field notes from her stay at a rest centre in Beaconsfield in October 1940.

Fremlin selected the rest centre at the Old Rectory based upon observations made from her discussions with evacuees in the area; her impression was that it was the least liked centre. When presenting herself at the centre, she admitted that she was not in fact an evacuee but that she was stranded and asked if she might be able to stay the night. The helper working at the centre agreed but insisted that she ought not spread this around. Quickly, Fremlin was taken into the confidence of the helper, who openly expressed disdain for the evacuees and gossiped about people currently sheltering there. For instance, after cheerfully bidding a woman good night, she turned to Fremlin and shared, '"That's a very difficult family" (nodding head in direction of door) "The most difficult we've had"'. Her chief criticism seemed to be the size of the family, with nine children. She said she thinks this is terrible. Regarding the same family, the helper went on to say,

> You can't grudge it to the poor things, of course; but do you know, I brought in a loaf this morning, and by this evening they had eaten the whole of it! And they've

had two tins of corned beef; and then the milk; look (shows pint bottle with half an inch or so at the bottom). That won't be enough for their breakfast; I suppose I'd better get them a quart tomorrow (sighs); They're a very difficult family ... I know they do what they can, poor things; she always tidies up and sweeps after their meals; but it's very difficult.[133]

Conversations with the inhabitants of the shelter, however, demonstrated that they were very aware of what the helper thought and said about them behind their backs. They described her as mean, stuck-up and stingy.

The rest centre helper openly expressed antisemitic views, yet frequently projected her racism onto others, attempting to distance herself from her expressions and judgements, 'I don't say anything against them myself, but they're so different from us – trousers and lipstick and head in a scarf – we aren't used to that sort of thing,' the helper explained. Similar expressions were echoed in indirects with the townspeople, some of whom admitted to holding antisemitic views. All seemed to understand that this was wrong and many considered themselves to be exempt from it, while simultaneously expressing it.

As in other places along the routes of flight from London's raids, many evacuees wandered the village by day, spending much time on park benches alone or with babies, as the rest centre and many other forms of accommodation turned people out first thing in the morning until 6 o'clock or so. A middle-aged woman sat alone on a bench and shivered. She asked a mass observer if it was half past six yet, but it was not. 'Oh, I'm so cold,' she said. She could not go back to her billet until 6:30.[134] The observer came across another daytime bench dweller and asked if his home had been bombed. This sparked a rambling reply that she recorded as follows:

Not a stone of it left, not a stone. I'd go back though – I'd go back and live there. Forty-six years I've been there – forty-six, not forty – It was a good business once ... (Rambles on about business – Inv [investigator] cannot hear much of what he says: 'Fifty waiters I had under me' And suchlike snatches are all she can follow).[135]

An observer stayed at a rest centre in Windsor and saw much the same as what was described in Beaconsfield, though tensions were not expressed in hushed side whispers in Windsor. There was incessant quarrelling between helpers and refugees. At breakfast, the helper suggested that it was not necessary that a baby should get an egg, which sparked the following very frustrated response:

blimey, if you was a baby you might think about wanting eggs or not, you might. Christ almighty, what is this? The desert or something. Is it necessary? My blessed life, I'd like to see you go without your daily egg, that I would. I'd like to push the shells down your arse, I would, the bleeding source of it all.

The observer summarized the general impression of the situation at the rest centre as follows: 'Inv amazed at low standard of life which existed in the rest centre. The people were completely demoralised … Women didn't care how they looked, what they said, what they did. There was incessant quarreling and marked racial hatred.'[136]

Returning to the functions that Mass Observation had identified for its wartime role, the emphasis was on finding the facts through multiple forms of documentation but also finding 'a human, non-bureaucratic solution for problems of civilian morale'.[137] Although *War Begins at Home* states that for the time being 'we unashamedly continue to document and describe rather than to conclude or recommend',[138] Mass Observation actively intervened by interpreting their day-to-day recordings of the war and its trials, bringing attention to intimate struggles, intonating a less-bureaucratic approach to ongoing problems and making recommendations when possible. One example of this concerning the difficulty for grieving and homeless civilians was discussed in the introduction to this volume. Though not all Mass Observation's work led to the outcomes it desired. For instance, Nina Masel's report on people's concerns about surface shelters provoked the Ministry to promote their supposed safety rather than providing the necessary deep shelters.[139]

In the case of Mass Observation's tracking of the flight paths out of London, we can find Harrisson drawing upon the investigators' field notes on the pages of the *New Statesman and Nation* when he described the 'inferior rest centres and plenty of unsympathetic touches' in reception areas. He conceded,

> There was real sympathy on the part of the country people, who felt that the cities had been through it, while the evacuees were more ready to make the best of things because this time they were glad to get away. The exaggerated stories of filthy evacuee behaviour, which did much to undermine the first scheme, were now conspicuous mainly by their absence.

But he gave the warning that 'the first flush of sympathy from hosts, relief from guests does not last indefinitely'.[140] There was much that needed to be understood and needed to be done. The failures of official plans, Harrisson insisted, were defined by the limits of planners' knowledge of what life was like on the ground and their bureaucratic exercise of care, 'If the Minister of Health had regarded this, the most rapid and terrific social arrangement in history, as a problem of human beings with prejudices and preferences and pride instead of human units with gas masks and identity labels, the story could have been very different.'[141]

3

# Lazy Dogs

While the number of animal companions destroyed at the beginning of the Second World War have only been estimated, anticipations of dwindling and uneven food supplies, evacuations and generalized anxieties about the care of animals in the context of the threat of air raids on civilian populations appear to have played their parts in prompting a sharp rise in the destruction of animal companions at war's commencement, as well as officials' concerns about how to deal with their corpses. Hilda Kean noted that 400,000 London dogs and cats were killed in the first week of September 1939, a number that circulated widely during wartime and was still recalled by respondents to Mass Observation surveys conducted two years later.[1] *The Times* cited what it called an exaggerated report of 2,000,000 dogs killed in Britain in the first week or two of the war but notes that the Royal Society for the Protection and Care of Animals (RSPCA) estimated that about 200,000 dogs were destroyed.[2] Contested figures notwithstanding, E.S. Turner wrote that, at veterinary clinics, there 'were queues of persons with pets to be put down. Outside the surgeries, the slain lay in heaps, mongrels and thoroughbreds alike, under tarpaulins.' Thus, the urgent problem of domestic pet corpses was raised in Parliament, with the Minister of Health being urged to propose a solution, possibly the creation of special trenches for burial or provisions for the bodies to go to municipal incinerators.[3]

Evacuation and air raid precaution (ARP) protocols set out in the anticipation of war were implemented quickly after Neville Chamberlain's declaration of war on Germany and, while air raids did not actually occur until several months into the conflict, the immediate shifts in the fabric of everyday life in Britain were profound, impacting the civilian home and neighbourhood in terms of shopping, cooking, leisure, labour, family living arrangements, sleeping habits and even the intricacies of home arrangement and décor. The role of the airplane in the Second World War foregrounded the significance of the home front over the front lines of battle. Later, under food rationing, some even astutely referenced the former as the 'Kitchen Front', after a Ministry of Food publicity campaign forwarding cooking and housekeeping tips under conditions of war, and hence it was apt of a Mass Observation diarist to describe the family-cook as the Kitchen Front's 'generalissimo'.[4] As a leaflet prepared in the first weeks of war by the National Canine Defence League (NCDL) illustrates, domestic animals, particularly dogs, were implicated in many of the everyday practices that needed adjustment on the home front and that sentiments linking the virtues of citizenship with the proper care of non-working animals were made imperative. Thus, leaflet no. 484, 'War-Time Dog Food', addressed its readers by framing the central problem as: 'Many dog-owners will be anxious to avoid depleting the national food supply but at the same time desire to feed their canine friends adequately.'[5] Insofar as their care was subject to revision under wartime imperatives – from those concerning blackout procedures, that constrained their movements, to ARP, that sometimes excluded them from shelter and differentially regulated their feeding – this chapter takes as its point of departure the observation that animal caregiving became a key site of formal and informal interventions influential in shaping the shifting and contested image of the good wartime citizen, while at the same time home front civil defence called for greater knowledge about non-working animals, their welfare and their shifting distributions.

Mass Observation collected various ephemera concerning the care of pets during wartime and, in 1941, it conducted surveys that sought access to attitudes about keeping dogs. Drawing from these, this chapter examines public rationalizations that intervened into the care for non-working animals during wartime and exercised subtle social control over everyday routines of feeding and managing other material and emotional resources. Struggles over the worthiness of pets' lives were animated through discursive appeal to a secular notion of sacrifice, which would, on the one hand, have citizens give them up and, on the other hand, acknowledge the self-sacrifice of citizens who preserved animals individually or as a species in the case of breeding. The discourse of sacrifice was supported by nationalist sentiments that revived an unresolved conversation from the wartime emergency of the First World War[6] and provoked debates over the utility or productivity of animals who do not work. The discursive construction of what could be considered animal productivity was marked by interpretive tensions. For instance, productivity could refer to an animal's labouring capacities, its potential as food, the security it provides, or its value for maintaining morale. Since Mass Observation's indirect interventions into the debate over the worthiness of pets' lives emphasized the ways in which pets enhanced morale and recognized that the keeping of non-working animals provided an outlet for the indirect communication of fears and difficult feelings that were often attributed to them, I argue that Mass Observation's work furnished arguments that supported the keeping of non-working animals by making appeal to everyday forms of care enacted in cross-species social bonds.

There is, however, a paradoxical element to Mass Observation's contribution. It arises from the commercial origin of their dog surveys, as these appear to have been carried out under a commission referred by the Advertising Service Guild for Bob Martin's Ltd, for whom Mass Observation embarked upon various inquiries throughout the 1940s.[7] As James Hinton has remarked with specific reference to interviews concerning the use of dog powders undertaken in the summer of 1942, some of the work that Mass Observation carried out for Bob Martin's was not clearly reconcilable with Mass Observation's insistence on demarcating their inquiries from that of strict market research by ensuring that their endeavours had the potential for findings with sociological significance.[8] As shall be shown, the Mass Observation surveys 'Dogs in London' and 'Provincial Dogs' do not suffer the same lack of distinction but instead shore up Hinton's dismissal of critiques of Mass Observation's commercial work which he claimed inaccurately present a story of the organization's decline.[9] Indeed, the dog surveys offer support to Hinton's observation that Mass Observation work conducted under commercial commission generally remained focused on social habit and did not necessarily constitute a departure from the early Mass Observation's social initiatives and critical orientations.

Insofar as Mass Observation survey prompts allowed for the extension of the discussion into domains that are rich for social inquiry, responses offer insights into public rationalizations that supported the indirect exercise of social control upon the everyday routines and values of wartime citizens. More specifically then, this chapter is concerned with how emergent formal and informal imperatives of caregiving for supposedly 'unproductive' animals, imagine social spaces such as the home and neighbourhood as discretionary sites in which informal asylum for social subjects (whether animal or not) needed to be deliberated on the home front. Further, this chapter charts the active interventions that Mass Observation proposed to the terms of such deliberations in their summary file reports. But as these surveys were conducted two years into the war, let us first go back to the start of the war to take stock of the considerations that would have pressed upon the caregivers and companions of non-human animals who were not engaged in socially recognized forms of labour or war work.

## Early days of war

It is apparent that some people were initially under the impression that the destruction of their animal companions was, or would become, mandatory, as one man remarked to a mass observer in 1941, 'I remember at that time they asked people to get rid of their dogs in the papers because of the food shortage. I know a lot of people who did get rid of them and now they wish they had them back.'[10] Such orders were never directly made, and the mass killing of companion animals in the first days of the war repeated, with greater numbers, a 'voluntary' rush to destroy pets during the Munich Crisis one year earlier.[11] The plight of companion animals should war come was already then registering in public discourse, with, for instance, kennels nestled in safe country locales offering spaces for town pets that would be removed from the dangers and alarming sounds of air raids, and Nina, Duchess of Hamilton, inviting animal evacuees to her Ferne in Wiltshire Estate.

The autumn of 1938 also saw the arrival of refugees from Germany and Austria, many of whom sought asylum for their beloved companion animals too. While the cost to quarantine newly arriving animals was too steep for some who fled, animal welfare organizations stepped in to help and used publicity to align the preservation of the lives of companion animals with humanitarian ideals. Our Dumb Friends League stressed that they opened their quarantine kennels as a matter of national and international 'duty'.[12] The NCDL established the Quarantine Fund for Refugee Dogs and likewise situated their campaign in humanitarian, as well as nationalist, terms by insisting:

> Many of these refugee dogs' masters and mistresses arrive in this country with little else but the clothes they wear and it speaks volumes for their affection for their canine friends that in some instances they have denied themselves necessaries in order to ensure that their dogs should breathe the free air of England. Seldom have we of the League derived more pleasure from aiding downcast dog-lovers than we have in extending a helping hand to these victims of racial and religious prosecution.[13]

Later, a pre-war ARP information brochure issued by the Home Office provided proscriptive messages to animal caregivers only in passing. In instructing heads of households on the procedures to follow at the sound of an air raid signal, provisions for domestic pets were addressed for the first time in the document as though the animals would be already absent by the time of war:

Pets should, if possible, have been sent away into the country at the first sign of danger. But if they are still in the house they should be taken into the refuge room, otherwise they may come into contact with gas, or get splashed by it, and contaminate you. But it should be remembered that animals will help to use up the supply of air in the room. To be on the safe side, count two dogs or cats as one person.[14]

The booklet gave no suggestion that animals be put down, but offered the implicit judgement that responsible caregivers would have already evacuated their pets from the towns – a precaution that had been recommended previously and was reinforced by this passage. In assuming the continued presence of animals in the household presented greater risk of contamination to humans and stressing that animals would compete with humans for air, the brochure presented what would seem to become over the duration of war a vivid image that would undergird the economic equation that presented human and non-human animals' access to the necessities of life – whether of air, food, shelter or attention – as a contest.

Notable among pre-war communications that addressed animal care in these uncertain times was the ARP handbook for animals that the Home Office issued in 1939. The opening line of *Air Raid Precautions for Animals*, ARP Handbook no. 12, was: 'Animals, like human beings, will be exposed to the risks of air attack in a modern war, and everyone will wish, both from practical and humane motives, to do what is possible to protect them and to alleviate their sufferings.'[15] From the outset, the handbook stressed that urban transport animals and domestic pets in industrial areas were at the highest risk of attack, but it provided advice for carers of livestock as well on matters such as how to prepare for and respond to gas, incendiary and high explosive bombs, as well as first aid and humane killing of incurably injured animals. For livestock thusly injured, it recommended the use of a captive bolt pistol and provided detailed instructions and diagrams that identified the exact shot locations for animals by kind. A subheading to the chapter on the destruction of incurably injured animals entitled 'Dogs and Cats' precedes the following sole paragraph:

> When an owner has been unable to send his dog or cat to a safe area or to make other suitable arrangements for its protection, he should consider the advisability of having it painlessly destroyed. During an emergency there might be large numbers of animals wounded, gassed, or driven frantic with fear, and destruction would then have to be enforced by the responsible authority for the protection of the public.[16]

Clare Campbell has referred to the above passage as the 'destruction imperative'[17] and suggested its role in the high death toll of companion animals at the start of the war. It is indeed possible that the handbook and other ARP documents gave the impression of a directive or signalled that such a directive would be forthcoming. Nevertheless, no direct orders were given to civilians to have their pets destroyed over the duration of the war.

It is significant, however, that this handbook clearly presented two options for the responsible management of companion animals in wartime: evacuation or consideration of humane destruction. Failure to secure evacuation for a pet, the handbook proposed, assigned responsibility to the carer to take the life of the animal – first, for its own protection by preempting the possible suffering that could be brought by injury or distress, and, second, for the protection of the public, since the animal's future behaviour might be unpredictable under anticipated emergency conditions. While the handbook did not issue an order to put down pets, neither in general nor in the case of those remaining in high-risk zones, it did indeed present evacuation or destruction as the moral equation that good citizens who have animals in their care ought to deliberate in advance of conditions of immediate emergency, frantic fear, incurable injury and frenzied behaviour that might endanger the public. The fact that the passage that presented this equation constituted the entire text provided under the subheading 'Dogs and Cats' in the chapter on the destruction of incurably injured animals suggested that carers ought not wait for injury, but kill in anticipation of conditions that might never be realized. In other words, the protection of dogs and cats meant ending their lives. To put it more starkly, the section marked urban, non-working dogs and cats as already dead.

## In the massacre's wake

Notwithstanding the lack of official instructions to destroy animals not engaged in socially acknowledged forms of work, the lives of hundreds of thousands of companion animals were taken in just a handful of days around Chamberlain's declaration of war. Hence, Kean has described this as a 'war on animals' and a massacre that occurred 'not through "enemy" action but because of the decision of their individual owners'.[18] Veterinarians were overwhelmed with the endless-seeming task of putting animals down as a preventative measure; one said the experience was 'dreadful and loathsome'.[19] The piles of bodies accumulating at available facilities were described at the time as so overwhelming that it was 'impossible to bear', the mechanisms for transporting them broke down, and receiving sites were overburdened. The situation was so dire that the National Air Raid Precautions for Animals Committee (NARPAC), a government initiative that subsumed several, sometimes at odds, animal welfare advocacy organizations and charities under official remit, urged people not to put their animals down unnecessarily. NARPAC objectives included first aid and, when deemed necessary, the painless destruction of animals, as well as the issuing of ARP identity tags for dogs and cats, but their primary task was: 'To protect the public from frightened, ferocious or gas-contaminated animals at all times of emergency and thereby relieve Police Officers and Civil Defence Personnel from the labour involved in handling such animals at times when they are fully occupied with duties connected to human beings.'[20]

Despite the high numbers of animals that were killed, whether to shield them from the threats of war or to respond to perceived social pressures concerning the distribution of scarce resources, the vast majority of pets endured the war and adapted to changes in routine, diet, leisure, spatial arrangements and family relations, along with their human companions.[21] Kean has stressed that, for many, 'there was never any question about destroying their own companion animals'.[22] Her research has informed her view that 'Often the animal-human relationship became closer than before the war. Knowing this, we can no longer accurately define that time as a "People's War" per se. On the Home Front it was a war experienced and shared by animals and humans alike.' Thus, Kean proposed 'The Animal-Human War' as a 'more accurate moniker for the Home Front of 1939–45'.[23] In this light, Howell and Kean have considered how 'this community under stress [was] both inclusive of and co-constituted by people's pets'.[24] In this respect, the loss of pets at the start of the war ought not to be viewed as a reflection upon them as merely disposable complements to human social organization. Rather, what Susan McHugh has observed about dogs – as having been subject to 'our confused and conflicted understandings of their significance' in our social relations – is perhaps relatable to companion animals generally. McHugh argued, 'Intersecting with humans' ideas of each other, the long histories of conflicting attitudes towards dogs' may inform the 'lived contradictions' that are inherent to the complex webs of meaningful social relations, marked as they are by 'maladies' and 'joys' shared between humans and animals.[25]

Acknowledging that war brought new concerns and demanded a re-patterning of daily routines of caregiving, animal welfare organizations and advocates circulated a large body of literature before and during the war that instructed pet owners on matters such as: feeding animals under the conditions of food rationing; management of 'hysterical' pets during air raids; and the exclusion of dogs from public air raid shelters. In the early weeks and months of the war, and partially in response to the mass killings of pets, a stream of calls for the preservation of non-working animals and advice for their care were given. Those who were old enough to have cared for dogs during the previous war may have recalled recommendations to feed them with boiled horse flesh, offal and bones, vegetable parings, fish-heads and any other leavings not considered fit for human consumption. The NCDL reissued these recommendations to the public at the start of the war.[26]

The RSPCA circular 'Animals and Air Raids' urged people not to have their pets put down and made simultaneous appeal to competing rationales for keeping pets during the war. On the one hand, it questioned the wholesale 'slaughter' of animals, noting the organization's opposition to such action. On the other hand, it subtly called upon readers' concerns about essential supplies during wartime, shifting the emphasis away from the food supply and placing it upon the diminished access to petrol by highlighting the burden of pet collection. To ameliorate caregiver's concerns about their pets during air raids, the leaflet offered practical measures; to this end, the third edition of the pamphlet recommended ear padding and drug management of nervous pets.[27]

The daily papers prompted reconsideration of both the popularly assumed risks and benefits of keeping dogs during wartime, with the former downplayed and the latter emphasized. For instance, readers of *The Times* were reassured and instructed with some precision:

> In an air raid dogs would be little worse off than their masters and mistresses, except that there is no effective protection for them against gas. No doubt the explosion of bombs and the noise of guns would terrify many that are what is called gunshy, but their nerves can be relieved by a dose of bromide of strontia in a little water.[28]

The article speculated that, despite the attention being given to the destruction of dogs, as the war progresses, there will be a rise in the demand for domestic dogs to guard the wives and families of absent service men. In a pre-war article appearing in *The Times* one year earlier, dog breeders and the public were urged that there will be plenty of food, such as 'meat offals, horseflesh, the carcasses of cattle and sheep that die, and on biscuits made from damaged flour', suitable to the maintenance of dogs and, therefore, the years of both financial and labour intensive investment in breeding kennels ought to be preserved if war breaks out, and without prejudice towards dogs based upon their breed's national origin.

The article assisted in prefiguring the association between animal caregiving and good citizenship by speculating that, in the event of war, those who keep dogs, 'having a sense of responsibility to the community, would bear uncomplainingly any regulations imposed, provided they realized that they were the outcome of a national need and not of panic'.[29] Yet the ways in which collective responsibility would be interpreted would be multiple and contested. On the one hand, preserving lives and breeds could be cast in nationalist terms. On the other hand, suggestions that animals disturbed by air raids could pose dangers to public safety would provoke the open judgement of neighbours who believed the keeping of pets to be irresponsible and a threat to community safety.[30]

Responsibility for the safety of others was a relation that could be enacted by humanely taking the lives of dogs in one's care as a preventative measure, since caregivers understood that they were assigned responsibility for the actions of their animal companions.[31] This underlines a contradiction that resides at the heart of pet-keeping to which Howell's study of the making of the modern, domesticated dog in the nineteenth century brought attention, 'The more that dogs were regulated, the more that they were accepted as domestic animals and good "citizens," so their legal status was enhanced, but this came only at the expense of becoming *property*.' In other words, the Victorian production of the non-working dog, removed from the economic domain and included as a member of the household to be embedded within companionate social relations, was paradoxically bound up with its legal status as an object of property.[32]

Wartime exacerbated mixed messages concerning the ethics of animal caregiving that characterized public discourse surrounding pets. With the range of products promoted to mitigate the sometimes vividly described potential horrors animals may be subjected to in wartime, some organizations and entrepreneurs may have fuelled, rather than soothed, feelings of helplessness that animal caregivers could experience. The fearful anticipations of air raids and gas attacks that had marked the years and months that approached the first days of war had extended implications for those who cared for furry and feathered dependents unable to use gas masks or to access public shelters. In the absence of gas masks for pets, other contraptions, such as the Frank-Heaton Protective Enclosure for small animals, became available for purchase. Alternatively, Bob Martin's Ltd offered caregivers do-it-yourself (DIY) instructions for preparing gas-proof containers at home. But animal advocates cautioned caregivers on solutions offered. While the brochure for the Frank-Heaton enclosure and Bob Martin's advice for DIY containers both carried the air of scientific and medical authority, the RSPCA urged people not to use these contraptions citing the possibility that the animals inside them may suffer starvation should the caregiver be injured and unable to return to tend to them.[33]

## 'Aeroplanes or Bacon?': calculations

The long-anticipated food rationing scheme saw its first implementation at the start of 1940, with sugar, butter, ham and bacon as the first items to fall under restrictions. The list would grow, as would instructions about the proper use of foods, and the regulation of many goods continued well into the post-war years. Heretofore, Lord Woolton, Minister of Food, would be a commonly referenced name, sometimes used to express vexation, even though he was well-regarded.[34] Exasperated Dewsbury shop attendant Kathleen Hey often addressed Woolton in her diary, as she did in July 1941: 'Oh, Lord Woolton! Could you be in our shoes for a single day! How much wiser you would be.'[35] By this time, eggs, milk and other items were rationed. But having an allowance of regulated foods would not guarantee their availability, and often customers went without. As Hey's diary repeatedly illustrates, a vocal few blamed shopkeepers. Though it was acknowledged that rationing was a mechanism that ostensibly mediated the distribution of scarce items at controlled prices, supposedly according to differential dietary needs, frustrations with the scheme and the shortages that necessitated it, could still be felt and displayed.

As food habits and tastes were stretched on the home front, there were alternatives and advice for managing the shifting challenges brought by shortages of favourite foods and key ingredients. Gert and Daisy, the comical Cockney cooks portrayed on BBC radio by sisters Elsie and Doris Waters, blended wartime tips with a sense of humour that listeners enjoyed, according to Mass Observation, because the characters successfully 'identify themselves and their problems with the genuine housewife'.[36] This identification failed to extend to the content of the advice that the programme offered because of a disconnect between the meals and the pragmatic realities that some listeners faced. According to a Mass Observation study, listeners perceived the meals to be too expensive and fancy and they required elaborate ingredients. Meanwhile, advertisements for products, such as Pyrex oven glassware, included handy tips, such as 'How *One Person's* meat ration can make a *Meal for Five!*'.[37]

Other publicity encouraged town residents to keep their own poultry and to grow vegetables where there had once been flowers. Sometimes encultured habits set firm limits, however, as Pam Hobbs suggests in an autobiographical account of her family's Christmas dinner in 1942 when they prepared their own backyard chicken, named Arthur. Arthur was described as a difficult bird, so aggressive that their other chicken reportedly feared him. When you fed him, you needed to carry a broom to keep him at a distance so as not to be pecked. If that was not enough, he had recently pecked at Pam's mother's bottom – an undignified scene that seems to have finalized the decision that he 'had to go'. A neighbour advised Pam and her mother on how to prepare the chicken for dinner. It was a two-day process that Pam found unappealing. Even so, she wrote that, on Christmas day, 'we drooled all morning as a heavenly aroma from the roasting bird wafted through the house'. The meal was finally served, 'But then, home-made paper hats on our heads, and paper chains made from magazine pages strung from the ceilings, implied a festive air we no longer felt. We sat in silence. Nobody wanted to take the first bite out of Arthur.'[38] Arthur's body was buried in the backyard instead before it occurred to the Hobbs that they could have offered the roast to a neighbour. Not to mind that the burial of a roasted chicken was in stark violation of the order not to waste food, an offense that could bring fines or even imprisonment. Upon reflection, the treatment of Arthur's body proved to be even more categorically blurry than the holiday meal: Was Arthur food or an uncompliant pet?

The implementation of rationing, the strains provoked by Nazi invasions of Holland and Belgium that sourced difficult to replace British imports,[39] as well as the order not to waste food, meant that from the first half of 1940 onwards pantries were less diverse, the contents of which could only selectively be shared with non-human members of the household. When cereals were no longer able to be used in the production of pet foods, dog biscuits became increasingly difficult to obtain, were lower in quality and went for a high price. The possibility that shopkeepers were capitalizing on the circumstances of rationing weighed on consumers' minds. For instance, an Oxford respondent to Mass Observation speculated, 'I think some people are making too much money selling dust instead of dog biscuits.' Another respondent from the same area asserted, 'I think there is profiteering going on in dog foods, some of them seem very expensive.'[40] Meat that was judged unsuitable for human consumption was marked for dogs with a green dye by regulation, which troubled some consumers who believed it to be poisoned. A shopkeeper remarked, 'They seemed to think that we had set up shop here specially with a view to murdering all their pets.'[41] Shopping for the foods that were allowed for pets meant additional stops, line-ups and sometimes the failure to procure the desired items due to shortages. Restrictions on what could be fed to animals also raised the spectre of the utility argument premised upon the division of productive and non-productive animals. For instance, while no milk could be given to cats, in 1941 milk powder was allowed to be given to cats engaged in productive work, such as protecting foodstuffs.[42]

The distinction between economically useful and non-useful animals did not give livestock reprieve, particularly chickens and pigs, who relied upon cereal imports. The Ministry gave feeding priority to dairy before other cattle, sheep, pigs and poultry, respectively. In August 1940, Lord Woolton conceded that those who kept poultry should reduce their flocks, regretfully acknowledging that they would face hardships as a result.[43] In the spring, he had said that pig clubs should not expect that the Ministry can help provide the required supplies in a food emergency.[44] Keepers of poultry, for instance, drew comparisons between availability of corn and dog biscuits,[45] one that would still be a matter of contention in 1942, when Lord Woolton received a postcard from Charles Elwell that respectfully inquired why he must destroy his 'productive chickens' when 'dog biscuits etc are still being produced for the, to a large extent unproductive, dog'.[46] To this, a public relations official replied on behalf of the Minister,

> The amount of material allowed for dog biscuits is strictly limited and if they were not manufactured people would feed their dogs on food fit for human consumption which is against the law … The whole question of dogs is very difficult and you will understand that if legislation about them were brought in it would be extremely difficult to discriminate between those which are really useful and valuable. I must remind you also that a certain amount of food is allowed to owners of hens and that some consideration is due to people who keep dogs.[47]

Sympathy for the dog-caregiver notwithstanding, consistent with biopolitical reason, it became common to calculate every action and every value, against a competing other. As *The Times* characterized the Ministry's position, 'Always in war there was the constant pull between demands for munition and food', thus, it was a matter of 'Aeroplanes or Bacon?'[48] Or, as another put it, 'Dog Food or Farm Help?'[49] In these tight equations, the interests of farmers and pet lovers came into frequent tension over the difficulties of securing food for animals. Hence, the most efficient use of resources with respect to the differential feeding of non-human animals was under debate, and these equations turned on the matter of utility. As the Ministry of Food considered how crucial it was to maintain a 'cat equilibrium', it became necessary to estimate the relative costs of cat subsistence and the loss of food from vermin left unchecked.[50] Similarly, if one racehorse ate the same amount of food as 125 hens in a day, as a farmer was quoted as insisting in *The Times*,[51] this assumed that the implication of worthiness would be found in the commonsense hierarchy of use. In any case, the same race horse-hen equation was used to make the reverse argument: 'Racehorses in training consume nearly 6,000 tons of oats a year. If this were fed to hens that would provide each person in the country with a quarter of an egg a year.'[52]

Implicitly, human animals were to be the beneficiaries of such determinations of worthy life that aimed to protect the nation though calculations that justified distinctions along species lines. This reasoning extended beyond the domain of the economy of food and to the economy of affection. Some vocally wondered if the time and care devoted to non-human animals was warranted in the nation's time of need. In August 1940, a reverend writing to the *Picture Post* agreed with a July letter to the editor in which the author had proposed to follow Germany's example by killing his three dogs to preserve the food they consume and to save children and emergency responders should the dogs become dangerous in a raid. Commending the hypothetical exchange of animal lives for abstract securities, the reverend wrote, 'I have often thought how much better it would be if people spent their love, money and time over children ... There are hundreds of children who would value the money and attention given to dogs.'[53] Following up in a subsequent issue, a third reader wrote to defend the value of the life of her own dog with appeal to the same logic that would have non-working dogs destroyed in a time of necessary austerity by making claim to the dog's efficiency and value by listing her uses as: companionate guard dog; skilled controller of vermin and rabbit hunter. On the latter points, the dog's record numbers of caught mice, rats and rabbits were given. 'For all this,' the letter argued, 'she costs about 6d. a week to feed. My guess is that the vermin she destroys would eat about a thousand times as much as she does in a year. Destroy her? I couldn't afford to do it!'[54] Production staff titled this letter the 'Economics of Dumb Friendship'.

Indeed, the economy of material resources was a matter of instrumental calculation, as publicity stressed that 'small savings make big totals. If in making tea the extra spoonful ... is cut out it will mean a total annual saving equivalent to 60 shiploads, while a waste of half an ounce of bread a day by each person means an annual loss of 30 shiploads of wheat.'[55] If this was the way in which goods were characterized, so too was other-oriented care, which stood in tenuous relation to presumed security. But as consideration of the disparaging stories that arose at the start of the first evacuation scheme illustrates, some humans do not necessarily come out of such calculations favourably. The link drawn between the cultural images of the poor town evacuee and the lazy biscuit consuming dog was anchored in animacy hierarchies that could be mobilized in the calculation of good home front economies of care; this will be the subject of the following chapter. My point here has been to show the prevalence of such rationalizations. Despite being frequently wielded, instrumental calculations remained a matter of interpretive contest, as we shall see elaborated in responses to Mass Observation dog surveys.

## Mass Observation dog surveys

In July 1941, NARPAC replaced the fibre identity tags they had previously issued for dogs and cats with a sturdier metal badge, corresponding with this was their national animals' day rally. In Manchester, the rally featured Alsatian dogs donning gas masks and laying telephone wires.[56] Since the laying of telephone wire was among the many crucial forms of labour that dogs had been employed to do for national armies in the West since the First World War, along with land mine detection, rescue and so forth,[57] the decision to highlight this performance was as strategic for its demonstration of canine labour capacity as it was for its novelty, given that the supposedly wasteful provisions for dogs were then so frequently debated. If brand new metal identity badges for dogs needed any justification, here dogs demonstrated that they too did their part. Later that month, Mass Observation launched its pilot survey, 'Dogs in London', which explicitly sought attitudes on keeping dogs during the war but provided deeper insights into caregivers' experiences and feelings. Investigators engaged Londoners, who either currently or in the past kept a dog, in conversation about: war difficulties and air raids, reasons for keeping, giving up and renewing dogs, as well as what kinds of assistance they believed was needed for their care in wartime. In August, Mass Observation followed up with a survey 'Provincial Dogs' in Worcester, which had not been blitzed, and in Oxford to provide a check on responses gathered in Worcester. Mass Observation also surveyed people who did not have dogs, as well as dog breeders and shops that catered to dog caregivers.

The file reports that summarize these surveys are unsigned and depart in tone and grammatical structure from those Tom Harrisson wrote. An unusual aspect of these reports is that they reference 'the problem' that initiated the studies, but never state or define the problem as such. The introduction to the pilot study asserts that dogs 'play a prominent part in British life' and identifies the relationship between the morale of caregivers and the perceived welfare of their dogs. We may only delineate the problem by considering how the reports are framed, the concerns that seem to inform the survey prompts, and by working backwards from the recommendations that the reports make, which largely concern the circulation of information on ARP facilities and treatments for dogs, the need for a 'dog slogan for the present time', and publicity to support 'goodwill for the dog'.[58]

In addition, Mass Observation conducted 'indirects', casual conversations that investigators struck in passing. One who conducted indirects often began by petting a dog and asking its human companion a question, such as, 'What is your dog?' or 'How do you find it trying to keep a dog in wartime?' When these approaches were well-received, the investigator followed up with contextualized, improvised comments and questions, such as, 'Have you made any air raid precautions for it?' or 'How do you get on with raids with him?' Indirects are more unstructured than interviews and provide more latitude in potential responses. Further, since the mass observer carrying out interviews in Euston at the same time suspected that some respondents cautiously formulated their answers, with some asking directly if the questions were for the RSPCA, people engaging in the indirects may have been less guarded than those interviewed. Having briefly situated the context of the Mass Observation dog surveys, we can now consider the themes that they brought forth and the interpretative work that Mass Observation did with them.

## No place for a dog

Although the preservation of pets' lives in wartime was generally considered debatable, the subjectivity of animals who do not work was nevertheless taken for granted in respondents' valuations of what was just or fair. Responses to the surveys often drew upon normative assumptions about what was fair or legitimate. Thus, respondents' deliberations concerning the proper provision of resources and care for non-working animals provide insight into the ways in which civic conduct was evaluated in the summer of 1941. Perhaps not surprisingly, a key consideration was geography, therefore, the concept of fairness arose repeatedly in responses and seemed to refer euphemistically to the either/or decision to evacuate or destroy town dogs. When asked whether the war would affect the decision to obtain or give up a dog, respondents frequently referenced their geographical locations as crucial to their decision, with urban contexts presenting a clear deterrent to getting a new dog, due to perceived difficulties in obtaining adequate food, reduced opportunities to exercise dogs, and air raids. The place-specific assertion that 'I wouldn't dream of buying another dog if I had to stay in London'[59] or 'I would not have a dog in London especially during the war. It is hard enough to get food for yourself let alone running around trying to find food for animals'[60] was more frequently put than the more general reference to wartime, 'I'd never buy a new dog in a war it would be such a bother',[61] and 'if you are a dog lover I don't think it is fair to have a dog during the war'.[62] Yet the weighing of difficulty of taking care of oneself and human members of the household against caring for animals extended beyond deliberations about one's own individual circumstances towards others who could be freely judged as irresponsible.

Regardless of the location in which the survey was being conducted, people frequently expressed that it was unfair to keep a dog in towns or specifically London, although only a few elaborated by specifying that it was either unfair to the dog, the community, or both. The following remark suggests the latter:

> I wouldn't keep a dog in London in any time. I don't think it is fair to the dog or your neighbours. If I was in the country I would have one as I like dogs. Nowdays [sic] you can't get meat for them to eat and this is what a dog mostly lives on ... I read in the papers some time ago that 400,000 dogs had been done away with. When you look at some of the streets you think it is a good thing, but still it does seem a lot.[63]

Although this respondent indicated that he would not keep a dog in London at any time, he reinforced his argument by indexing wartime conditions, lack of meat as the central part of a canine diet, and the ruins of bombed out streets which signified the threat of violence to, or perhaps from, dogs. Though air raid destruction suggested to the speaker that it was perhaps a good thing that many London dogs had been put down at war's start, he wavered a bit: 'still it does seem a lot'. Lack of space, time and food, as well as the threat of raids contributed to the perception that 'London was not the place for a dog',[64] and the war was not the time.

Thus, some London respondents who kept dogs implicitly justified themselves when questioned by Mass Observation investigators. Characteristic unsolicited justifications included: 'I don't really feel it's fair to have a dog in London but I'm so fond of him I can't really bring myself to part with him unless I heard of a really good home'; 'I had him before it began you see so naturally I couldn't do anything'; and 'I haven't had this dog long, I didn't really want to have him in the first place because I don't think dogs are right in London, but he had no home ... I couldn't think of him being killed ... so I said I would take care of him'.[65] Indeed, these self-justifications and other responses to survey questions suggest personal sensitivity towards the persistence of the belief that it was not fair to keep dogs in London, or that 'people should be forbidden to have [dogs] in large towns',[66] and responded to the expectation that keeping dogs at the supposedly wrong time and place – in wartime and/or in towns – would be open to social disapproval. As such, mass observers were made privy to such expressions during their interactions. For instance, an Oxford woman reported that she knew someone who got rabbits and chickens from London to feed to their dogs, an action that she depicted as 'quite wicked' and something deserving of imprisonment.[67] Likewise, Mass Observation diarist Pam Ashford frequently cast judgements upon her office co-worker Margaret for her undisciplined care of the indulgent dog Dandy, who allegedly ate a Cadbury milk chocolate bar every day and even took butter on his dog biscuits. If that were not enough, Ashford was incensed that Dandy had taken over Margaret's rations, having 'six fresh eggs a week and has his helpings of liver daily'.[68]

While most respondents to the survey kept dogs or were supportive of keeping them, the survey subject matter provided a platform for folks to make disapproving judgements about others. For instance, several people expressed that, while it would be alright for people with more space and resources to keep dogs, those with fewer resources were selfish in doing so. One person remarked that 'whatever way you look at it you must have a house and a bit of a garden before you can keep a dog. I don't hold with these upstairs flats.' Another suggested, 'Beside that with raids and the bombing I don't think it is right for people to keep them in small houses and flats', while this respondent was more explicit that proper pet-keeping was a matter of class when noting that 'you have to be rich really to have a dog in London – then you know they'll be taken care of properly'.[69] Speaking about a stranger with a large dog to whom the mass observer had been conversing previously, a person said, 'I don't think people ought to keep big dogs like that unless they live in the country where it can get its proper exercise. And anyway they do too much damage to people's gardens. It's not fair to the dog – let alone anything else – to keep it in the town.'[70]

A particularly significant, although not widespread, suggestion was that people keeping dogs during the war misdirected their time and efforts where more pressing home front responsibilities were concerned. One woman argued that dogs are best to keep in times of peace. During the war, 'only invalids and shirkers' have the time to care for dogs properly, she insisted. More subtly, another remarked, 'I wouldn't have a dog myself because I find I have enough to do to look after a family.'[71] Therefore, the qualities that undermined the value of dogs who did not work could extend to their human caregivers who presumably made smaller contributions to the national effort by virtue of their dedication to supposedly lazy dogs. Hence, biopolitical logics that informed the value of animal lives could have the potential to inform differential value to human lives as well. We will see more suggestions of this kind, but as such judgements raise questions about what kind of contributions animal caregivers made to the nation and the war effort, we should turn to the two most central themes in the Mass Observation dog survey responses: sacrifice and utility.

## Secular sacrifice

As we have already seen, the biological life of the companion animal, or the animal who does not work, was debated during the Second World War, and this debate continued, though reframed, conversations from the First World War and the Munich Crisis. In times of perceived crisis, pets could be characterized as luxuries and threats to the food supply so that it seemed appropriate to suggest that 'Really patriotic people wouldn't have pets while the war's on.'[72] While Mass Observation investigators did not explicitly raise the question of the life of the dog in wartime, and in fact seemed to avoid it by inquiring instead about conditions in which people would give up or sell their dogs, the question of animal life remained intractable, and some respondents addressed this problem bluntly. Where this was the case, two themes whose contours were sharply drawn in responses to Mass Observation surveys are the logic of secular sacrifice and the notion of utility. While this section will address sacrifice, these two closely linked themes mutually supported each other and contribute to a broader biopolitical rationale activated on the home front around the notion of care for the common good or the national effort, as realized in the enacted values of the imagined good wartime citizen.

The destruction of non-working animals was often posed directly in terms of sacrifice. In other words, if one was to have a non-productive animal destroyed, this was an action done for the good of the whole. For instance, a man from Hendon reasoned that 'farmers need a dog but ordinary people don't have to have a dog at all. They only keep them because they like them in which case it's not too much to ask them to sacrifice them.'[73] In this reasoning, the preservation of the life of a pet was a preference that ought to be renounced for the common good. This can be seen again in the following rationalization given:

> [Food] is so short for ourselves that it's not right to give it to animals – especially animals which are for the most part useless. If a dog's fed on unusable scraps

then all would be well and good ... I dare say two dogs eat about as much as one pig. I reckon there's about a million dogs in London – that's one dog per 8 people. That would feed 500,000 pigs to feed the people of London.[74]

The theme of sacrifice then resonates with the perception that people who kept animals for companionship rather than for their labour, did so for their own pleasure at the expense of the common good in a period of crisis. This perception was referenced even in responses from people who kept pets or were sympathetic. For instance, an elderly woman defended her own decision to keep her dog, 'a lazy old thing', who she complained had the very bad habit of sleeping in every day. For her, the company of a dog was 'the only pleasure nowadays' and surely, she insisted, God 'wouldn't begrudge that'.[75] Following this logic in the opposite direction, a Hendon man compared keeping a dog with entertainments such as sport and cinema or the consumption of luxury items, such as cigarettes and liquor:

> I can't get beer when I want it – or fags. It's the same with lots of other things. Lots of people have had to give up sport ... I know some of the poorer people who have had to give up going to the pictures but people who can't keep dogs won't give them up – & they are the people who ought to be made if necessary to give them up – the people who can't keep them.[76]

Yet one woman remarked compassionately to a mass observer, 'I feel rather sorry for people who keep pets – they seem to have everybody down on them – the Govt. as well – for using up the nation's food in a non-productive manner.'[77]

It is worth lingering on the logic of sacrifice for a moment. In her work concerning the labour of laboratory animals, Donna Haraway has addressed the common appeal to secular sacrifice as a way of justifying the pain and death that laboratory animals endure as part of the research of which they are co-producers. The concept of sacrifice, Haraway points out, relies upon its demarcation from homicide, or, in other words, the assumption that 'only human beings can be murdered'.[78] Its religious origin was connected with offering and exchange, as well as the strict separation of sacred and profane things, however, the concept of sacrifice has translated well into secular humanist discourse that places the presumed to be bounded and self-possessed human individual within a taxonomy of the living, which is mediated by a 'moral order of representation' that grants differential attributions of free will and responsibility to entities.[79]

According to Haraway, following Jacques Derrida, the logic of sacrifice produces the very distinction between the human animal and the non-human animal.[80] Indeed, Derrida was troubled by the philosophical claim that the animal cannot respond and 'seems deprived of all possibility, in fact, of all power of saying "Here I am" and of responding, hence of all responsibility' so that 'the animal doesn't die'. That is, the animal doesn't die even if it is put to death since it can be put to death 'without committing murder, without "Thou shalt not kill" concerning it'.[81] For Haraway, the attribution of responsibility and mere reaction to humans and animals respectively, casts animals – not as situated in 'webbed existences' of 'multiple beings' in mutual relations[82] – but as non-responsive, as capable only of their unidirectional use according to the rational calculation of the common good. Thus, the concept of sacrifice justifies the taking of non-human animal lives whenever the equation between their preservation and the greater good of knowledge production, resource distribution and so forth is presented in either/or terms, such as the calculations presented above did.

In analysing responses to the surveys, however, Mass Observation reversed the direction of sacrifice by interpreting comments supportive of those who kept pets in wartime in terms of the self-sacrifice of those who had not destroyed their pets. A man noted that 'for some people it would be literally impossible to give up their dogs ... They go mad over them without rhyme or reason. Well, you can't help admiring them in a way.' Another put it more directly by arguing, 'There's a certain amount of self-sacrifice attached to keeping a dog in peacetime – but even more so in wartime.'[83] Following up, Mass Observation suggested that sufficient survey responses re-positioned the caregiver as the object of sacrifice for the good of the animal and recast the negative relationship between the keeping of pets and commitment to the national war effort.

## But are they useful?

As noted earlier, the expectation that animals ought to be sacrificed was tied to the problem of utility, the aspect to which I turn now. Hence, several respondents acknowledged that there was a relationship between the food supply and dogs in wartime, noting, as one respondent did, that 'a pet's a luxury eating up the country's food. A farmer's sheep dog is different – dogs that earn their keep.'[84] Therefore, the perceived utility, productivity and instrumentality of dogs strengthened the legitimacy of the subsistence they were afforded: 'They might only be given scraps I know but if the scraps were given to a pig there'd be more food for a nation. If a dog was wholly useful I shouldn't say anything – but then no dog is. Well – sheepdogs are I suppose – & police dogs – any working dog. But there aren't many working dogs.'[85]

The demarcation between useful and useless dogs continued an unresolved conversation from the 'the wartime emergency' of the First World War, when, as Howell has noted, 'the key institutions of dog breeding, and the association between dogs and Britishness, were called into question as never before'.[86] Howell observed that, at that time,

> defending dogs by no means equated to defending *all* dogs. Fancy journals and correspondents often enthusiastically joined in the attacks on *stray* dogs, for a start. *The Country World and Illustrated Kennel News* ... called for an embargo on the breeding of such evidently useless animals, for 'By so doing, they will strengthen the Government's hands in dealing with this question, eliminate the mongrel, to the ultimate advantage of the Fancy'.[87]

While the line between useful and useless dogs was activated again in the early years of the Second World War, it was defined differently though remained contested. For one thing, the 'mongrel' was positioned on firmer ground in this war. Mass Observation stressed that mongrels were the quintessential British dog and noted the vernacular morale-boosting language people used to describe mongrels' handling of air raid stresses. Thus, Mass Observation noted, 'Mongrels seem "to take it" better than thoroughbred dogs.' Though some respondents described their dogs as adversely impacted by air raids, most said that their dogs had become used to them. One London resident even said that their dog enjoyed them, and another shrugged the question off by reporting that the dog has pretty good morale. 'The strongest symptoms of air-raid effects were noted by the owners of Alsations [sic] and Pekes',[88] thus, Mass Observation aligned the ordinary mongrel with the confidence and stability that good morale supported in civilians on the home front.

The degree and nature of a companion animal's utility was a recurrent and explicit device brought to bear by both animal advocates and those who believed that keeping pets during wartime was harmful to the war effort, as 'feeding the brutes only impedes the war',[89] and, less frequently, to the animals themselves. It was at times thought that death was kinder than war, as a Hendon woman explained, 'Well, it doesn't seem right that dogs should be made to suffer man-made horrors – raids & such like. Dogs didn't cause it. It would be kinder to put them to sleep. But otherwise I don't see why people shouldn't keep dogs.'[90] As noted, however, utility was variously defined. Often, utility referred more strictly to economic productivity, such as the vital work of a farmer's dog. Dogs, whose recognition as pets is a relatively recent historical development,[91] had found themselves counted in these kinds of equations before. For instance, Kathleen

Kete has shown that the tax on dogs legislated in France in 1855 was in part premised upon the assumption that there was an inverse relationship between the food supply and the dog population: 'Two classes of dogs were recognized: useful ones and useless ones, working dogs and luxury dogs.' According to Kete, 'Utility was defined in economic terms. The purpose of the tax was to limit dog ownership to those for whom it was a means of making a living, shepherds and blind people and the like, and to those with the means to care properly for a pet.'[92] But if a dog's utility was defined in strictly economic terms, then Kete argued that nineteenth-century pet keeping allied the dog's 'affective properties…with a new notion of utility'.[93]

But as some forcefully argued during the Second World War, utility could as easily be ascribed to the companionship that an animal gave to its carers. This is indeed what a non-dog owner from Neasden did when underlining the social and emotional contributions of dogs as valuable, 'A person's dog is often the most precious possession – some lonely old people have their only companion in their dog.' Another non-dog owner from Hendon, while still accepting the logic that utility justifies the lives of pets, appealed to the contributions of dogs both on the home and hot fronts of war to defend their being allowed to live:

> Well, I know dogs are unpopular nowadays. I know when I had mine some people were down right rude to me. And it's grown worse lately. It's foolish really. Probably dogs do more to uphold morale among their owners than anything else. Dog messengers on the front always have done a lot of good in wartime. Surely they have earned the privilege of being allowed to live for all of their kind.[94]

The morale support that could be offered by companion animals became a crucial point forwarded by individuals and organizations that defended animal life during the war.

Mass Observation itself drew from surveys to produce and mobilize a version of this argument in their summary file reports, although they did not construct it explicitly as an argument of utility. Drawing from the survey responses, Mass Observation underlined that many non-dog owners who speculated upon the difficulties of keeping dogs during wartime expressed admiration for carers' demonstration of devotion. 'Feeling is definitely generally sympathetic to dog keeping in wartime. There is a widespread appreciation, even among those who have never had a dog and never intend to have one, of the part a dog can play in individual or family life, and even of the particular value that this part may constitute in wartime.'[95] Mass Observation emphasized the emotional and companionate significances of dogs in the context of families separated by the war through home-loss, service and evacuation. As one woman put it, 'It's surprising really what marvelous company a dog is – I have been all alone in the house since my husband went and the children were evacuated – and that dog's been wonderful company.' Pragmatically, dogs offered security for women living alone. Another woman explained that her dog was more important during the war, especially 'during the winter and the blackout, when you hear of so many blackout robberies'.[96]

But Mass Observation stressed that the value of dogs stretched beyond pragmatic instrumentality by remarking upon what they called an increased 'pro-dogism', which they defined as an emotional, egalitarian and companionate attachment between dogs and humans. 'This increased pro-dogism,' Mass Observation argued, 'is largely "emotional", mainly based on the feeling of the dog as a companion or member of the family.' While Mass Observation cast this as a 'predominantly female feeling' or bond, which was less evident in responses from men, who seemed to 'value dogs especially for their utility or their sporting qualities – factors rarely taken into account by women',[97] their attention to this companionate bond was critical to the connection that Mass Observation forged between non-working dogs and wartime morale.

## Conclusion

The central force of the Mass Observation dog surveys resides not only in what they can reveal about how lives were categorized for deliberation in the distribution of care during the war, a subject that will be examined through a different lens in the next chapter, but also in the innovative way that they approach public feelings that were in large part sublimated. Indeed, one of Mass Observation's claims was that people communicated their fears and difficult feelings indirectly by attributing them to their companion animals.[98] This was perhaps most palpable where Londoners were asked, 'Does [the dog] mind you leaving him when you have to take shelter?' Many replied affirmatively, for instance: 'Yes, he minds a hell of a lot'; 'Well, I think he does (mind) but there isn't much that can be done about it'; 'Yes, he kicks up an awful row ... It makes me upset, but I don't know what to do about it.'[99] This question interrogated the human caregiver's interpretations of their dog companion's feelings while taking account of the significant bond between human and dog by bringing attention to the difficult scenario that the formal exclusion of dogs, often appreciated as members of the family, from public shelters.

Acknowledging Chris Pearson's observations that there is a 'deep and extensive history of human-canine cooperation and cohabitation' and that attachments between humans and dogs are 'fragmented, multifaceted, contested, and contingent'[100] in character, underlines that leaving a companion animal behind at the call of the air raid signal was no minor matter for many Second World War domestic animal caregivers. As Martin Alexander has noted in the context of the occupation in France, the welfare of animal companions impacts people's responses to emergencies – a reality that more recent environmental emergencies have brought to the attention of emergency planners.[101] Further, both the question and answers of some respondents seem to tacitly accept in practice that companion dogs possess selfhoods. Leslie Irvine's research has elaborated how dogs and cats exhibit each of the aspects of selfhood (as defined by Herbert Mead) – a category usually reserved for human subjects.[102] To take a more cautious line, however, animal companions play crucial parts in human narratives of selfhood and, as Colin Jerolmack has observed, establish a bridge between places, times, cultural practices and (human and non-human) significant others in those narratives.[103] Thus, Mass Observation survey responses to the question about whether dogs minded being left behind when human companions took shelter, at minimum, offer access to human narratives concerning the extent to which the two mutually defined that scene.

Hilda Kean's *The Great Cat and Dog Massacre* addresses the 'war on animals' during what has been called the Phoney War, the months between the war's declaration and evacuation from Dunkirk. Informed by attentive archival research of animal advocacy organizations, as well as personal correspondence, diaries and so forth, Kean asked: For whom were the first several months of the war 'phoney'? Situated in Animal Studies, Kean's work and its methodological provocations that encourage shifting animals to the centre of historical study[104] challenged 'the popular memory of the "Good War," the unified "People's War"'.[105] Even though, as Kean observed, more animals than humans lost their lives, she noted that 'the written accounts in diaries of keeping or evacuating an animal tend to be more numerous than those including accounts of killings. This can, of course, be interpreted in various ways – including the lack of significance of such an event for the diarist.'[106] As the Mass Observation survey responses show, some respondents clearly saw the lives of companion animals as expendable, yet few discussed putting their own animals to death due to the war, and therefore, the silences that Kean referenced can be found there as well.

How can we make sense of the silences that Kean observed, along with the concern for animals expressed not only in diaries, informal conversation, but in public discourse and forms of social organization represented in the numerous agencies devoted to the care of animals in wartime and without? Perhaps stoicism could account for these silences. Or perhaps social indifference to the lives of companion animals could explain the mass killings of animal companions, but the Mass Observation surveys suggest that such indifference was not widely held. Instead, I suggest that it might be useful to ask how care itself is connected to the abandonment of loved ones. The concept of secular sacrifice that was applied to the lives of animals in rational calculations drew upon bureaucratic forms of care that privileged the preservation of life at the abstract level of the population, a totality which includes animals as precarious sub-categories always undergoing slippage. This is the lens through which we might approach this kind of abandonment and its silences in the following chapter concerning confused animacies.

In a report of January of 1940, Harrisson wrote that 'History has told too much of the story of armies and bloody battles, not enough of the story of boredom and broken hearts.'[107] Mass Observation's commercial work on dogs in wartime provides the stuff of everyday life just as quirky as its initial promise to study beards. From Mass Observation's topic collection on dogs in wartime, we know that, in the early 1940s, Nip was a fashionable town dog's name, while Spot was most popular in Worcester. The collection introduces us to an innovative dog named Tim who apparently could, at the whim of his carer's request, scratch his own name in the dust on the ground.[108] Further, by reformulating the companion animal's instrumentality for the production and support of their caregiver's positive feelings, it suggested a different answer to the question of a non-working dog's usefulness. The contents of the dog surveys indeed tell of many things, from boredom and broken hearts to difficult deliberations over the question of life itself to loving (sometimes lazy) companion animals – both human and not.

4

# Confused Animacies on the Home Front

In June 1940, British readers were informed that Germany had ordered pet dogs be put down to preserve the food supply.[1] As mentioned in the previous chapter, a heated debate over the preservation of the lives of British dogs carried on in the letters section of the *Picture Post*, when one reader provoked others by calling for Britain to follow Germany in killing its dogs. To illustrate further, I attend with more detail to this surface polemic. 'Let's have no more nonsense about gas-masks for dogs, rules and regulations about dogs in or out of shelters. Kill them all off and be free of the whole responsibility,' wrote this reader, who asserted that the position was consistent with their love of dogs, which was no less than that of the 'old ladies and country gentlemen' who would likely protest this view. Admitting to keeping three dogs, the reader insisted that 'rather than to risk them taking fright in a raid, maybe tripping up firemen or ambulance workers or biting frightened children, I'll kill them myself'. In a final justification, the letter weighed the utility of the wartime diet these three dogs consumed with that of the waning grain supply that sustained hens. 'Germany has already ordered her 3 million dogs to be killed,' the letter reminded readers, 'Let us follow suit. Leave the cats – they keep down the rats and mice.'[2] As we saw, a letter of response from a reverend published two issues later offered support to the original correspondent who 'proposes to kill the three [dogs] he owns to save the food they consume, to avoid their biting frightened children, and tripping up firemen and ambulance workers, etc', judging it to be 'most sensible'. This response recast the predicament in zero-sum terms, love and material resources are spent on either animals or children: 'There are hundreds of children who would value the money and attention given to dogs.'[3] A third letter responded directly to the initial one. It opened denouncing 'nonsense' about gas masks for dogs by asking in retort, 'What *is* all this nonsense about destroying our dogs?' Here another argument of utility and exchange was presented, but this time it favoured the dog's preservation by listing her uses. She is described, in the emotionally distant terms of breed, as 'a pedigree wire-haired bitch'. The dog's uses included security and companionship in the absence of the writer's husband, as well as vermin control and rabbit catching. In the case of the latter two, the letter provides numbers to illustrate the dog's efficacy and sums up, 'For all this she costs about 6d. a week to feed. My guess is that the vermin she destroys would eat about a thousand times as much as she does in a year. Destroy her? I couldn't afford to do it!'[4]

In adjudicating the life of dogs with reference to their potential disruption of emergency operations, the anticipated irrationality and suspected danger of their fearful responses to raids and the efficiency of allocating food to them, these letters struggled over the relative worth of lives by drawing not only upon the forceful rhetoric of use and competing justifications for keeping or killing animals who do not work, but on the very crucial matter of care: care for the proper distribution of food allocated according to tacit distinctions and the hierarchy of species; care for the presumed optimization of safety and affection for children; and care for the unimpeded operations of emergency personnel whose tasks were oriented towards the preservation and protection of life. In other words, a biopolitically informed notion of care animated and underpinned the struggle that unfolded in these letters. Thus, the kind of care to which this debate appealed aimed to fortify the strength of the population by dividing it into parts and drawing priorities between these parts in the relative weighing of, for instance, the tasks of essential workers, the integrity of frightened children, and the competing claims of dogs, cats, hens, rats and mice with respect to the protection of the nation.

The line drawn between human and non-human life is neither singular nor static. Therefore, acknowledging that this line is culturally informed and subject to revision particularly in times of crisis, this chapter tracks the blurring within and between the categories of human and animal in home front discourses that surrounded pets and evacuees, as well as children who remained behind and were considered generally unhouseable. Moreover, this chapter examines the ways in which the lives of impoverished evacuees and companion animals were differentially elevated and lowered in response to the threats posed to the life of the nation during the war. It considers these subjects in relation to Mel Y. Chen's theoretical interventions into the concept of animacy hierarchy, which denotes structures that order different forms of life and other material, in this context, according to presumptions of relative 'sentience, agency, ability, and mobility'.[5] Following Chen's consideration of the ways that animacies are conceived and ordered in different cultures and histories underlines that multiple animacy hierarchies can be simultaneously in operation, this chapter provisionally sketches emergent and shifting home front animacy hierarchies that imperfectly mapped onto each other. This problem requires interrogation into some of the ways that social subjects, human and non-human, were categorized and ordered with respect to the affordances of informal care. Namely, it concerns how care itself could make distinctions between lives by seeking to make qualitative differences between them precisely to save life through its fortification – a dilemma that resides at the heart of state racism as Michel Foucault defined it.

Thus, this chapter operates as a hinge that weaves together conceptual threads from chapters two and three, while anticipating the closing chapter's observations about the perceived agency of slum housing, by examining how discourses surrounding companion animals and displaced persons strengthened, countered and stretched dominant assumptions about animacies during the war. Posthumanist scholarship informs critique of biopolitical thought by interrogating the distinction between human and non-human animals and highlighting the conceptually troubled ways in which the lines that distinguish human from non-human animals have been underpinned in the traditions of Western thought – although it is crucial to acknowledge that not all cultures situated within geographies associated with the so-called West share this cosmology, and, as Zoe Todd has argued, Indigenous ways of being and knowing have without credit informed post-humanism's questioning of these demarcations.[6] Meanwhile, Western religion, philosophy and science have drawn and attempted to maintain the animal-human distinction by appealing to several slippery properties.

Sunaura Taylor has noted the emphasis on walking upright as a key human trait, one that has enjoyed both moral or scientific purchase. Among Taylor's examples is Saint Isidore of Seville, who in the sixth century characterized humans' erect posture as a gesture towards God. Charles Darwin is here too, since, although he problematized the distinction, he nevertheless granted to bipedalism the human's unique evolutionary departure from other animals. Harriet Ritvo also regretted that Darwin's theory of evolution, despite its removal of a divine creator and decentring of human beings with respect to other animals, did not in any practical sense disrupt the metaphors that underpinned naturalist discourse, even if it was to come under the new disciplinary indexes of biology and zoology. As Ritvo noted, the theory of natural selection decentred human beings biologically, but it retained and underlined human intellectual superiority. She argued that evolutionary theory's speculation on the survival of the fittest made a stark impression upon readers perhaps because it seemingly justified the hegemonic positioning of humans within the natural order and may have been useful to the articulation of a range of social concerns.[7]

Posture would figure centrally in the teleological narrative of progress presented in the ubiquitous visual representation of evolution, *The March of Progress*. Introduced in 1965, it remains a hegemonic representation of the development of civilization, despite its inherent conceptual problems, its blatant racism and ableism.[8] Of her own experience, Taylor wrote:

> In my life I have been compared to many animals. I have been told I walk like a monkey, eat like a dog, have hands like a lobster, and generally resemble a chicken or a penguin. These comparisons have been said both out of mean-spiritedness and playfulness. I remember knowing that my kindergarten classmates meant to hurt my feelings when they told me I walked like a monkey, and of course they did. I wasn't exactly sure why it *should* hurt my feelings, however... I understood that they were commenting on my inability to stand completely upright when out of my wheelchair – my failure to stand like a normal human being. I understood that being told I was like an animal separated me from other people.[9]

The criterion of upright posture for membership in the category of human fails to hold the ontological distinction that it is meant to secure, as it imposes breaks within categories of human and non-human alike. Hence, as Taylor noted, difficulty arose in the seventeenth century in categorizing anthropoid apes. With reference to anatomist Edward Tyson's 1699 illustration of *Homo Sylvestris*, a chimpanzee standing with the aid of a walking stick, Taylor asked, 'If an ape who stands upright (even with the help of a mobility device) can be seen as more human, what happens to humans who do not or cannot stand upright?'[10] Taylor also addressed travel writings depicting women of colour engaged in forms of labour that required stooped postures as less than human; in the case of Richard Ligon, he also took the opportunity to comment upon the women's breasts in these postures, likening the women labourers to a 'kind of insect with an abundant number of legs'.[11] Social conventions, relations and labour have shaped differential human postures. In *The Road to Wigan Pier*, George Orwell dedicated a long passage to the ways that the two- to three-mile travel that miners embarked upon each workday in passages where 'You have not only got to bend double, you have also got to keep your head up all the while so you can see the beams and girders and dodge them when they come. You have, therefore, a constant crick in the neck, but this is nothing to the pain in your knees and thighs.'[12] The description goes on painfully, but what it illustrates is the moulding of postures that this form of labour does. Thus, forms of labour can make postures inconsistent with a criterion of human categorization and then be put to work in racializing and racialized terms, breaking up human subpopulations into race, gender, ability and class. Indeed, there is political utility in the blurring lines that such processes impose within and between categories insofar as they are mobilized to justify ongoing colonial practices, as well as the hidden incarcerations or public entertainment spectacles of heterogeneous bodily forms, movements and so forth.

According to Cary Wolfe, social subjects have been evaluated or defined in terms of their supposed capacities for reason and language, and this has implications for diversity not only in relation to posture and movement. Drawing from Temple Grandin, Wolfe emphasized that it does so for different sensorial capacities as well. The domain of the visual – by which is meant a culturally coordinated, perspectival visuality attributed to humans – has been privileged due to its perceived tie to reason. Yet this belies the more photographic seeing that occurs for some people whose sensorial experiences are atypical (such as with some forms of autism, as for Grandin) and afford heightened visual and tactile access to the world and underlines 'that what we traditionally think of as disability can be a powerful and unique form of abledness'.[13]

Chen has given attention to how language and communication furnish the 'primary criteria' for marking separation between animals and humans, noting that this relies upon the dismissal of the possibility of animals' languages (a relatively recent exclusion, which is of considerable interest to Chen as a linguist). Chen offers insight into the deep political implications of assigning (narrowly conceived) language the task of dividing animacies,

> Language's status among creatures, human and not human, continues to be hotly debated among humans, for as a register of intelligence, judgment, and subjectivity it is a key criterion by which lay, religious, and expertly scientific humans afford subjectivity – and sentience – to animate beings both within and beyond the human border. Who and what are considered to possess 'language,' and the qualities afforded to it within that location, are factors that influence how identification, kinship, codes of morality, and rights are articulated, and how affection and rights themselves are distributed; and hence how ranges of human-nonhuman discourses such as disability, racialized kinship, industrial agriculture, pet ownership, and 'nature' itself are arbitrated.[14]

Language has been a messy arbiter. Presented 'immutably in humans' terms', it affords the production of multiple divisions between kinds of animacies. Yet these divisions come to possess social meanings that are observed and acted upon through the political distributions and articulations that Chen enumerates. The force of these divisions emphasize that the conceptualization of animality, a paradoxical and 'flexible rubric that collides with and undoes any rigid understanding of animacy', to garner exclusions and misrecognitions bolstered by 'its humanist formulation and from its strange admixture between science and racist imperialism'[15] shore up its force as a 'primary mediator, or crux'[16] for defining both human and animal.

On language, Kalpana Rahita Seshadri has stressed that 'the withholding of access to the law-speech nexus' through the practices that mark the 'sacrosanct dividing line between human and non-human' by limiting what forms of communication will be recognized as 'meaningful and credible speech' serves 'to consign the other to silence'.[17] Silence, or the perceived inability to respond, also receives the attention of Jacques Derrida, whose text lingers on Jeremy Bentham's question, 'Can they suffer?':

> With this question – 'Can they suffer?' – we are not undermining the rock of indubitable certainty, the foundation of every assurance that one could, for example, look for in the *cogito*, in *Je pense donc je suis*. But from another perspective altogether we are putting our trust in an instance that is just as radical, although essentially different: namely, what is undeniable.[18]

What is troubling to Derrida about the distinction brought by philosophers, such as Descartes, Kant, Heidegger and Levinas, between response and mere reaction (the latter of which they attribute to non-human animals), is less that animals may be denied the capacity of response (or responsibility) but that humans are granted it. Or, more precisely, they give it to themselves.

Humans grant the capacity of responsibility only to themselves with some reservations; reservations that impose breaks within the categories of human and non-human alike. The not too historically distant inclusion of humans in menageries, circuses and zoos provoked Yi-Fu Tuan to pose the reminder that 'humans too can be treated and "valued" as curiosities and pets'.[19] Tuan's historical observations additionally illustrate that pets are effects rather than pre-existing beings merely adopted into domestic relations. Tuan posited that dominance, coupled with affection, produced the pet as now known.

The borders made by the 'rubric' of animality in the discourses surrounding evacuees and non-working animals reveal a symbolic twinning of impoverished children and animals whose care was judged not to be economical in austere conditions. At the same time that hundreds of thousands of household animals were put to death at the start of the war and evaluated in terms of their relative use, evacuees who began their trek on 1 September 1939 were widely described in their receiving communities as animalistic and domestically untrained. Often, the nouns used to reference them, as well as supposedly unhouseable children who were left behind, were names that served to animalize them: dog, pest, mite, rat, locust, urchin (hedgehog) and waif (lost property or stray animal).

In a seemingly softer, less common twist, some critics opposed evacuation, conceiving it as a form of desertion. Indeed, according to Patricia Y. Lin, this was how many evacuees who were later sent overseas under the auspices of the Children's Overseas Reception Board to Dominion countries such as Canada, Australia, South Africa and New Zealand understood the hostilities they felt when they returned to Britain five years later. 'Although many evacuees contributed to the war effort while abroad by sewing clothing, sending food packets, and in the case of those eligible, by joining the Forces, as well as through their unique diplomatic position of being "ambassadors of Britain", they were seen by many British people to have "run away from the conflict".'[20] But the charge of desertion was not just for those who went overseas – it was levelled at evacuees who remained in Britain. Staying put was considered a productive 'test' of youngsters' citizenship growth. Therefore, evacuees could be seen not only in reference to their ostensible filth but also as undutiful – as 'rats deserting the ship'. Berry Mayall and Virginia Morrow pointed out that, along these lines, *The Lady* magazine argued that 'children should be thought of, not as "charming pets to be kept away from real life".'[21]

The image of evacuee children as deserting rats streaming from danger zones resonates with the first evacuation's official title, 'Operation Pied Piper'. As Lisa Farley has observed, the scheme's appropriation of the title of the legend, *Pied Piper of Hamelin*, is curious, as it 'tells the tale of a stranger who is hired by the town's mayor to rid the town of rats. Through the seductive tune of his pipe, the piper marches the dutiful rodents beyond the city limits.'[22] The most memorable aspect of the tale is that the piper led all the children away, but less often remembered is that the piper only returned to lead the children away after the town defaulted on its debt to him for removing the pests in the first migration. Farley offers that 'the official code name of the rescue mission, "Operation Pied Piper," reveals something more dubious than its intended aims.'[23] Farley's emphasis is on the negative psychic effects of separation as worked out in British psychoanalysis, which underwent considerable development during the war. Farley wrote,

> it is perhaps not a coincidence that the earliest critiques of 'Operation Pied Piper' came from psychoanalysts – Susan Isaacs, John Bowlby, and Winnicott among them – whose training it was, after all, to read the underside of conscious intention ... these British analysts seemed to be asking: what unspoken meanings – such as loss, betrayal and abandonment – are held within the evacuation's legendary namesake? What cannot be spoken in what is officially being said? What happens

if we cast the adults charged to care for evacuated youth in the ambiguous position of 'Pied Piper'?[24]

To this, perhaps one more question might be added: to which of the two migrations from the tale's setting in Hamelin did the evacuation's operation code refer?

Rats, children or charming pets? So many symbolic connections were drawn between children officially compelled to migrate from danger zones, pests who needed to be kept down and animals that should be given a better death – a calculated death – rather than to suffer from lack of food, excessive noise, or the terror of bombing. When do the symbolic blurs extend beyond the poetics of metaphoric language use and point to the entangled logics of biopolitical calculation of the common good and the production of breaks into the order of life? The production of such breaks was the first of two parts of a process that Foucault had called state racism; the second is dependent upon the activation of animacy hierarchies that order categories, though they do so according to shifting rationales. With respect to animacy hierarchies, Chen offers,

> to consider the biopolitical ramifications wrought by these separated categories is extremely complex, since 'humans' are not all treated one way and 'animals' are not uniformly treated another way. This is why the statement that someone 'treated me like a dog' is one of liberal humanism's fictions: some dogs are treated quite well, and many humans suffer in conditions of profound indignity.[25]

Before going on, I'd like to return to the common formulation of comparative worth made about non-working animals discussed in chapter three. These tended to rely upon calculations concerning the relative productive value of different forms of life. These revealed that the distinctions were neither stable nor shared, and, although animal kinds could be subject to orders of value, each would be subject to internal division. For instance, Ritvo's historical account noted that in the Victorian period horses were considered most noble animals only secondarily due to their appealing appearance and graceful movements but primarily due to their perceived servitude. Yet we know that wartime debates separated horses, their value determined in part by use during wartime, with race horses considered most expendable. Horse meat became a source of food for dogs, whose wartime existence was itself exposed to the demand of justification against suggestions of the kind that was made at a meeting of the National Farmers' Union in East Yorkshire County, where it was suggested that 'a dog which tended sheep and killed rabbits and rats earned its food, but many dogs in towns were of no value'.[26] The imperative of use as an effect of calculation

**Figure 4.1** Animals, in the service of Man, Poster issued by the National Savings Committee, c. 1945.

could mean advocating for the killing of animals perceived to threaten the food supply. This logic may compel one to kill, as in the case of the 1943 Grey Squirrels Order, which made it compulsory to destroy grey squirrels if they were on your property, while authorizing anyone else to come onto your property to kill them.[27]

Indeed, the measure of animal worth in terms of use was not unique to the Second World War. For instance, in giving attention to human and animal interactions in England in the nineteenth century, Ritvo observed that service was a crucial trope in early popular zoological texts. Whether by providing resources, such as hides, for the manufacture of commodities, or through labour ensured by domestication, animals were evaluated largely in terms of the wide range of utilities and resources they offered to humans. Animals also rhetorically served to underpin and reinforce not only a scheme of natural order but also that of a social hierarchy '[d]escribed in terms that suggested human servants, domestic animals provided the standard by which other animals were to be judged. But some domestic animals offered better models of the relations between human superiors and inferiors than others'.[28] Ritvo explained that, although sheep and oxen were acknowledged for their hard labour and even their capacity to demonstrate a bond with a human, they were not afforded the status that an animal such as a horse enjoyed. Ritvo found in the musings of naturalists and zoologists that the horse secured this higher status through its demonstration of servitude and recognition of human superiority. But, Ritvo insisted, the dog, even more than the horse, demonstrated its commitment to serve:

> It was the dog's 'ungrudging love' for man that made it 'delight to serve' him. Again and again naturalists expressed their admiration for this 'humble and laborious servant,' whose single-minded devotion inspired its 'conqueror' with feelings close to the 'esteem,' normally reserved for human beings … The dog understood and accepted its position so thoroughly that it did not resist punishment if it failed in its duty; it might even lick its master's hand as he delivered the corrective blows.[29]

The dog's subordination to humans was assumed to be a primary instinct and so immediate that naturalists called into question societies that had not domesticated the dog. In fact, where the dog was not domesticated, the civility of the society was doubted, and the intelligence of both the dogs and humans was dismissed; on this point, Ritvo cites Darwin's observation that English dogs are very intelligent, but dogs found in Polynesia or China are quite stupid.

Dogs then could be made to bear the marks, and serve as markers, of nations and peoples, a point supported by Susan McHugh's observation that animal narratives can be 'inseparable from shifts in the politics and sciences of species, such that questions about animal narratives come to concern the formal and practical futures of all species life'.[30] David Williams argued that, with respect to the historically ambiguous category of the human, dogs have occupied an ambivalent ontological position as neither merely animal nor quite fully human. Thus, Williams remarked that '[r]epresentations of dogs have often been used to figure cultural change and negotiate the borderlands in-between'.[31] When an article published in *The Times* that advocated for the preservation of dogs during the Second World War made the added qualification that this should be done without prejudice towards dogs based upon their breed's national origin, it acknowledged a tenuous citizenship attributed to them. While the rights of citizenship may not have formally extended to dogs, they may be called upon informally to bear negative aspects of national responsibility, as dachshunds were in the Great War when they were kicked and stoned in the streets, and their caregivers were suspected of 'treasonable sympathies'.[32] Thus, in 1938 readers would be urged:

> To-day prejudice should not be extended against harmless dogs because of their country of origin ... One may point out that by this time they are surely entitled to the rights of naturalization, and that in any case it is unfair to condemn dogs because they are of foreign extraction. Dachshunds should be the last to come under the ban [on breeding] because we have had a considerable share in their making. When they first came to us they were exclusively in Germany and Austria for sporting purposes. We exhibited them before the Germans did, and our Dachshund Club preceded theirs by some years.[33]

This effort to thwart the temptation to treat individual dogs considered of German breed as punishable alibis for the enemy state and nation simultaneously reinforced the tie between breed and nationalism by recasting the dachshund fancy as more properly British. Nevertheless, as one report from Brighton attested, some dachshunds did face verbal abuse in symbolic substitution for the Nazi state during the Second World War.[34] But as the previous chapter has shown, the divisions that could be drawn between dogs worth keeping and dogs better to be given death were multiple and stretched beyond the overt racializing that breed distinctions make. For instance, Mass Observation's study found that smaller dogs were preferred during wartime for several practical reasons, and, as *The Times* reported, 'it has been suggested to some owners of big dogs that they are guilty of an unpatriotic action'.[35]

The wartime subordination of larger, or especially, non-working dogs hinged upon spatial and subsistence considerations. There were, other, more subtle, intertwining animacy hierarchies at play. A man responding to a mass observer provided a familiar rationalization that drew species comparisons that relied upon an implicit hierarchy of kinds:

> [Food] is so short for ourselves that it's not right to give it to animals – especially animals which are for the most part useless. If a dog's fed on unusable scraps then all would be well and good . . . I dare say two dogs eat about as much as one pig. I reckon there's about a million dogs in London – that's one dog per 8 people. That would feed 500,000 pigs to feed the people of London.[36]

Such rationalizations vitalized other divisions and implicated assumptions of value ascribed differentially, subordinating non-working dogs to pigs, and both were cast in terms of their necessary sacrifice to sustain human life.

Even when the companionate function of dogs was privileged, hierarchies were maintained. For example, a woman responding to the Mass Observation dog survey demarcated the kind of companionship she shared with her dog from that of other dog-human relationships by asserting,

> I've no patience with these people who pet and coddle their dogs, feed them on chicken and champagne and take them to bed with them. That's not company – it's only trying to find some way to fill their wasted idle hours, bought by an independent private income . . . I think it's disgraceful the way some monied women feed their dogs – better than the majority of the slum people. Some slum people would be glad to lead a dog's life.[37]

This remark granted that the company that a dog offers is of considerable value but insisted that not all companionate animal-human relationships were equal, authentic or moral. The ordinary dog-human relationship was not the same as that of the pampered dog and the idle, monied woman, according to this speaker, who drew this new line by underscoring that the struggle for food was not simply one between dogs and humans that would make its final appeal to the species distinction. Yet the species distinction was crucial to the moral force of the speaker's words that described the independently wealthy woman filling of her wasted hours by coddling and taking to bed a dog to whom she fed chicken and champagne – an image that resonated with the representation of the lonely woman, a recurring motif of presumed threat in Home Intelligence documents.[38] The speaker brought attention to what would appear to be an inappropriate cross-species intimacy and indulgence – a woman's improper displacement of intimacy, affection and duty.[39]

Nevertheless, the main struggle dramatized in this remark was a classed one that at times crossed the species line. In other words, some people and their dogs ate better than some other people and their dogs. Indeed, this comment acknowledged that, in practice, rights and resources were not always distributed according to the species hierarchy, but it also upheld the species line distinction between human and animal and suggested that some animals might be sacrificed as a remedy for problems of distribution. Another woman told Mass Observation, 'those people who feed their dogs on the fat of the land should be imprisoned for sabotaging the war effort. And I mean it. Some of those rich society dames feed their dogs on stuff that which would be a feast for a poor man.'[40] While these were angry remarks, they acknowledged that access to material resources, as well as affection, was in some circumstances differentiated less by species than by other markers of difference.

Staying with these comments and pushing them somewhat further, the concept of animacy hierarchy helps to make sense of the rhetorical move that these respondents made with respect to the usual argument that companion animals were not useful and therefore could be sacrificed in times of crisis and austerity. We can see that species itself did not serve as a pivot in this discourse. Instead, conceptions of relative animacies between and within human and animal categories, as contested as they were, served as slippery and substitutable anchors for determining the relative worth of contested lives or ways of living. Rather than arguing that the animals were indeed useful for the company they provided or for bolstering wartime morale, these speakers recast the human figure – in both cases the wealthy, but lonely, woman – as useless and a threat to the war effort. Even here, despite their claim to companionship as a form of utility equal to that of the food supply, the comments engaged the same biopolitical rationale to the extent that utility remained central to the calculation of what was good for the nation. What is illuminating is the ongoing production of breaks within and between animal categories and that utility was the concrete and constant arbiter in these opposing rationalizations over what was imperative and what could be sacrificed for the common good.

If I may return to the critique that Haraway made of the secular uses of the notion of sacrifice treated in the previous chapter, her aim was not to block instrumental use, even in the experimental lab context where many animals suffer and die. She argued that all relations, including those between human beings, are to some degree situated within relations of use. She asserted that 'there is no way of living that is not also a way of someone, not just something, else dying differently'. Further, not all such relations need to be objectifying or oppressive. Instead, she advocated for acknowledgement of the 'consequential relationships' of 'co-presence' in which human and non-human animals are situated in admittedly asymmetrical relations of use that can be cooperative. Rather than relying upon the culturally privileged hierarchy implied in the 'secular salvation' that is presumed to arise from practices of sacrifice premised upon 'sufficient reason' to calculate the means to best support the supposed 'greater good', we might all become better at both killing and dying. Here she effaced the commandment Thou shalt not kill and substituted the post-humanist imperative: 'Thou shalt not make killable.'[41]

If keeping a dog in a home front town could elicit social disapproval from neighbours and strangers alike, Kathleen Hey's diary shows that having a baby in wartime could also provoke gossip, whispers weighing the judgement of parents who would willingly bring a child into anticipated future suffering. Thus, after visiting a new baby and her parents who were subjects of their acquaintances' quietly exchanged judgements, Hey wrote in her diary, 'So little Hazel makes her debut to a somewhat disapproving world but her parents love her and that's all that matters.'[42] Hey does not bring utility into the matter.

The evacuee in the popular imaginary produced through evacuation stories approximated the cultural figure of the 'wild child', or feral child, whose fascinating presence has haunted literary inheritances and colonial discourses. Like the so-called 'wolf' girls, Kamala and Amala, who were presented to the world as feral children apparently discovered in a wolf den by a missionary in India in 1920, evacuation rumours and stories constructed the evacuee as undomesticated and thus as having a constitution that was impervious to the order of the British home. In her discussion of the wild child, Seshadri observed that such a child is 'not merely homeless; it is unhomely (unheimlich) and always already undomesticated, feral, unhoused – unable to be housed'.[43] It was this ostensibly unhomely characteristic of the evacuee that the most shared and most widely travelled evacuation stories emphasized. 'If you say two words to them they turn round and swear at you. I've seen a lot of dogs with better manners,' a Blackpool landlord reported to a mass observer about local evacuees.[44] Another told a mass observer that the people of his community initially understood it to be their duty to accept evacuees. For his part, he admitted that he had already requested that the two girls they received, aged seven and ten, be removed due to the extra work he feared they would make for his wife. Already, they had resolved to give the children their meals separately because their manners were 'ruffianly'.[45] An evacuated mother angrily remarked of her circumstances, 'That bitch [the hostess] couldn't smile to save her bloody life. Puts us food in the back kitchen as if we was dogs.'[46] In chapter two, we saw that the table manners and difficulties of bed wetting led to charges that evacuees were not house trained and that some of them appeared to their hosts as incompatible with the furnishings and other markings proper to the home. Names attributed to them, whether affectionately or not, often animalized them. When the *Northampton Independent* playfully described a little boy who had never seen a cow before and could not pronounce the word recognizably, it referred to him as an 'urchin',[47] a word that alludes to a hedgehog and has an unpleasant etymology that extends to behaviour and destitution, while forging an inherently immoral link between the two.

Amy Bell has also remarked upon frequent comparisons onlookers made of working-class families to animals during the war. For instance, while observing a mother and her two children huddled amongst rags in a tube shelter during the blitz, it struck Peter Conway that this family 'seemed barely human. I could not help thinking, as I looked at them, of a monkey mother with her young; and there was nothing disparaging in the thought. It was, I think, the pathetic suggestion of near-humanity and protection.'[48] Therefore, animalization was not reserved exclusively for evacuees, but it knew how to divide.

Marie Paneth's study *Branch Street* frequently employed animal metaphors to describe the sixty presumably 'wild' and lawless children in her care who remained in their impoverished neighbourhood during the war. I turn briefly to Paneth's text because it frequently animalized the ostensibly unhouseable children she sought to engage, describing them as lions, weasels, or as emerging from liars.

From the start, Paneth described a raucous group of boys who taunted and tested her on her first evening by insisting that she tell them how babies are made. To the open disapproval of on-looking colleagues, she eventually complied with the request, rationalizing that doing so would foster trust and demonstrate that she would not be rattled by such challenges. Paneth wrote, 'Standing there, in the midst of the boys, I had the sensation of being confronted by a nest of young wild animals. They bristled with mischief and expectation. I did not want to turn away from them, but to go through with it, though I knew that the setting for a talk of that kind was rather unfavourable.'[49] Paneth painted a picture of herself as the tamer of wild things to whom she must demonstrate her strength and establish herself as leader. Although chastised by a social welfare official for giving in to the boys' demands, Paneth insisted to her superior that, as a foreigner and one not dependent upon this endeavour for her income, she had nothing to lose in taking these risks, and thus she would continue to pursue her methods, even if it resulted in her dismissal. Reluctantly, the welfare officer agreed to let the pedagogical experiment continue.

Indeed, Paneth showed that, after the difficult initial meeting with the children, she gained a measure of the children's trust, and following that the girls were confiding with her and making inquiries of their own. 'We had a succession of good evenings. There was definite improvement,' Paneth wrote,

> The wild animals were tamed apparently; everybody was glad and optimistic. It was also true, however, that everyone was experiencing the feelings of the tamer who leaves the arena after a performance with freshly imported lions … We did not know yet whether the animals would still attack us and raise their claws to scratch and bite – bite people whom a moment ago they seemed to appreciate.[50]

Similar accounts that had portrayed the children's instincts over reason and reactions over response, applied to any offerings made, whether bits of coloured paper and ribbons that the children apparently tore at, and gifts that they received, which they 'snatched' before abruptly running off. One boy, who Paneth referred to throughout as the little leader, 'ran away with his box like a weasel'.[51] The children were depicted as unpredictable, untrusting and ruled more by shifting mood than reason.

When a dispute between the play centre staff and some of the older children escalated, some of the children barricaded themselves in the basement, 'the only place in the house which could have reminded them of their own lairs in the street', since they were reportedly accustomed to taking up condemned, rat infested basements as their hidden play areas. Paneth suggested to readers, 'It was as if, on the verge of behaving nicely and normally as citizens, they were doubly sensitive. As if the evil in them, attacked, took refuge in the outer symbol of their lawlessness, the empty uninhabited room.'[52] The attribution of animality to the children here shifted to evil, as an essential characteristic, which was housed in infested and condemned architecture (a pairing between active dwellings and passive inhabitants which will be taken up in this volume's next and final chapter). Despite Paneth's radical art pedagogy, permissive form of care and her desire to understand and meet the children where they were at, the difference remained a repellent force, perhaps because it was stubborn, and Paneth wished to be the one to eliminate it.

Therefore, Paneth did not critically evaluate the implications of her characterization of a child who was adopted by a neighbourhood woman. Paneth judged the child to be so beautiful that 'In Branch Street she resembles a being from another world. In fact, that is probably what she is. She was not born in Branch Street … Eileen has had the rare bad luck to be a child adopted by a Branch Street woman, for the money's sake, of course.'[53] For the others, however,

Most probably it is too late. Even if we could get them out into the country, away from their homes and the street which made them what they are, and could give them the most healthy and carefully selected surroundings, we could not make good of what they have missed during the first thirteen years of their lives, nor undo what they have had to endure in the way of evil.[54]

A common characteristic of evacuation stories, as well as Paneth's account of impoverished children left behind, is their capacity to elicit the feeling of disgust. In his book *The Anatomy of Disgust*, William Ian Miller described disgust as an emotion that mobilizes social hierarchies, while assigning differential locations within those hierarchies to those who provoke and feel it. Miller offered, 'The emotions that constitute our experience of being lower or lowered – shame and humiliation – exist in a rough economy with those passions which are the experience of reacting to the lowly, failed, and contaminating – disgust and contempt'.[55] Disgust, he observed, is also a profoundly paradoxical emotion as it simultaneously draws us towards and drives us away from its object; the object of disgust is compelling and repelling in the very same instance. The emotion of disgust plays a containing or bordering role, as it draws the contours of not necessarily the body but the self. The voluntary blurring or breaching of these borders 'marks privilege, intimacy, duty, and caring'.[56] Furthermore, Miller pointed to the intertwined relationship between expressions of disgust and moral judgement, remarking that 'moral judgement seems almost to demand the idiom of disgust. *That makes me sick. What revolting behavior! You give me the creeps*'.[57]

In one circulating rumour, evacuated children reportedly 'stripped several gardens of flowers, like a horde of locusts'. So unruly were these insect-children, it was said that even the youth hostel would not take them.[58] So often described as verminous, in this account, evacuees became inseparable from insects and parasitic infestation. Indeed, this was not an expression of a new sentiment. Children from impoverished families and communities had been described in this way even by those determined to protect society by saving such children, as the Bolton's Queen Street Mission which articulated in 1908, 'if children who are only pests to their mothers are not otherwise cared for and saved, they will most assuredly become pests to society, the hooligans of tomorrow and the despair of Church and State'.[59]

Miller insisted that emotions are never experienced in pure and singular form. Seemingly contradictory intonations of feeling mingle together. Contempt is one such contradictory emotion that can often accompany disgust. Miller characterized contempt as an emotion that historically shifted to support the coming of Western democracy by distributing more or less evenly the strategies of indifference that manage it, as well as 'the style of tolerance captured by the saying "live and let live"'.⁶⁰ Unlike contempt, which Miller suggested can promote, and is necessary to, acts of care and kindness or even love, disgust blocks such orientations insofar as it admits to perception of threat, and, therefore, it can 'lead to disproportionate responses; it often seeks removal, even eradication of the disgusting source of threat. But there is an ambivalence in the desire to eradicate. Like those we hate, those who disgust us define who we are and whom we are connected with. We need them too – downwind.'⁶¹

Therefore, the internal tensions that animated emotions and contempt and disgust may inform the ambivalence of charitable and humanitarian efforts to save and protect pets, the verminous, the insect, as well as the morally corrupted pests that concerned the Bolton Queen Street Mission and its 'From the Slum to the Sea' initiative that annually brought thousands of children from Bolton slums on excursions to the beach in the 1930s. 'From the Slum to the Sea' was framed as 'a battle against ignorance, misery, cruelty, a battle fought in vile surroundings on behalf of children with stunted bodies, poisoned minds and starved souls', and, as Francesca Moore argued, represents how middle-class women philanthropists engaged in 'race work' that was fed with an 'eugenic impulse'.⁶²

This hinge chapter has addressed how ambivalent conceptions of animacy crossed species lines to make hierarchies that were contested, context-specific, and shifting. I have also brought attention to the mutually paradoxical symbolic space that some children and non-working animals occupied in the negotiations of these implicit animacy hierarchies. I hope also that I have maintained that the discourse concerning use and sacrifice, although messy and shifting, was tied not only by the notion of utility but also an orientation of care, the concept that Miller tied to contempt.

5

# Careless Homes Cost Lives

Eileen Potter did not get a full night's sleep. The air raid siren whirred at 3.00 am, Monday, 4 September 1939. Drained, she sat on the stairs, the designated safe space, until the all-clear signal. In the morning, she arrived at the office where she was ordered to evacuate to Dorchester with a family, several small children and a nurse. All were whisked straight away to the station. On the train, she shared her lunch – sandwiches, an apple and a bar of chocolate – with the family, who had none of their own. In Dorchester, a kind woman invited her to billet at her home, where Potter could have a quiet space in the separate garden house. There, an exhausted Potter was offered a bath and, without visit or delay, sent to bed. The thought of rest promised respite from an overwhelming day. In the room allotted to her, Noel Coward waltzes played over the wireless, and a tray with tea and honey and piece of cake was delivered to her in bed. In her diary, she recorded 'a vague inclination to lapse into sentimental tears'.[1]

The division of a single apple amongst hungry travellers fleeing their homes at the start of war, the stranger's offer of shelter, the waltzes floating from the wireless left on for a weary traveller, the tea and cake – these were acts of care that made a difference. They made a difference in a context in which words perhaps fail to register contradictory feelings. Potter's diary pages do not tell us what she said, thought, or felt as a she portioned her sandwiches, apple and chocolate. She relayed not a single word from her host, only mentioning the subtle acts: the offering of the bath and the release from weighty social obligations that allowed her to go straight to bed. The wireless and the tea and cake seemed to originate from the host's consideration of Potter's circumstances, and these small acts anticipated what might sooth a guest under the circumstances. The tears these acts, or just the whole sum of experiences, nearly provoked for Potter were undoubtedly mixed ones. The shock, exhaustion and uncertainty were surely part of it, but the feelings were intonated with recognition of kindness and gratitude for it.

Pam Hobbs, an eleven-year-old evacuee, tried to make her discomfort discreet when the warm, elderly couple who billeted her in an ivy-covered Kirk Langley mansion excitedly informed her that they had invited her parents (of much humbler means), for a week-long visit in July 1941. Her dissembling was perhaps less subtle than she imagined: It's not allowed for parents to visit. Dad will probably be too busy. It will be too difficult for them to get train tickets. Mom surely cannot make the trip alone. Immersed in her life at Ivy House, cared for by 'Aunty' Min, 'Uncle' Fred, their maid, Vera, and followed around faithfully by a little piglet named Mardi, Pam felt the prospect of this visit an unwelcome intrusion upon her new life.[2] She had already almost come to resent letters from home peppered with accounts of rationing and bombs:

> I no longer hovered around the end of the drive waiting for the postman ... Accounts of queueing, and attempts to make meals from few ingredients, Mum's ongoing war with the local wardens about chinks in the blackout, were described with humour. But the truth was I read her news with a twinge of guilt, because a part of me didn't want to be there sharing the shortages and bombs and all of the other worrisome stuff going on at 19 Kent.[3]

Even if Pam's attempts to thwart the visit were less than subtle, her foster parents seemed not to notice. Uncle Fred went to Derby and bought the tickets himself, just in case. Pam's elder sister Vi took time away from the factory to accompany her Mom on the journey. The two arrived from Leigh-on-Sea in their best formal clothing. Pam's mother presented Min with clippings from her rosebushes, 'You seem to have everything already,' she coupled her offering with an implicit apology, 'so I didn't know what else to bring.'[4] Mom had insisted that Vi not smoke at Ivy House: 'It wasn't ladylike. These people weren't factory workers.' But, bright and early on the first morning, Vi and Min were found out in the garden smoking and drinking tea together. Whether she intended it, Min put to ease some of Mom's worries about the difference of habit, '"This is a vice the girlies don't know I have," she admitted, tucking her Players packet back into her apron pocket.'[5] Min sent Pam's mom home with fresh butter, a ham that was surely larger than she could have gotten on the ration, and eggs too, which Vi packed in her gas mask case so they would not break on the journey. Watching them depart, Pam was awash with regret for trying to prevent the visit.

## Being careful

If care, as noun, denotes provision and attention, these acts most certainly constitute those things. As a verb, care suggests feeling relations, potentially one-directional, of concern or affection. As noted in the introduction, care feels like a good word, perhaps most often associated with 'attentive conscientiousness or devotion'. Less often, it seems, the word care comes to refer to the circumstance of being encumbered with worries or troubles.[6] Thus, we are sometimes advised by well-wishers to let go of our cares. Or we are bidden to take care, which seems to exhort that we take our burdens with us. Warren T. Reich observed that care has two conflicting meanings: burdensome worry and attentive provision. He noted that, while Virgil gave shape to care's encumbering nature when noting that vengeful Cares placed their couches near to Grief and pale Diseases at the threshold of the underworld, Seneca stressed care as the path to goodness. Reich suggested, however, that this contradiction was resolved positively in the myth of Cura, who shaped a human being out of earth.

After Cura shaped a creature from earthen clay, she entreated Jupiter to breathe spirit into its lifeless form. Having granted this request, Jupiter objected when Cura wanted to name the creature after herself. Each felt that their contribution justified that it should have their own name. Tellus interrupted the dispute, insisting that the creature should carry her name – after all, it was moulded from her own body. Acting as the ultimate arbiter, Saturn gave it the name of homo, assigning its soul to Jupiter and body to Tellus after death, but granted the creature's life itself to Cura. 'The positive side of care dominates in this story,' Reich argued, 'for the primordial role of Care is to hold the human together in wholeness while cherishing it.'[7] A lovely thought, surely. But do these two senses of care, attentive devotion or 'solicitude' and burden of worries, really stand in sharp contradiction? Are they two distinct orientations?

Being attentive to the other's desire or need – whether that be for the beauty contained in a rose cutting or the flavour, sustenance and novel convenience that come with scarce foods – requires that one imagine from the other's position. Yet such acts of care can bring pain insofar as they depend upon a faulty imagination of the other. When the image of the other is wrong, or perhaps even a little too accurate, acts of care can feel like barbs or manifest in harm. Sometimes care can be a weapon. Or, when one is attentive to the other's position – as Pam was when she imagined the austerity of her parents' meals at home, while delighting in her own – this can crystallize guilt into cooling affective distance. The fact that there can be beauty in acts of caregiving does not elide the troubling fact that care is often born of asymmetrical relations, a point that Didier Fassin underlined in relation to humanitarian efforts. Likewise, Yi-Fu Tuan, in his elaboration of the making of pets and even the social positioning of women and children, insisted that the relation of care is usually forged in 'bonds of inequality'.[8] Thus, Tuan, who observed that 'The word *care* so exudes humaneness that we tend to forget its almost inevitable tainting by patronage and condescension',[9] does not let the carer dwell too long or comfortably in feelings of goodness but locates care in the uneasy tension between domination and affection.

The observation that care arises in relations of asymmetry has relevance for other interpretations of the myth of Cura that are not as warm as Reich's reading. For John T. Hamilton, the myth of Cura relays a story of indebtedness for the gift of life. Hamilton wrote, 'Human being (*homo*) is portrayed … as a creature endowed with multiple donations from the gods: a form, a body, a spirit, and a name. These provisions are not freely given but rather impose a series of obligations or debts' that will be paid at death, when Cura (care) will no longer possess it.[10] In death, when Saturn's judgement grants its body back to earth and its spirit back to Jupiter, the creature will be carefree, apart from care, *se-cura* – secure. Hamilton, who was interested in the relationship between the two words – care and security – that seem to share much more than their etymological relation, observed that an implication of the Cura myth is that security, 'a concern to be without concern',[11] finds its true realization only in death.

## Dwelling between care and security

Mass Observation argued that preparations for air war were so extensive that they transformed Britain's social structure by re-ordering the family, leisure, sex, shopping, civil authority and the home itself.[12] Insofar, as responsible homemakers were to orient their actions and emotions to the war effort specifically and to the population's interests generally through strategies of 'passive civil defence' that targeted the home and community,[13] they were endowed with tasks of biopolitical regulation. Biopolitics is concerned with the management and enhancement of life; not just individual life but the life of a population.

Jennifer Purcell noted, 'Whatever one did, or wanted to do, if it was done well and if it was deemed useful to the nation in its hour of need, it was important.'[14] Wartime civil defence imperatives endowed each action of the homemaker with forceful agency in the war effort. They warned: be careful what you say, as careless talk costs lives; be careful how you feel, because your resilience will bring us victory; be careful what you do in the kitchen because every scrap of waste kept saves lives; be careful how you travel or spend time indoors at night because no light should be seen from the sky; be brief on the telephone lest you interrupt vital communications; make-do and mend so that you do not squander scarce resources. These imperatives addressed citizen-subjects assumed to be responsible and agential. Like careless talk, homes could be careless and cost lives by going unfortified, being wasteful or infused with despondent emotions.

But at the same time that civil defence imperatives endowed each action of the homemaker with forceful agency to contribute to victory, there was another side to discourse surrounding the wartime home. There were some homes that were careless in other ways, and these, as material-spatial structures, possessed agency greater than that of their poor occupants. It was implicitly suggested that slum dwellers stood quite apart from the active wartime citizens that Air Raid Precaution (ARP) publicity was designed to engage.

Public discourse on the slum and its dangers was not novel to the Second World War, but negative evaluations of the first official evacuation, Operation Pied Piper, which sits at the intersection that Hamilton underlined between care and security, brought cause for the re-consideration of housing issues, as well as existing health and welfare services. Studies that followed up on the problems of evacuation assumed a perplexing distribution of agency to social and material actors, with the most destitute of the working classes presented as less agential than the built environments they inhabited. The striking language that characterized these studies, published in the early 1940s, produced a sense of urgency surrounding matters of social welfare, education, health and morality. Yet the broader context within which the dissemination of findings and recommendations occurred is relevant to their reception, especially with respect to the question of why affective disciplinary considerations of the post-war home could consume a nation at war. Examining the release of the County of London Plan, Frank Mort has argued that military successes in the summer of 1943 'not only marked a turning point in allied operations, they also intensified policy debates about postwar construction'.[15] Mort also situated these discussions in those raised by the Beveridge report and the white paper on state education, arguing, 'Almost all of the wartime programs for reconstruction, on social insurance, education, and the welfare state, achieved their expansive, collectivist impact partly by defining those groups [of people and places excluded from the plans] outside as well as inside the new social consensus.'[16]

In this concluding chapter, I extend the examination of how the Mass Observation movement recorded and shaped the logics of care that became central to the daily routines of civil defence to the problem of the ostensibly careless home as an animated built environment, asking how Mass Observation treated the relationship between homes and inhabitants. To begin, however, more must be said about how careless homes were imagined and their relationship to negative responses to evacuation.

## The careless home and its 'problem family'

Evacuation was first and foremost an expedient ARP strategy that saved lives and helped to preserve essential services in wartime emergencies. Researchers who studied it often explicitly referred to evacuation as an experiment, and recognized that it provided opportunities for interventions into perceived internal threats beyond the strict context of war,[17] ones similar to those that had motivated interwar initiatives to train working-class women about hygiene and nutrition.[18] Thus, negative reactions to evacuees became entangled with interwar fears about class, differential birth rates, race and the supposed decline of civilization at the same time that evacuation opened a space upon which a blueprint for a post-war Britain could be drawn and perhaps be built into the bodies of displaced children.

Eugenics advocates were vocal in the interwar years and exploited interwar anxieties by stressing that the differential birth rate would lead to the decline of civilization.[19] The debates that evacuation precipitated provided additional fodder for advocates of eugenics, whose concept of the 'problem social group' was refunctioned as the 'problem family'.[20] John Welshman has argued that 'the "problem family" was the inheritor of social attitudes that stretched back to the late nineteenth century and beyond', as well as to Charles Booth's well-known concept of 'the submerged tenth' often referenced in debates about mental deficiency.[21] The 1943 report *Our Towns: A Close Up* arose from the collaborative research and consultation of voluntary and professional contributors, who did not share a unified perspective on the matters to which it attended, thus it combines critical and conservative assessments and recommendations. Welshman attributed the report's influence to its contradictory character, since 'it echoed interwar debates about behaviour and citizenship, but also reflected the ideas that would shape the welfare state in the postwar years'.[22] Despite its internal contradictions, *Our Towns* promoted the concept of the problem family, describing it as 'always on the edge of pauperism and crime, riddled with mental and physical defects, in and out of the Courts for child neglect, a menace to the community'.[23] The so-called problem family was thus brought further into power's grasp so that more work could be done upon the working classes to free them from the supposed 'slum mind' and the contaminating dangers it posed by its 'gravitational pull'.[24] But Welshman also pointed to the connection between the concept of the problem family and the kind of process noted in the introduction to this volume, that of privatization and professionalization of politics, by showing that 'reports published about "problem families" tell us little of value about the families themselves and rather more about professional rivalries and connections' – those of the volunteer, the social worker and the doctor.[25] Each belonged to arenas that enjoyed expansion during and after the war, and reactions to the first evacuation scheme opened the space for these growing territories as well as their reach into the intimate lives of citizens, and welfare initiatives continued in distancing mothers from the collective life associated with working-class communities.[26]

Although derived from eugenic discourse in the first place, the new concept of the problem family appealed to the Eugenics Society, which later struck its own committee in 1947 to study it. Its chair, Charles Blacker, believed that adult members of problem families could not be educated due to their subnormality. While other organizations and individuals advocated different forms of education or even training in domesticity through the example of practical help, a *Lancet* article cited the home as an obstacle to the latter by arguing that 'to treat the family members and ignore the home would be "to treat the symptoms and leave the focus of disease untouched"'.[27] From that point of view, inhabitants were the symptoms, while the home was the source of a disease.

According to Matthew Hollow, the blitz, which struck many of the places from which the often-maligned children and mothers were evacuated, 'transformed the idea of re-building Britain from a loosely defined and vaguely desirable objective into a coherent necessity',[28] while placing environments and their effects under more intense scrutiny. *Our Towns* had attributed not only the spread of deadly illnesses, such as diphtheria and tuberculosis, but also 'warped character' and delinquency to overcrowded slums. The home and environment were granted the capacity to 'aggravate the serious and growing problem of the dull child', who would 'grow up to produce most of the problem families of the next generation including many of the feeble-minded'.[29] Good homes, on the other hand, could perhaps rehabilitate problem families – or, some of them, since *Our Towns* had suggested targeting rehousing initiatives towards what it called 'grey rather than black families'. While it described 'grey' families as unwholesome, they were considered capable of improvement, the 'black' ones were characterized as unmovable and impervious to new influences.[30] In either case, a crucial answer was proposed in the report's emphasis on the need for nursery schools, which would remove children from the home and serve as 'the only agency capable of cutting the slum mind off at the root and building the whole child while yet there is time ... they [the nursery years] are in fact those years which give the best hope of influencing three generations – the child, its parents and its offspring'.³¹

Debates over post-war housing imagined built environments that could save ostensibly eroded lives and cast some working-class populations as passive objects to be worked upon through training, surveillance and discipline built right into housing and community development schemes.³² Hollow has argued that the blitz provided vast, flattened-out, "socially empty" spaces in the centres of Britain's main cities upon which planners could project their visions for the future'.³³ From the planning perspective, the flattening of metropolitan spaces, overcrowded, out-of-date, of poorly mixed function, provided both opportunity and justification for extensive, utopian re-imagining of spaces. Thus, 'it would not be overstating things to suggest that a great many planners positively relished the opportunities that the Blitz had provided them with', pointing to a town planner's reference to Nazi bombers as effective 'site-clearing agencies' and architect Clough Williams-Ellis's unrestrained assertion that 'today [our cities] are all swept away, to the undisguised delight of the more enlightened citizens and of the very able city architect'. But, of course, the blitz did more than hit 'an already existing chaos',³⁴ it wiped away homes, communities, as well as lives. It made strikes upon the places from which children and mothers were evacuated.

The main tension in public discourses that centred on slum districts and strategies of, what Francesca Moore has called 'biological and social defence', rested upon debate about the determining capacities of heredity and environment to produce 'dull' children who would parent the next generation.³⁵ Environmental explanations appealed to progressive people, as well as to moderate eugenics advocates, who tended to support selective pro-natalism and welfare reforms, but still assumed the existence of a significant sub-population whose members posed inheritance risks. The distinction between heredity and environment, as well as the ways that they could interact, was often presented in blurry and opaque ways, and appeals to environmental factors did not necessarily depart from eugenic projects. Even in the mid-1930s, the Eugenics Society had been stressing the marriage between heredity and environment as potential threats to child welfare. Richard Overy observed, 'The preoccupation with race improvement did not preclude a genuine desire to ameliorate the conditions of pauperization and chronic ill-health',³⁶ hence, social welfare and exhortations towards the care of vulnerable or disadvantaged subjects require attentive interrogation insofar as they responded to some of the demands of the eugenics movement at the same time that they, as Nikolas Rose remarked, appealed to

**Figure 5.1** We've great things to do, keep on Saving, Poster issued by the National Savings Committee, c. 1944.

advocates who saw these causes as 'progressive and humanitarian, in touch with the latest scientific evidence'.[37]

A critical aspect of the opaque constructions of circular causality between heredity and environment is their similarity with the more flexible and relational conception of the body in the nineteenth-century discourse of impressibility, which 'indexed the agential responsiveness of the nervous system to external stimuli'. According to Kyla Schuller, the presumed state of unimpressibility, or mere reaction, was a racializing attribution, while '[i]mpressibility was understood to be an acquired quality of the refined nervous system that accrues over evolutionary time through the habits of civilization that transform animal substrate into the cultural grounds of self-constitution'.[38] Since it referred to a state that involves reflection and the capacity for attachment, impressibility departed from the meaning of impressionability, which denoted a passive state that 'characterizes how a living body is acted on by the animate and inanimate objects of its environment'.[39] This distinction has its roots in Jean-Baptiste Lamarck's evolutionary theory and Thomas Malthus' theory of population. In the 1920s, Ernest William Barnes, Bishop of Birmingham, advocated positive eugenics with appeal to the theory of 'chemical Lamarckism' or 'germ-weakening', which was thought to be 'caused by inner-city overcrowding'.[40] Although Lamarckism was relatively marginalized, the Soviet Union adopted a variant in the late 1920s, thus, according to Patrick Merricks, it came to influence some British socialists who were more open to theories that emphasized environment over genetics.[41]

I raise this because it illustrates the eugenic impulse of biopolitical regulation. Biopolitics and eugenics are historically intertwined. The term biopolitics arose in the twentieth-century interwar period when classical conceptions of the state were challenged by the growing belief that the state was a living organism whose existence would be determined by the relatively homogenous genetic heritage of its population and that social ills have their origin in biological factors.[42] Although Germany's National Socialists were not alone in holding this view, the Nazi expression of biopolitical thought in overtly racist terms alarmed observers and initiated a flurry of scientific counter-discourses on race that placed new emphasis on cultural or ethnic 'types'. In Britain, the 1935 book *We Europeans: A Survey in 'Racial' Problems* showed that the biological concept of race could not be supported scientifically. Its authorship is formally attributed to the well-known zoologist, Julian Huxley and Alfred C. Haddon, an ethnologist, even though, as Tony Kushner, following Barkan, has pointed out, Charles Singer, a science historian, and Charles Seligman, an anthropologist, were contributing authors. In excluding their names, the presumption was that the participation of two Jewish scholars would open *We Europeans* to the criticism of bias or lend 'ammunition to antisemites at home and abroad'.[43] Approaching the subject matter through systematic study and multiple disciplinary lenses, *We Europeans* demonstrated that

> When, in fact, the differences which go to make up these commonly accepted distinctions between 'racial stocks' and nationalities are more strictly examined, it will usually be found that there is very little in them that has any close relation to the physical characteristics by which 'race' in the biological sense can be distinguished ... it will generally be found that the distinctive qualities upon which stress is laid are cultural rather than physical, and when physical they are often introduced by climatic and cultural conditions.[44]

The re-accentuation from race to culture had paradoxical impacts on biopolitical thought and vernacular expressions of difference that often implicated and contributed to the ongoing relational shaping of social classes and cultural identities. Indeed, *We Europeans* forcefully denounced the use of the word race on scientific grounds. On the one hand, this work had the positive impact of further weakening the perceived veracity of racial typologies but did not eliminate racialized hierarchies or biological preoccupations and the attachment of social meaning to them.[45] On the other hand, the racialization of culture lent fuel to existing and tumultuous inter-cultural prejudices within Europe, and perhaps to prejudices already existing within Britain in its persistently drawn analogy between the domestic undeserving poor and, with some exception, the imperial other.[46] Thus, when Kushner observed, 'A less optimistic reading [of *We Europeans*] would point to the continuation of racial thinking alongside anti-racism',[47] he underlined that racial thinking has no need for the noun race or a substance to which at different historical moments it denotes.

Prejudices rearticulated in cultural or ethnic terms were widened and sharpened during the war, as understandings of culture, race and state were undergoing reconceptualization. Hence, with respect to biopolitical assumptions, social ills could be assumed to be found in cultural contagions of immorality, uncleanliness, laziness and uncivilized manners within a nation's population. This informs the perplexing demarcation of agential capacity between the sub-populations addressed by ARP publicity, presumed to be responsive, and those that were conceived to be suggestible, impressionable, merely reactive and presented as an effect of 'slum' dwellings.

## Mass Observation

While discourse circulated about lively but careless homes and environments capable of imprinting themselves on inhabitants characterized as less lively and in need of discipline, Mass Observation reported the resourceful and creative patterns by which people lived when in overcrowded, dilapidated built environments and sought to bring attention to existing structural constraints. Attributing a single perspective to Mass Observation is not possible, since the movement's participants were multiple, and its apparent coherence was produced through the framing of problems, the methods used and the centralized production of written reports overseen by its organizers. Mass Observation was relatively silent on eugenics. Yet Mass Observation's organizational structure shifted over time, especially after Harrisson was conscripted and gradually became more removed from its operations. So, while it did not directly address eugenics in its reports and publications of the period (its work often indirectly challenged eugenic assumptions), a notable exception to this can be found in *Britain and Her Birth-rate* (1945), prepared under the auspices of the Advertising Service Guild and under David Ferraby's direction and primary authorship.[48] It responded to the assumption that new homes might make more babies. Eager to show that they could make effective interventions into the social problems of the time, some planning professionals proposed that reconstruction could address the falling birth rate. Lewis Mumford's articulation of this attributed town planning with a 'sympathetic magic' by which 'the impulse to bear' will be bestowed upon women.[49] While *Britain and Her Birth-rate* produced detailed inquiries and recommendations that ran counter to prevailing assumptions at the time, it was an instrument for, and product of, demographic racism and thus stands apart from the other Mass Observation work.[50] In this respect, rather than the commercial work or even the covert intelligence operations for the Ministry of Information, it is the birth rate text that marks a discrete departure from Mass Observation's founding critical aims in 1937 and the ultimate fracture in the project of the early Mass Observation.

Kushner argued that the dangers of the concept of race, 'racism, nationalism and the position of minorities inside and outside of Britain' were from the beginning among the central concerns of the Mass Observation project. According to Kushner, Mass Observation's inclusion of antisemitism among its (at first glance) idiosyncratic list of objects of investigation (taboos about food, eyebrows, behaviour in bathrooms), illustrate that its founders recognized 'race' as a form of superstition that was 'a key feature of European society and culture and that antisemitism was at the heart of it'.[51] While their project was not free of the ubiquitous biopolitical assumptions that have historically furnished modern rationality, Mass Observation consistently pushed against administrative and technocratic approaches taken to the lives of social subjects and aimed to 'record the impacts of these world shaking times in terms of the ordinary people in this country'.[52] Mass Observation challenged renderings of some working classes as passive, impressionable objects to be worked upon or corrected, and Harrisson stressed that their fieldwork had demonstrated that class differences were not inherent, but relational, regional, overlapping and overall unstable.[53]

Concerning housing, Mass Observation made three mutually connected moves. First, it consistently argued what it had since its conception: before treating a problem as an administrative or planning one, sincere and sound inquiries into social realities must be undertaken.[54] Planning needed to be responsive to real social patterns of living and, as Harrisson would remark, 'For pity's sake let us make sure that this time we remember minds as well as bodies, babies as well as baths, people's hopes and fears and beers as well as their taps and switches and pedestrian crossings.'[55] Thus, Mass Observation contended that, while planners may reshape needs, they must first utilize the social sciences to know the minds of the people from whom they live at a distance. Second, Mass Observation's studies highlighted the ways that everyday life was lived in creative ingenuity even in constrained circumstances. Third, against the tendency of planners to give priority to abstract notions and speculative paper plans that treat people anonymously and with indifference, 'as if they were numerical units to be redistributed into a larger cubic capacity of air with a larger number of adjacent bathrooms',[56] Mass Observation advocated for consideration of the complex lives of individuals as situated within their personal and social bonds, eschewing the bureaucratic forms of care that social reformers, planners and architects exercised in dialogues on housing.

If, for instance, suburban housing estates had been designed to create new microcosms of surveillance and control to alter the patterns of social life, Mass Observations showed how inhabitants of one estate made the bus one of its central social sites. Its jovial tenor would sometimes approximate that of the old neighbourhood pub, which was deliberately absent from the estate – an absence that drew criticism from Mass Observation, given that the pub was a key social site.[57] Harrisson, who had lived in Letchworth, a model for the Garden City, for almost two years to 'learn what sort of Utopia this was', reflected, 'For myself I can only say that in none of the places in which I have lived have I found less feeling of community, more individual loneliness.'[58] So much for utopia then.

Brian Lewis has noted that housing costs prevented Letchworth from attracting residents from different social classes, and 'to the dismay of the directors became famous for a motley, outspoken collection of smock-and-sandal-wearing, hat-and-glove-discarding freethinkers, vegetarians, teetotalers, feminists, Esperanto enthusiasts ... all in pursuit of the simple life'.[59] Ever cautious about architects' and planners' schemes, Harrisson once boasted that Mass Observation's preliminary results on housing 'provided enough ammunition to blow a lot of architectural assumptions from here to Port Sunlight'[60] – the playful reference was to the community that the Lever Brothers had built for their soap factory workers in Wirrel, Merseyside, where 'in the country with good houses for the workpeople to live we get a more settled body of workers', William Lever had reasoned, and 'a still further improvement in the workpeople of each succeeding generation'.[61]

Mass Observation's contributions to debates on rehousing Britain offer a more complex view of working-class home dwellers. While Mass Observation did not directly respond to the subtle discursive renderings of impressionable inhabitants and morally agential homes, the organization was clearly dissatisfied with plans that aimed to 'rearrange people', and assumptions that 'ordinary people want better ones than they live in'.[62] Mass Observation organizers discussed plans to carry out a study that would 'make people think again about what they are reconstructing, who they are reconstructing, why they are doing it'.[63]

In their *Enquiry into People's Homes*, published by the Advertising Service Guild, Mass Observation argued as they had in other instances that successful plans must 'depend on the people'.[64] They insisted upon the leadership that housewives, as the primary 'homebuilders', could provide to planners and architects. They estimated that a post-war housing shortage would demand several million new homes in addition to the mass need for existing home refitting to meet habitation standards. Therefore, they approached working-class housewives for open-ended interviews that they promised would bring about visions of the home as '*spontaneously* raised by [working-class] housewives themselves'.[65]

It observed in people's comments the social significance of the kitchen, noting also that this was the room that had been becoming smaller in new designs. Many of those interviewed had only a kitchenette and living room. One woman said: 'We need an extra room here. The kitchen is only a scullery, and it's hard work to keep one room nice for sitting in and eating in.' Another offered, 'If the food's on the table and someone calls, you've got nowhere to ask them in if you want to talk private, you've got to stay on the doorstep.'[66] Melanie Tebbutt has stressed the social significance of the best room or parlour for those who had one – its limit could operate as a border between visitors and the goings on of the deeper home interior – but its reserve could make a site of imagination and hope too.[67] Mass Observation also followed women in their housework routines, tracking how the lay-out of the residence implicated the duration and difficulties of the labour involved and the strategies that they used to mitigate inconvenient spatial arrangements that require the housewife in the course of daily tasks to walk 'several hundred yards, going from room to room, upstairs, downstairs, and out into the yard or garden'[68] and inadequate sinks and storage that increased labour by forcing the washing, drying and putting away of only a few dishes at a time over several cycles. *People's Homes* provided multiple detailed findings concerning the needs and desires of housewives that could inform the blueprints of post-war homes, but some ambiguity arose where interviewers appeared to be disappointed in the interviewees' responses, for example, when they did not seem to view their communities as potential sites of civic engagement. At the policy level, Mass Observation stressed the social structure, asserting, 'This is not so much a housing problem as the general political and social problem of establishing a national minimum standard of living, below which no person or family should be allowed to fall. No such national minimum would be adequate unless it included a minimum standard of housing space and amenities.'[69]

The participatory fieldwork of Mass Observers who embedded themselves in shelters during the blitz gave accounts of a provisional kind of homemaking and make-do domesticity, which lead to their article 'The Tube Dwellers', published in 1943. The question it posed at the time was: Why do thousands of Londoners essentially live in the tubes so long after the area had experienced what had been the last serious raid? Mass observers watched as some people would leave the tubes in the early hours of the morning only to line up to mark places for their families for the next evening. They held that people were now not merely sheltering in the tubes, but living in them. This can only be understood, the article suggested, by considering what was happening in the tube shelters almost two years prior. What brought people to the tubes during the winter of 1941 and 1942 'was not merely a desire for safety ... During that winter this country saw the first stages of the formation of a new community; perhaps one of the strangest communities in recorded history.'[70]

In fact, Mass Observation's investigators had long been watching the development of these communities and making policy recommendations to protect them. In a report to Home Intelligence in October of 1940, Mass

Observation raised concerns about the effects on morale of queuing for tube shelters for long periods. Noting that, as winter approached and the weather worsened, this matter required urgent attention. Mass Observation recommended that allocated spaces would help to alleviate the strains this placed especially upon children. Yet it critiqued plans that had been recently announced in Middlesbrough and cautioned that any policy meant to alleviate this problem must be careful not to take an 'inhuman approach' by breaking up shelter communities that have spontaneously been built.[71]

Going back to old notes of field visits during the blitz, the 1943 article remarked that what was initially 'chaotic and undisciplined' tube life, marked by squabbles over spaces and intimate quarrelling between family members occurring in full view, grew into a community – a new society, for which a 'code of unwritten laws' was actively negotiated. 'Each shelter,' according to Mass Observation, 'became more and more a self-sufficient community, with its own leaders, traditions and laws.'[72]

During the blitz, some people avoided the tube shelters, considering them to be populated with rough or rowdy sorts, but Mass Observation argued that 'the real explanation seems to lie not so much in the character of the individuals as in the complete novelty of the social set-up. With the disappearance of all ordinary ways of life it was only to be expected that some of the ordinary canons of behaviour should also have been set aside.'[73] Back in the wintery evenings of the blitz, tube-dweller norms were in a state of collective making. If people originally sought out the tubes for safety, by 1943 they continued to go for the new life to be had there, the social group and 'family atmosphere' that had emerged. Some had traded 'solitary bed-sitting rooms with a gas ring' for the light and sociality of the tubes.[74] For housewives, a considerable amount of household duties could be avoided if the family spent its leisure time and took meals in the shelter. Some people surprised themselves, forging new social skills and talents for organizing and cooperating with others. Auntie Mabel, a shelter marshal, knew everyone and everyone knew her. Such a person provided an anchor in the 'family atmosphere' that Mass Observation found still thriving in April of 1943. At that time, however, it noted that some of these tube communities were beginning to show signs of disintegration as people moved back to their homes and new internal rhythms. But not just yet – in the meanwhile, a mass observer at a North London shelter was encouraged by tube community inhabitants to 'Come an' have a look at our newest baby, he's only three weeks old.'[75]

Thus, as the cameras of ordinary life that mass observers in 1937 had set out to become, they rendered snapshots that captured aspects of life often missed. If the tube shelters seemed miserable and disordered to passers-by or the infrequent user (and they did), mass observers could find something in them beyond the bickering and dramatic struggles over territories marked out with sometimes tattered blankets. As they did in other contexts as well, Mass Observation sought and found the social glue that held apparently unlikely social bonds together, while emphasizing the creative liveliness of social subjects and communities along the way. The experiences in tube shelters were too heterogeneous and shifting to describe as simply bad or good, end of story. Social life is fuller and messier than that. With the plethora of facts it sought and presented in different forms to different audiences, Mass Observation frequently interrupted prevailing and official narratives at the time. What Derek Sayer argued about Mass Observation's *May the Twelfth* (the publication of day surveys on the coronation of King George VI and Queen Elizabeth), which took a form quite different from the publications that followed, is in many ways also relevant to its more conventionally composed works:

> Mass-Observation's 'subjective cameras, each with his or her own distortion,' bring 'society' to visibility not as a singular reified abstraction but in a multiplicity of images shot by a multitude of differently situated observers – something that is always in flux and can never be described either in its totality or independently of the biases of one or another point of view. These images are not put forward as illustrations of a thesis or evidence supporting an argument. *They are the argument.* The point is not to make the world artificially coherent in order to render it comprehensible.[76]

During the Second World War, civil defence strategies were saturated with profound social contradictions insofar as they were intertwined with aspirations towards social engineering and population control. Civil defence imperatives re-ordered everyday life and promoted regimes of caregiving for each other, the domestic landscape and the ideal of the nation, according to indifferent, biopolitical logics. Through exhaustive study of everyday life throughout the war, Mass Observation's participatory movement continued what it set out to do in 1937, to find out what really put people on tenterhooks, locate contemporary superstitions, map public feeling and enhance the conditions for a vibrant public sphere that could rest upon the dynamics of distributed communication rather than the flattened one-directional transfer of information that routinely positioned ordinary people as receivers of elite messages to which they were expected to defer. Like the pieces of an apple shared among strangers on a train, eggs delicately packed in a gas mask case so they won't break, waltzes playing on the wireless at the end of a long and uncertain journey – the work Mass Observation did then, the alternative futures it imagined, the archive it left us – it was a kind of care.

# Notes

## Imperatives: A Preface

1 The National Archives (TNA), Home Office (HO) 186/113, Draft of War Emergency Instructions: What You Should Know and What You Should Do, probably June 1939, 1.
2 TNA, HO 186/113, The Protection of Your Home Against Air Raids, Leaflet, 1938, 1, 9.
3 Ibid., 13–19.
4 Churchman's Cigarettes collectible card series, Air Raid Precautions, No. 17: Extinction of Incendiary Bomb (Transferring the Bomb to the Redhill Container), Replica, Edinburgh: Memorabilia Pack Company.
5 TNA, HO 186/113, The Protection of Your Home Against Air Raids, Leaflet, 1938, 19.
6 Greene, *The Ministry of Fear*, 26.
7 TNA, HO 186/113, The Protection of Your Home Against Air Raids, Leaflet, 1938, 6–7.
8 TNA, HO 186/2247, War Gas Leaflet, Ministry of Home Security. Available online: http://www.nationalarchives.gov.uk/education/resources/home-front/source-3c (accessed 5 January 2019).
9 This is how Wells described the Great War in his 1933 speculative future history, 'The Shape of Things to Come', which predicted the outbreak of a second world war in 1940. Kindle locations 170893, 170947.
10 TNA, Board of Education 136/112, Shena D. Simon, 'The Children in War-Time: How to Rebuild the Educational System', London: Worker's Educational Association, 1940, 4.
11 Isaacs et al., *The Cambridge Evacuation Survey*, 1, suggests that these plans were shared and negotiated with local authorities in the twelve months prior to the first evacuation. Titmuss, *Problems of Social Policy*, however, notes a much longer period for the discussion and drafting of various civilian protection plans in government department committees from as early as the 1920s, as '[t]he first shadowy outlines' of the picture of a future war were sketched by the impacts of German air raids in the First World War, which injured 4,820 and killed 1,413, Kindle locations 213, 278. See also Harrisson, *Living Through the Blitz*, 34.
12 Titmuss, *Problems of Social Policy*, Kindle location 280.
13 Turner, *The Phoney War*, 75.

14 Lindqvist, *A History of Bombing*, 27.
15 Greene, *The Ministry of Fear*, 64–5.
16 Lindqvist, *A History of Bombing*, 27.
17 Greene, *The Ministry of Fear*, 65.
18 Lindqvist, *A History of Bombing*, 5 and 82–3.
19 Grayzel, *At Home and Under Fire*, 37.
20 Holman, '"Bomb Back, and Bomb Hard"', 400.
21 Grayzel, *At Home and Under Fire*, 36.
22 Holman, 'The Shadow of the Airliner', 499, 500.
23 Hamilton, *Theodore Savage*, 51.
24 Ibid., 69, 73.
25 Quoted in Robinson, 'Invisible Targets, Strengthened Morale', 356.
26 See Stradling, *Your Children Will Be Next*.
27 Brown, *J.D. Bernal*, 122.
28 Ibid., 131.
29 The Keep (TK), Mass Observation Archive (MOA) 26 Mass Observation Organisation and History, 1/3 Bulletin Drafts, MO Publications – reviews and comments, Draft of April 1938 bulletin, 2.
30 Quoted in Stradling, *Your Children Will Be Next*, 8.
31 'This is War!' *Picture Post* 1.10, 3 December 1938, 26.
32 'A Realistic Plan for A.R.P.' *Picture Post* 2.3, 21 January 1939.
33 Quoted in Shapira, *The War Inside*, 33.
34 Grayzel, *At Home and Under Fire*, 3.
35 Noakes, '"Serve to Save"', 735.
36 Titmuss, *Problems of Social Policy*, Kindle location 263–306.
37 TNA, HO 186/113, 'Public Defence: Some Things You Should Know if War Should Come', Public Leaflet No. 1. Lord Privy Seal's Office. June 1939. Excessive purchases of food were discouraged in instructions prepared to be issued in a war emergency in the draft of War Emergency Instructions, 'What You Should Know and What You Should Do'. Undated.
38 TNA, HO 186/113, Letter from Lord Privy Seal to Mr. Eady, 1 May 1939.
39 TNA, HO 186/113, 'Public Defence: Some Things You Should Know if War Should Come', Public Leaflet No. 1. Lord Privy Seal's Office. June 1939. A later formulation of this statement in a document prepared for issue in an emergency removes the direct reference to the life of the nation and instead proposes: 'The work of the country must be carried on so far as possible', Draft of War Emergency Instructions: 'What You Should Know and What You Should Do'. Undated, probably late spring 1939.
40 TNA, HO 186/113, Letter drafted in the Lord Privy Seal's office. Unaddressed, probably April 1939.
41 Rose, 'Women's Rights, Women's Obligations', 278.

42 National panellist quoted in TK, MOA File Report (FR) 2 Government Posters in War-Time, 18 October 1939, 35.
43 Respondent quoted in TK, MOA FR 2 Government Posters in War-Time, 18 October 1939, 73.
44 TK, MOA FR 2 Government Posters in War-Time, 18 October 1939, 78–9.
45 Ibid., 86–7.
46 Ibid., 94.
47 Ibid., 91.
48 Saint-Amour, *Tense Future*, 7.
49 Ibid., 8.
50 TK, MOA FR 3 The Public Information Leaflets, 18 October 1939, 11.
51 National panellist quoted in MOA FR 3 The Public Information Leaflets, 18 October 1939, 12.
52 Ibid., 18.
53 MOA FR 3 The Public Information Leaflets, 18 October 1939, 16.
54 Orwell, *Coming Up for Air*, 27.
55 TK, MOA Diarist (D) 5390, 1 September 1939. Selected diary entries from this Glasgow secretary are abridged from 29 August 1939 to 28 October 1940 in Garfield, *We Are at War*. The name Pam Ashford is the pseudonym Garfield gave to her, and I am following this convention. Not all the quotations used here are included in the book, however.
56 TK, MOA D 5390, 6 September 1939.
57 Orwell, *Coming Up for Air*, 237.
58 TK, MOA D 5390, 20 September 1939.
59 Ibid., 3 September 1939.
60 Trevelyan, *Indigo Days*, 109.
61 Purcell, *Domestic Soldiers*, 2–3.
62 TNA, HO 186/113, The Protection of Your Home Against Air Raids, Leaflet, 1938, 5.
63 TNA, INF 13/17/6, She's in the Ranks Too. Poster. Central Office of Information.
64 Imperial War Museum (IMW), Posters (PST) 20030, ARP – Serve to Save. Poster designed by F. Gardner, HMSO, 1939.
65 IWM PST 2983, When you go out don't crow about…the things you know about, Abram Games. War Office. 1945.
66 IMW PST 13953, Keep it under your hat! Careless Talk Costs Lives, John Gilroy. Poster, 1941.
67 IWM PST 0142, You never know who's listening! Careless Talk Costs Lives, Fougasse (Cyril Kenneth Bird), Poster, Ministry of Information, 1942.
68 TNA. EXT 1/116/2, Look before you sleep. Poster. Extracted from INF 13/215 Ministry of Information and Ministry of Labour flyers.
69 Tom Wintringham, 'Against Invasion: The Lessons of Spain', *Picture Post* 7.11, 15 June 1940, 17.

70 'The Beauty of Britain', *Picture Post* 7.12, 22 June 1940, 16–17.
71 This phrase marked a series of National Savings posters for the campaign that 'helped finance the war effort by promising aspiring British savers affluence and stability once the war was over'. See Slocombe, *British Posters of the Second World War*, 88.
72 IWM PST 2916, Use Spades Not Ships – Grow Your Own Food, Abram Games, Poster, HMSO, 1942.
73 IWM PST 20697, Help Win the War on the Kitchen Front: Above all avoid waste, Ministry of Food, Poster, date unknown.
74 IWM PST 14778, Save Kitchen Scraps To Feed The Hens! Poster. HMSO, Poster, 1939–1945.
75 TNA. INF 13/299/24, This Means You, Central Office of Information, Poster, 1942–1947.
76 TNA. INF 13/299/42, What Mrs Housewife can learn to do, Central Office of Information, Poster, 1942–1947.
77 The wartime character of the squanderbug as a saboteur of the war effort was used to promote thrifty behaviour. It appeared on posters and in cartoons. In 1943, Phillip Boydell designed a poster urging frugality in the form of a Wanted Poster depicting the squanderbug. See Slocombe, *British Posters of the Second World War*, 49.
78 Donia Nachshen designed the two posters for the Board of Trade in 1942: the first was the well-known Make-do and Mend, the second urged designs that could be tailored for children's growth. See Slocombe, *British Posters of the Second World War*, 73.
79 TNA, INF 2/72, How to Make Your Linens Last Longer, Central Office of Information, Poster, 1940–1945.
80 Bailey, *Can Any Mother Help Me?*, 91, 93.
81 Harrisson, *Living through the Blitz*, 19.
82 Shapira, *The War Inside*, 27.
83 Harris, 'War and Social History', 22.
84 Quoted in Bell, 'Landscapes of Fear', 172.
85 Harrisson, *Living through the Blitz*, 20.

# Introduction: Read, Listen, Obey and Keep a Good Heart

1 These are four of nine direct imperatives that appear in a Home Office draft of war emergency instructions. The National Archives (TNA), Home Office (HO) 186/113, Draft of War Emergency Instructions: 'What You Should Know and What You Should Do', probably June 1939.
2 Noakes, '"Serve to Save"', 735.
3 Grayzel, *At Home and Under Fire*, 3.
4 Noakes, '"Serve to Save"', 735.

5 See University of Liverpool Social Science Department, *Preliminary Report on the Problems of Evacuation*; University of Liverpool Social Science Department, *Our Wartime Guests*; Mass Observation, *War Begins at Home*; Wagner, 'Evacuation'; Crosby, *The Impact of Civilian Evacuation in the Second World War*; McLaine, *Ministry of Morale*; Rose, *Which People's War?*
6 TNA, Board of Education 136/112, Minister of Health, Memorandum on Evacuation, 11 April 1940, 7. See also University of Liverpool Social Science Department, *Our Wartime Guests*; Isaacs et al., *The Cambridge Evacuation Survey*.
7 The Keep (TK), Mass Observation Archive (MOA) File Report (FR) 79 Public Feeling about Aliens, 25 April 1940; FR 174 Refugees, 6 June 1940.
8 Warren T. Reich. 'History of the Notion of Care', The History of Care, Georgetown University. Available online: http://care.georgetown.edu/Classic%20Article.html (accessed 21 June 2018).
9 Fassin, *Humanitarian Reason*, 191.
10 Tuan, *Dominance and Affection*, 163.
11 Stevenson, *Life Beside Itself*, 3.
12 Ibid., 84.
13 Mass Observation, *War Begins at Home*, 306–11.
14 Ibid., 295.
15 Ibid., 313.
16 Turner, *The Phoney War*, 113. See also Kean, *Animal Rights*; *The Great Cat and Dog Massacre*.
17 'Friends for the Lonely: Companionship of Dogs', *The Times*, 13 June 1938; 'Dog Breeding in War Time: Plenty of Suitable Food', *The Times*, 3 October 1938; 'Dogs in War-Time: Exaggerated Reports of Destruction', *The Times*, 2 October 1939. Entrepreneurial enterprises also advocated for keeping pets by targeting goods for wartime.
18 TK, MOA FR 838 Provincial Dogs, 20 August 1941. Despite Mass Observation findings that, where pets were concerned, strains on the food supply were more pronounced in some reception areas than in towns.
19 TK, MOA TC 79 Dogs in War Time 1939–42, 1/E Survey of non dog owners – August 1941.
20 TK, MOA FR 804 Dogs in London, 29 July 1941, appendix III, point 1.
21 Several sources stress the relationship between citizenship and everyday life, for instance: Morgan and Evans, *The Battle for Britain*; Lin, 'National Identity and Social Mobility'; Cunningham and Gardner, '"Saving the nation's children"'; Rose, *Which People's War?* and 'Women's Rights, Women's Obligations'; Jerolmack, 'Animal Practices, Ethnicity, and Community'; Purcell, 'The Domestic Soldier'; Noakes, '"Serve to Save"'; Grayzel, *At Home and Under Fire*.
22 Purcell, *Domestic Soldiers*, 77. One of the Mass Observation diarists removed her child who had suffered abuse and neglect.

23 Critiques of this consensus include Rose, *Which People's War?* and Lowe, 'The Second World War'. Rose emphasized wartime, while Lowe focused on wartime and post-war, particularly regarding welfare state development and frames the ways that the thesis of consensus has been challenged in historical and political science scholarship to show that it had limitations and shifted across time and context. Lowe's article sought to clarify the thesis of consensus, in part, through a productive elaboration of the terms consensus and welfare state (showing the former's inheritance from the functionalist organic analogy), as well as through a historical unpacking of the wartime and post-war consensus for which Lowe found 'conflicting chronologies' between accounts. At the level of popular consensus during the war, Lowe suggested that 'A general feeling of "social solidarity" would also appear to have been an "artificially manufactured myth"', 157, 175.
24 Addison, *The Road to 1945*, 18.
25 Brooke, *Reform and Reconstruction*, 8.
26 Harris, 'War and Social History', 24.
27 Calder, *The People's War*, 34.
28 Ibid.
29 Harris, 'War and Social History', 31–2.
30 Ibid., 26–7.
31 Todd, *The People*, 131.
32 Ibid., 133.
33 Ibid., 148.
34 Nicolson, *Diaries and Letters 1939–1945*, 57.
35 Cannadine, *Aspects of Aristocracy*, 219.
36 Summerfield, 'The "Levelling of Class"', 201.
37 Rose, *Which People's War?*, 2.
38 Ibid., 21.
39 Ibid., 6.
40 Ibid., 24–5.
41 Ibid., 18.
42 Wiggam, *The Blackout in Britain and Germany*, 2.
43 Summerfield and Peniston-Bird, 'Women in the Firing Line', 236–7.
44 Ibid., 232.
45 Langhamer, '"A Public House is for All Classes, Men and Women Alike"', 437.
46 Ibid., 437.
47 Purcell, 'The Domestic Soldier', 153.
48 Ibid., 154.
49 Summerfield and Peniston-Bird, 'Women in the Firing Line', 232.
50 King, 'Future Citizens', 394.
51 Ibid., 393.

52 Ibid., 399.
53 Quoted in ibid., King's parentheses.
54 Mayall and Morrow, *You Can Help Your Country*, 129.
55 Rose, *Which People's War?*, 18.
56 TNA, HO 186/113, Draft for leaflet, 'What Will an Air Raid Be Like?', 1939.
57 Bell, 'Landscapes of Fear', 155.
58 Calder, *The People's War*, 61 and 69. In a personal letter written to his sister in November 1939, Chamberlain speculated that the war would end by the spring of 1940, as the Germans would come to see victory as not worth its cost. Public opinion varied, but Mass Observation found that one in five surveyed in autumn 1939 thought that the war would be over within six months. Officially, the plans were designed for a three-year war.
59 Welshman, 'Evacuation and Social Policy During the Second World War', re-examined the role of the initial 1939 evacuation of children in policy changes with emphasis on children's health and welfare policies. Despite Titmuss's overly optimistic expectations for the National Health Service, Welshman agreed with his contention that 'evacuation profoundly altered attitudes to state welfare, and led to significant policy changes', 53.
60 Fassin, 'The Biopolitics of Otherness'; 'Compassion and Repression'; *Humanitarian Reason*; also Walters, 'Foucault and Frontiers'.
61 Fassin, *Humanitarian Reason*; Lemke, *Biopolitics;* Hilton, MacKay, Crowson and Mouhot, *The Politics of Expertise* (hereafter Hilton et al.).
62 I only provide contours here that complement the aspects of Mass Observation's history that give context for this book's subject matter. For a comprehensive history of early Mass Observation, see Hinton, *The Mass Observers*.
63 Mass Observation, *First Year's Work*, 66.
64 TK, University of Sussex Special Collections (SxMS) 71 Charles Madge Archive 1/3/1, autobiography, 67.
65 Hubble, *Mass Observation and Everyday Life*, 5.
66 Sayer, *Making Trouble*, 59.
67 TK, MOA 26 Mass Observation Organisation and History, 1/1/2, Letter 'Anthropology at Home' to *New Statesman and Nation*, signed by A Midwife.
68 Mass Observation, *Britain*, 7–8.
69 Hubble, *Mass Observation and Everyday Life*, 254, n.9.
70 Highmore, *Everyday Life and Cultural Theory*, 2 and 17–18.
71 Hubble, *Mass Observation and Everyday Life*, 3.
72 Ibid., 9–11.
73 For a sense of the scale of participation, Sheridan, Street and Bloome, *Writing Ourselves*, 35, reported that 2,500 people responded to directive replies during the war, there were more than 500 diarists who submitted their accounts of their lives, and 150 of them did so during September 1939, the first month of the Second World War.

74 Hall, *Worktown*, 2.
75 Hinton, *Nine Wartime Lives*, 17.
76 Sheridan, Street and Bloome, *Writing Ourselves*, 46.
77 Ibid., x.
78 David Pocock quoted in Sheridan, Street and Bloome, *Writing Ourselves*, 45.
79 TK, MOA 41 Publicity Relating to Mass Observation, 3 Press Cuttings, Tom Harrisson, 'Mass Observation Reveals – How the First Six Months of War Have Changed – Your Life', *Sunday Graphic*, 31 March 1940.
80 Ibid.
81 Curzon, *Mass-Observation and Visual Culture*, 2.
82 Penny Summerfield, 'Mass-Observation: Social Research or Social Movement?'; Hubble, *Mass Observation and Everyday Life*, 1.
83 TK, MOA 26 Mass Observation Organisation and History, 1/2 Notes on Mass-Observation Techniques and Services, November 1948, 8.
84 Hubble, *Mass Observation and Everyday Life*, 1. Summerfield, 'Mass-Observation', 448, sums up the initial vision as 'information is power'.
85 Hinton, *The Mass Observers*, 162–4; Sheridan, Street and Bloome, *Writing Ourselves*, x.
86 Summerfield, 'Mass-Observation', 442, discusses some of these motivations.
87 TK, MOA 41 Publicity Relating to Mass Observation, 3 Press Cuttings, Harrisson. 'Public Opinion & The Refugee', *World Review*, 45.
88 TK, MOA 4 Mary Adams Papers (1939–42) 7/3, Public Reaction to Alien Internment Order of May 12, 1940. Home Intelligence reported, 'Surveys conducted in the third week of April showed that partly as a result of the press campaign 90% of those interviewed thought drastic action had become an urgent necessity', and also attributed this to people's fears of parachutists, 14 May 1940.
89 TK, MOA 41 Publicity Relating to Mass Observation, 3 Press Cuttings, Harrisson. 'Public Opinion & The Refugee', *World Review*, 45.
90 TK, MOA 26 Mass Observation Organisation and History, 1/1/1, Madge, 'M-O Panel and its function', 18 January 1940.
91 Quoted in Sheridan, Street and Bloome, *Writing Ourselves*, 34.
92 Ibid.
93 Haraway, 'Situated Knowledges', 592.
94 Ibid., 593.
95 Ibid., 585.
96 Ibid., 589.
97 Summerfield, 'Mass-Observation', 444.
98 Trevelyan, *Indigo Days*, 97.
99 TK, MOA 26 Mass Observation Organisation and History, 1/1/1, Madge, 'M-O Panel and its function', 18 January 1940.

100 TK, SxMs 71 Charles Madge Archive 9/2/2, Letter from Charles Madge to John Maynard Keynes, 17 April 1940.
101 TK, SxMs 71 Charles Madge Archive 1/3/1, autobiography, 122.
102 Quoted in Hinton, *The Mass Observers*, 133.
103 Hubble, *Mass Observation and Everyday Life*, 14.
104 Hubble, *Mass Observation and Everyday Life*, 14.
105 The often-cited study of reception of early war posters addressed in the book was initiated at the request of the MoI in late September 1939; however, the Ministry retracted this offer one week later, stating that they were unable to contract an outside agency. Having already begun the work, MO saw the study to completion. See TK, MOA FR 2 Government Posters in War-Time, 18 October 1939, 1.
106 Mass Observation, *War Begins at Home*, v.
107 Cited in Marcus, 'Introduction', 8.
108 Hubble, *Mass Observation*, 166.
109 Harrisson, *Living Through the Blitz*, 297.
110 Hubble, *Mass Observation and Everyday Life*, 3.
111 Hinton, *The Mass Observers*, 3.
112 TK, MOA 26 Mass Observation Organisation and History, 1/1/1, Harrisson Memo to Madge, 18 January 1940.
113 See, for instance, *New Formations* volume 44, edited by Laura Marcus, and dedicated to the Mass-Observation Project, which places emphasis on the poetic, psychoanalytic and artistic aspects of their approach.
114 Sayer, *Making Trouble*, 62–3.
115 Highmore, *Ordinary Lives*, 92.
116 TK, MOA FR 360 US 18, 1 August 1940, 1.
117 During the Munich Crisis, Mass Observation, *Britain*, 103 and 224–5, revealed the gap between public opinion – of the 'everyman' – and official representations of the nation as unified in support of the agreement: 'The month of September, 1938, will provide the historian of the future, or even of next year, with a supremely illuminating insight into sense and statesmanship and the *status quo*. But if, as has been the custom in the past, the historian accepts as statements of fact the numerous published assertions as to what the public of England are thinking about it all, he will, as so often before, be a typically lousy historian.' In the same volume: 'Everything points to a position where we know as little about personal needs and individual ideals as we do about wider social feelings and mass responses. Everywhere we turn in the British scene, we are faced with no data, or data utterly inadequate for any scientific or long-term judgments about our society and culture.'
118 Mass Observation, *Britain*, 235.
119 Marcus, 'Introduction', 9.
120 Sheridan, Street and Bloome, *Writing Ourselves*, xi.

121 Highmore, *Everyday Life and Cultural Theory*, 143–4.
122 TK, MOA 26 Mass Observation Organisation and History, 1/1/1, Madge, 'M-O Panel and its function', 18 January 1940. Madge, offering a rushed internal report on his panel initiative, noted further that, although the panel is not necessarily representative, 'The intellectual influence of M-O has been largely because it has set to collect knowledge for the benefit of as many people as possible as soon as possible: I know it [the panel] has not got out enough results or reached enough people to justify this properly, but the idea has been strong enough to win a lot of support. I think myself that this idea rather than the spy or superior "anthropologist" idea has been the reason why it has caught on.' The last part is a shot at Harrisson (the reference to spying alludes to the Home Intelligence work, the anthropologist in scare quotes to Harrisson's self-representation), however, their correspondence at this time should be understood in its context, which was both personal and professional and produced under conditions of considerable strain.
123 Fassin, *Humanitarian Reason*, 1.
124 Ibid.
125 Ibid., 3.
126 Ibid., 6.
127 Ibid., 25.
128 Ibid., 31.
129 Sayer, 'White Riot', 101.
130 Ibid.
131 Cox, Lienesch and Jones, 'Beyond Economics'.
132 'PM Commits to Government-wide Drive to Tackle Loneliness'. Press release, Gov. UK, 17 January 2018. Available online: https://www.gov.uk/government/news/pm-commits-to-government-wide-drive-to-tackle-loneliness (accessed 10 February 2018).
133 Anushka Asthana. 'Loneliness is a "Giant Evil" of Our Time, Says Jo Cox Commission', *The Guardian*, 10 December 2017. Available online: https://www.theguardian.com/society/2017/dec/10/loneliness-is-a-giant-evil-of-our-time-says-jo-cox-commission (accessed 10 February 2018).
134 Fassin, *Humanitarian Reason*, 4.
135 Titmuss, *Problems of Social Policy*, Kindle location 458.
136 Fassin, *Humanitarian Reason*, 4.
137 Ibid., 259.
138 Hilton et al., *The Politics of Expertise*, 3.
139 Ibid., 210.
140 Fassin, *Humanitarian Reason*, 226.
141 Stevenson, *Life Beside Itself*, 6.
142 Shukin, 'Transfections of Animal Touch', 492.

143 Imperial War Museum (IWM), Art.IWM PST 14158, Coughs and Sneezes Spread Diseases, Poster, Henry Mayo Bateman, Central Council for Health Education, Ministry of Health, Her Majesty's Stationary Office, Britain, 1942.
144 Foucault, 'Society Must Be Defended', 254. For more on this subject, see Campbell, *Improper Life*; Esposito, 'Community, Immunity, Biopolitics', 83–90.
145 Foucault, 'Society Must Be Defended', 255.
146 Ibid., 258.
147 Ibid., 256.
148 Ibid.
149 Ibid., 258.
150 Repo, 'Governing Juridical Sex', 89–91, 103.
151 Repo, *The Biopolitics of Gender*, 3.
152 Ibid., 4.
153 Schuller, *The Biopolitics of Feeling*, 17.
154 Walters, 'Foucault and Frontiers', 143.
155 See Soloway, *Demography and Degeneration* and Overy, *The Twilight Years*.
156 TNA, HO 186.1419, Meeting with representatives of the National ARP Animals Committee regarding the question of animals in the evacuation towns, 5 November 1942.
157 THA, HO 186.1419, Letter to R.L. Tufnell, MP, 19 November 1942.
158 TNA, HO 186.1419, Meeting with representatives of the National ARP Animals Committee regarding the question of animals in the evacuation towns, 5 November 1942.
159 TNA, HO 186.2075, NARPAC Report on the Service for Urban Areas, 9 April 1942, 2.
160 Chen, *Animacies*, 13.
161 Ibid., 29.
162 The multiplicity that is clearly signalled in the concept of animacy hierarchies more explicitly underlines the heterogeneity of the politics of life, therefore the former concept will be used more centrally in the volume.
163 Pearson, '"Four-Legged *Poilus*"', 732.
164 Kean, *The Great Cat and Dog Massacre*, 143.
165 Wolfe, *Animal Rites*, 8.
166 Arendt, *The Origins of Totalitarianism*, 230–1.
167 Kean, *The Great Cat and Dog Massacre*, 4.
168 Chen, *Animacies*, 127.
169 Seshadri, *HumAnimal*, ix.
170 Ibid., x.
171 Ibid., 25.
172 Chen, *Animacies*, 3.
173 Ibid., 159.

174 *Our Towns*, xiv.
175 Haraway, *When Species Meet*, 70–3.
176 TK, MOA FR 785-6 Blitz Information – The Lifeline of Civil Defence, 14 July 1941, 180. This file report was drafted as an article submitted for publication in *Local Government Service*. Page numbers in reference to this file report refer to those given in the typeset proofs of that article, which show that some revisions were made to the original report.
177 Ibid., 183.
178 Ibid., 180.
179 Foucault, *History of Sexuality, v.1*, 92–5.
180 TK, MOA FR 785-6 Blitz Information – The Lifeline of Civil Defence, 14 July 1941, 183.
181 Ibid.
182 See Hamilton, *Security*, 10–13.
183 Ibid., 11.

# 1 Keeping Watch Over the Population

1 Addison and Crang, *Listening to Britain*, 1.
2 The Keep (TK) Mass Observation Archive (MOA) 4 Mary Adams Papers (1939–1942), 4/2/1, Home Intelligence Report on Home Front Propaganda, n.d.
3 Addison and Crang, *Listening to Britain*, xii.
4 The National Archives (TNA), Ministry of Information (INF) 1/263, Wartime Social Survey Policy and Organisation, Home Intelligence: Mass Observation & Wartime Social Survey, 12 September 1940, 1. See also Addison and Crang, *Listening to Britain*, xiv and McLaine, *Ministry of Morale*, 51–2.
5 Home Intelligence quoted in Addison and Crang, *Listening to Britain*, xiv.
6 TK, MOA 4 Mary Adams Papers (1939–1942), 4, Special Intelligence Reports, Mass Observation Policy & Finance, Letter from Adams to Waterfield. 12 March 1940.
7 TNA, INF 1/263, Wartime Social Survey Policy and Organisation, Home Intelligence: Mass Observation & Wartime Social Survey, 12 September 1940, 1.
8 TNA, INF 1/250, Planning Committee – Minutes of Occasional Meetings and Reports, Home Morale Emergency Committee, Report to Policy Committee. 4 June 1940, 1.
9 TNA, INF 1/263, Wartime Social Survey Policy and Organisation, Wartime Social Survey Organisation File OEPEC Paper No. 530, 9 October 1940.
10 Adams in Addison and Crang, *Listening to Britain*, xii; Nick Hubble, *Mass Observation and Everyday Life*, 179–80. Mass Observation, *War Begins at Home*, v.
11 Hajkowski, *The BBC and National Identity in Britain*, 5.

12 Mass Observation, *War Begins at Home*, v.
13 Harrisson, *Living Through the Blitz*, 297.
14 McLaine, *Ministry of Morale*, 2–3.
15 TNA, INF 1/263, Wartime Social Survey Policy and Organisation, Home Intelligence: Mass Observation & Wartime Social Survey, 12 September 1940, 1.
16 Heimann, *The Most Offending Soul Alive*, 3.
17 Hubble, *Mass Observation and Everyday Life*, 14.
18 Foucault, '"Omnes et Singulatim"', 302.
19 Purcell, *Domestic Soldiers*, 115.
20 Foucault, *'Society Must be Defended'*, 253.
21 Foucault, *The Birth of Biopolitics*, 224–5.
22 Ibid., 216.
23 Foucault, '"Omnes et Singulatim"', 303–7. See also Rose's use of the term pastoralism and its distinction from my use of pastoral power derived more directly from Foucault, in Rose, *Governing the Soul*, 265.
24 Stevenson, *Life Beside Itself*, 84.
25 Mass Observation, *War Begins at Home*, 72.
26 Addison and Crang, *Listening to Britain*, 92.
27 Ibid., 88.
28 Cited in Marcus, 'Introduction', 8.
29 TK, MOA File Report (FR) 473a Experiment in Gauging any Daily Morale Fluctuations (Series IV), 30 October 1940.
30 TK, MOA 4 Mary Adams Papers (1939–1942), 4/2/1, Appendix to Home Morale and Public Opinion – A review of some conclusions arising out of a year of Home Intelligence Weekly Reports, Stephen Taylor, 1 October 1941.
31 McLaine, *Ministry of Morale*, 10.
32 Ibid., 7.
33 While the activities of the MoI depended upon a wide range of reciprocal observations, communications, and analyses, including correspondence with members of the public, due to secrecy and security, the degree of this reciprocity was not as significant as it was for the MoI paper salvage campaign, which was 'dependent upon a delicate balance between popular and government action'. Irving, 'Paper Salvage in Britain During the Second World War', 375.
34 Harrisson, *Living Through the Blitz*, 13.
35 TK, MOA FR 89 Morale Now, 30 April 1940, 1.
36 TK, MOA Topic Collection (TC) 1 Housing, 5/A, Harrisson, Review of Poverty and Progress by Seebohm Rowntree (Longmans). *World Review*, October 1941, 59.
37 TK, MOA FR 89 Morale Now, 30 April 1940, 1.
38 TK, MOA 26 Mass Observation Organisation and History, 1/2, Madge, M-O Panel and its Function, 18 January 1940.

39 TK, MOA 41 Publicity Relating to Mass Observation, 3, Press Cuttings about Mass-Observation, Harrisson's article, 'You Don't Have to Smile', appeared with slightly altered titles in several newspapers: *Evening Standard*, 16 May; *Yorkshire Evening Post*, 19 May; *Belfast Telegraph*, 19 May 1941.
40 Harrisson, *Living Though the Blitz*, 278–9.
41 TK, MOA FR 466 Fourth Weekly Report for Home Intelligence, 24 October 1940, 3.
42 TK, MOA FR 89, Morale Now, 30 April 1940, 11.
43 Harrisson, *Living Though the Blitz*, 279.
44 Addison and Crang, *Listening to Britain*, 76.
45 Mass Observation, *War Begins at Home*, 423–4.
46 Home Intelligence Report 27 May 1940 in Addison and Crang, *Listening to Britain*, 41.
47 TK, MOA FR 360 US 18, 1 August 1940, 4.
48 TK, MOA FR 466 Fourth Weekly Report for Home Intelligence, 24 October 1940, 4.
49 TK, MOA FR 89 Morale Now, 30 April 1940, 11.
50 Mass Observation, *War Begins at Home*, 66.
51 TK, MOA FR 89 Morale Now, 30 April 1940, 16.
52 Ibid.
53 Ibid., 4.
54 Ibid.
55 Ibid., 7.
56 Ibid., 6.
57 TK, MOA FR 459 Third Weekly Report to Home Intelligence, 18 October 1940, 6.
58 TNA, INF 1/250, Planning Committee – Minutes of Occasional Meetings and Reports. Report of Planning Committee on a Home Moral Campaign, n.d. probably June 1940, 1–2.
59 TK, MOA FR 1 The Five Channels of Publicity, 11 October 1939, 4.
60 Briggs, *The History of Broadcasting in the United Kingdom*, 584.
61 Tebbutt, 'Listening to Youth?', 17–18.
62 Burns, *The BBC*, 19 and 21; BBC Written Archives Collection. BBC Audience Research Reports. Part 1: BBC Listener Research Department reports, 1937–c.1950: a guide to the microfilm edition with an introduction by Siân Nicholas, University of Wales Aberystwyth, 7–8.
63 Nicolson, *Diaries and Letters*, 111–12; BBC Audience Research Reports. Part 1: BBC Listener Research Department, 1937–c.1950, 8.
64 McLaine, *Ministry of Morale*, 25.
65 Hall, 'The Social Eye of the *Picture Post*', 101.
66 'Black-out: A Symbol of the War Which Mustn't be Photographed', *Picture Post* 5.5, 4 November 1939, 13.
67 TK, MOA FR 129 Summary of News Belief and Disbelief, 22 May 1940; FR 65A Preliminary Report on Newsletters, 4 March 1940.

68 Trevelyan, *Indigo Days*, 101.
69 TK, MOA FR 65A Preliminary Report on Newsletters, 4 March 1940, 4.
70 TK, MOA FR 89 Morale Now, 30 April 1940, 13.
71 TK, MOA FR 197 Letter to S.C. Leslie, Chief Public Relations Officer, Ministry of Supply, 13 June 1940, 3–5.
72 Ibid., 2.
73 Ibid., 6.
74 Malinowski's essay is published in Mass Observation, *First Year's Work*, 81–121.
75 TK, MOA, Diarist (D) 5390, 5 September 1939.
76 Ibid., 9 September 1939.
77 Letter to *Picture Post* 5.13, 30 December 1939, 43.
78 TK, MOA FR 439 First Weekly Report for Home Intelligence, 4 October 1940, 10.
79 TK, MOA FR 449 Second Weekly Report to Home Intelligence, 11 October 1940, 12.
80 TK, MOA FR 459 Third Weekly Report to Home Intelligence, 18 October 1940, 9.
81 Turner, *The Phoney War*, 269; Freedman, *Whistling in the Dark*, 38.
82 TK, MOA 26 Mass Observation Organisation and History, 1/8, Correspondence, Madge to Geoffrey Thomas, 13 September 1939.
83 Coast and Fox, 'Rumour and Politics', 223.
84 Tebbutt, *Women's Talk?*, 11.
85 TK, MOA FR 4 ARP Instructions, 18 October 1939, 5; Mass Observation, *War Begins at Home*, 68.
86 TK, MOA FR 4 ARP Instructions, 18 October 1939.
87 One exception to this in social psychology is Tamotsu Shibutani's *Improvised News*. Critical synthesis and intervention within social psychological treatment of rumour in the closing of the twentieth century largely come from the symbolic interactionist perspective. See, for instance, Miller, '"Snakes in the Greens" and Rumor in the Innercity' and, later, Miller 'Rumor: An Examination of Some Stereotypes'. Other disciplines, such as history, have generally taken a much richer approach to rumour than social psychologists leaning towards either of its two overlapping sides of psychology and sociology.
88 TK, MOA FR 4 ARP Instructions, 18 October 1939.
89 TK, MOA FR 1 The Five Channels of Publicity, 11 October 1939; FR 4, 18 October 1939.
90 Mass Observation, *War Begins at Home*, 71.
91 TNA, INF 1/250, Planning Committee – Minutes of Occasional Meetings and Reports, Home Planning Committee Sub-Committee on Anti-Gossip, 14 March 1941.
92 TK, MOA 4 Mary Adams Papers, 4/2/1, Home Planning Committee, Sub-committee appointed to report on action to counter Haw Haw, 30 January 1941.
93 Freedman, *Whistling in the Dark*, 71.

94  Addison and Crang, *Listening to Britain*, 202.
95  TNA, INF 1/257, H.7 Home Morale, Letter from Kenneth Clark to Wilfred Greene, 9 July 1940.
96  TNA, INF 1/257, H.7 Home Morale, Notes for brochure, The Fifth Column – How it Works.
97  TK, MOA FR 360 US 18, 1 August 1940, 5.
98  Fox, 'Careless Talk', 949.
99  McLaine, *Ministry of Morale*, 82.
100  Freedman, *Whistling in the Dark*, 39.
101  Fox, 'Careless Talk', 949.
102  McLaine, *Ministry of Morale*, 3.
103  Freedman, *Whistling in the Dark*, 67.
104  Maggie Joy Blunt's (pseudonym) Mass Observation diary entry, 3 December 1939, in Garfield, *We Are at War*, 113.
105  Waugh, *Put Out More Flags*, 136.
106  TNA, INF 1/250, Planning Committee – Minutes of Occasional Meetings and Reports, Report of Planning Committee on a Home Moral Campaign, probably June 1940, 3. McLaine, *Ministry of Morale*, 48.
107  Christopher Hollis, 'Minister of Information: Alfred Duff Cooper', *Picture Post* 7.9, 1 June 1940, 16.
108  McLaine, *Ministry of Morale*, 3.
109  Ibid., 86.
110  TK, MOA 41 Publicity Relating to Mass Observation, 3 Press Cuttings about Mass-Observation, Denis Dunn, 'Laugh This Off', *Sunday Graphic & Sunday News*, 22 January 1939.
111  TK, MOA FR 210 Arrest of an Observer, 19 June 1940.
112  Marcus, 'Introduction', 15–16.
113  Addison and Crang, *Listening to Britain*, xvi.
114  TK, MOA 4 Mary Adams Papers (1939–1942) 4 Special Intelligence Reports, Mass Observation Policy & Finance, Letter from Adams to Waterfield, 12 March 1940.
115  TK, MOA FR 333 Press Campaign Against Duff Cooper, 8 August 1940, 5.
116  TNA, INF 1/263, Dr. Stephen Taylor, Home Intelligence, Short Account of WSS in Response to Request from Francis Williams, 5 September 1941.
117  TK, MOA FR 333 Press Campaign Against Duff Cooper, 8 August 1940, 5–6.
118  TNA, INF 1/250, Planning Committee – Minutes of Occasional Meetings and Reports, Home Morale Emergency Committee. Report to Policy Committee, 4 June 1940, 1.
119  Foucault, *Security, Territory, Population*, 193.
120  Ibid., 169.

121 TNA, INF 1/263, Wartime Social Survey Policy and Organisation, Home Intelligence: Mass Observation & Wartime Social Survey, 12 September 1940, 1.
122 TK, MOA FR 477 Fifth Weekly Report for Home Intelligence, 1 November 1940, 5.
123 TK, MOA 41 Publicity Relating to Mass Observation, 3 Press Cuttings about Mass-Observation, 'Negatively at Home', *Eastern Daily Press*, 30 September 1940.
124 TK, MOA FR 486 Sixth Weekly Report for Home Intelligence, 8 November 1940, 23.

## 2 Verminous House Guests and Good Hosts: Evacuation Stories

1 McLaine, *Ministry of Morale*, 2 and 28.
2 Grayzel, *At Home and Under Fire*, 17.
3 Mass Observation, *War Begins at Home*, 305.
4 The Keep (TK), Mass Observation Archive (MOA), Topic Collection (TC) 1 Housing, 1/A The Housing Centre 1939–40, Harrisson's notes, 24 October 1939, 6.
5 Mass Observation, *War Begins at Home*, 304.
6 Ibid., 313.
7 Stevenson, *Life Beside Itself*, 3–7.
8 Mass Observation, *War Begins at Home*, v and 24.
9 Ibid., 20–1.
10 TK, MOA TC 5 Evacuation 1939–44, 1/I Reactions to Arrival of Evacuees, October–December 1939, Joke told in Windsor pub, October 1939.
11 'Diary of the War: No. 4', *Picture Post* 4.13, 30 September 1939, 20.
12 Mass Observation, *War Begins at Home*, 3.
13 TK, MOA TC 5 Evacuation 1939–44, 1/D Evacuation of schools, September–October 1939.
14 'How the War Began', *Picture Post* 4.11, 16 September 1939, 16–17.
15 Ibid., 14.
16 TK, MOA TC 5 Evacuation 1939–44, 1/C Evacuees' departure, September 1939. Victoria, 1 September 1939.
17 TK, MOA TC 5 Evacuation 1939–44, 1/I Reactions to Arrival of Evacuees, October–December 1939. I have replaced surnames with initials.
18 MacKay, *Half the Battle*, 46.
19 TK, MOA TC 5 Evacuation 1939–44, 2/A Evacuation Report. 28 October 1939.
20 TK, MOA TC 5 Evacuation 1939–44, 1/I Reactions to Arrival of Evacuees, October–December 1939.
21 TK, MOA TC 5 Evacuation 1939–44, 1/D Evacuation of schools, September–October 1939, St Albans, 6 November 1939.
22 University of Liverpool, *Our Wartime Guests*, 5.

23 TK, MOA File Report (FR) 20 Recording the War, 29 January 1940, 2.
24 University of Liverpool, *Our Wartime Guests*, 5.
25 Ibid.; Cunningham and Gardner, '"Saving the Nation's Children"', 334.
26 Mass Observation, *War Begins at Home*, 312.
27 University of Liverpool, *Our Wartime Guests*, 5.
28 TK, MOA TC 5 Evacuation 1939–44, 1/E General comments on success of evacuation scheme, September–December 1939.
29 Turner, *The Phoney War on the Home Front*, 77.
30 TK, MOA TC 5 Evacuation 1939–44, 1/D Evacuation of schools, September–October 1939.
31 Quoted in Titmuss, *Problems of Social Policy*, Kindle location 2690.
32 Mass Observation, *War Begins at Home*, 301.
33 Hobbs, *Don't Forget to Write*, 69.
34 TK, MOA TC 5 Evacuation 1939–44, 1/B Receiving Evacuees September 1939.
35 TK, MOA Diarist (D) 5390, 1 September 1939.
36 University of Liverpool, *Our Wartime Guests*, 8.
37 TK, MOA TC 5 Evacuation 1939–44, 1/H Romford: a neutral area, 29 October 1939.
38 Turner, *The Phoney War*, 80.
39 Scrubb's Ammonia advertisement, *Picture Post* 5.3, 21 October 1939, 56.
40 Titmuss, *Problems of Social Policy*, Kindle location 2737.
41 Quoted in Sheridan, *Wartime Women*, 58.
42 TK, MOA TC 5 Evacuation 1939–44, 1/E General comments on success of evacuation scheme, September–December 1939.
43 'Diary of the War: No. 4', *Picture Post* 4.13, 30 September 1939, 17.
44 Letter, *Picture Post* 4.13, 30 September 1939, 44.
45 TK, MOA TC 5 Evacuation 1939–44, 1/I Reactions to Arrival of Evacuees, October–December 1939.
46 TK, MOA TC 5 Evacuation 1939–44, 1/E General comments on success of evacuation scheme, September–December 1939.
47 University of Liverpool, *Our Wartime Guests*, 8.
48 Mass Observation, *War Begins at Home*, 318.
49 TK, MOA TC 5 Evacuation 1939–44, 1/E General comments on success of evacuation scheme, September–December 1939.
50 TK, MOA TC 5 Evacuation 1939–44, 1/B Receiving Evacuees September 1939.
51 Quoted in Sheridan, *Wartime Women*, 58.
52 Mass Observation, *War Begins at Home*, 309.
53 TK, MOA TC 5 Evacuation 1939–44, 1/M Press Cuttings, '15 Boys – Bang Go the Chairs', *Daily Herald*, 28 November 1939, 7.
54 Quoted in Isaacs et al., *The Cambridge Evacuation Survey*, 192.
55 TK, MOA D 5390, 9 September 1939.

56 Titmuss, *Problems of Social Policy*, Kindle location 2963.
57 TK, MOA TC 5 Evacuation 1939–44, 1/L Printed material on evacuation 1939–41. *The Spectator*, 22 September 1939.
58 Turner, *The Phoney War*, 85; Mass Observation, *War Begins at Home*, 316.
59 TK, MOA TC 5 Evacuation 1939–44, 2/A Evacuation Rumours. 11 September 1939.
60 TK, MOA TC 5 Evacuation 1939–44, 1/E General comments on success of evacuation scheme, September–December 1939.
61 Mass Observation, *War Begins at Home*, 331.
62 TK, MOA TC 5 Evacuation 1939–44, 1/D Evacuation of schools, September–October 1939, 6 November 1939.
63 TK, MOA TC 5 Evacuation 1939–44, 1/E General comments on success of evacuation scheme, September–December 1939. Mass observer relays: 'I saw one mother rather hysterically remove her child from playing near trees as she was afraid they might fall.' Regarding reactions to rivers and farm animals, see Mass Observation, *War Begins at Home*, 315.
64 Mass Observation, *War Begins at Home*, 316.
65 TK, MOA TC 5 Evacuation 1939–44, 1/L Printed material on evacuation 1939–41. W. Beach Thomas, 'Country Life', *The Spectator*, 22 September 1939, 409.
66 Mass Observation, *War Begins at Home*, 331.
67 Quoted in Isaacs et al., *The Cambridge Evacuation Survey*, 75.
68 Quoted ibid., 78.
69 Quoted ibid.
70 Quoted ibid., 77.
71 Ibid., 177.
72 Ibid., 128.
73 Ibid., 153.
74 Mass Observation, *War Begins at Home*, 302.
75 Ibid., 316.
76 Ibid., 311.
77 TK, MOA TC 5 Evacuation 1939–44, 1/E General comments on success of evacuation scheme, September–December 1939.
78 Mass Observation, *War Begins at Home*, 312.
79 TK, MOA TC 5 Evacuation 1939–44, 1/E General comments on success of evacuation scheme, September–December 1939.
80 Ibid.
81 Mass Observation, *War Begins at Home*, 330.
82 Visser, *The Rituals of Dinner*, Kindle locations 1072 and 1143.
83 TK, MOA TC 5 Evacuation 1939–44, 1/E General comments on success of evacuation scheme, September–December 1939.
84 Visser, *The Rituals of Dinner*, Kindle location 1709–15.

85 TK, MOA TC 5 Evacuation 1939–44, 1/E General comments on success of evacuation scheme, September–December 1939.
86 Mass Observation, *War Begins at Home*, 321–2.
87 TK, MOA FR 174 Refugees, 6 June 1940.
88 Welshman, 'Evacuation and Social Policy', 33.
89 Diarist Tomlin (pseudonym), 10 October 1939, Garfield, *We Are at War*, 52.
90 TK, MOA TC 5 Evacuation 1939–44, 1/E General comments on success of evacuation scheme, September–December 1939.
91 TK, MOA TC 5 Evacuation 1939–44, 2/A Evacuation Rumours, 11 September 1939.
92 Ibid., Evacuation Report, 28 October 1939.
93 Mass Observation, *War Begins at Home*, 327–8.
94 Ibid., 329.
95 Titmuss, *Problems of Social Policy*, Kindle location 2834.
96 INF 13/171 6, 'She's in the ranks too!' Ministry of Health, Evacuation Poster.
97 Rose, *Which People's War?*, 118.
98 Ibid., 124.
99 Ibid., 119.
100 TNA, ED 136/112, Memo discussing the repeal of plans to prosecute parents, 16 October 1941.
101 TK, MOA TC 5 Evacuation 1939–44, 1/M Press Cuttings, 'Odyssey', *Star*, late issue, 28 November 1939.
102 TK, MOA TC 5 Evacuation 1939–44, 1/M Press Cuttings, 'Evacuees Hike 30 Miles', Source unknown. November 1939.
103 TK, MOA TC 5 Evacuation 1939–44, 1/M Press Cuttings, 'They Were Seven and Homesick', *News Chronicle*, 15 November 1939, 3.
104 TK, MOA TC 5 Evacuation 1939–44, 1/M Press Cuttings, 'Evacuees Hike 30 Miles', Source unknown. November 1939.
105 Welshman, 'Evacuation and Social Policy', 33.
106 Mass Observation, *War Begins at Home*, 295.
107 TNA, ED 136/112, Shena D. Simon. 'The Children in War-Time: How to Rebuild the Educational System'. London: Worker's Educational Association, probably early 1940, 7–8.
108 Pomfret, 'The City of Evil and the Great Outdoors', 417.
109 TK, MOA TC 5 Evacuation 1939–44, 1/B Receiving Evacuees September 1939.
110 TK, MOA TC 5 Evacuation 1939–44, 1/M Press Cuttings, 'The Lighter Side of Evacuation: Scores of Amazing and Amusing Incidents', *Northampton Independent*. 8 September 1939.
111 Ibid.
112 Ibid.

113 TK, MOA TC 5 Evacuation 1939–44, 1/E General comments on success of evacuation scheme, September–December 1939.
114 Ibid.
115 Letter, *Picture Post* 5.4, 28 October 1939, 48.
116 Quoted in Myers, 'The Ambiguities of Aid and Agency', 32.
117 Quoted ibid., 33.
118 Ibid., 37.
119 Ibid., 39.
120 Headmaster of Winchester College quoted in Mayall and Morrow, *You Can Save Your Country*, 88.
121 TK, MOA TC 5 Evacuation 1939–44, 1/L Printed material on evacuation 1939–41, Evacuation: Why and How? Public Information Leaflet, No. 3, Privy Seal's Office, July 1939.
122 Foucault, *Abnormal*, 316–17.
123 Mass Observation, *War Begins at Home*, 295.
124 Ibid., 313.
125 Fassin, *Humanitarian Reason*, 226.
126 Rose, *Which People's War?*, 107.
127 TK, MOA TC 5 Evacuation 1939–44, 1/K Miscellaneous notes and correspondence on evacuation, September–December 1939. War-time Directive, no. 3, November 1939.
128 TK, MOA TC 5 Evacuation 1939–44, 1/L Printed material on evacuation 1939–41, Harrisson, 'The Third Evacuation', *The New Statesman and Nation*, 9 November 1940, 460.
129 TK, MOA TC 5 Evacuation 1940–44, 2/J Reception of refugees, October 1940: A40/A44 routes out of London. Refugees Worcester, 18 October 1940; 2/L Reception of refugees, October 1940: A30.
130 TK, MOA TC 5 Evacuation 1940–44, 2/L Reception of refugees, October 1940: A30, 3 October 1940.
131 TK, MOA TC 5 Evacuation 1940–44, 2/P Panel on local situation, Little Eversden, October 1940.
132 TK, MOA TC 5 Evacuation 1939–44, 1/L Printed material on evacuation 1939–41, Harrisson, 'The Third Evacuation', *The New Statesman and Nation*, 9 November 1940, 461.
133 TK, MOA TC 5 Evacuation 1940–44, 2/J Reception of refugees, October 1940: A40/A44 routes out of London. Communal Rest Centre at the Old Rectory, Beaconsfield, 8 October 1940.
134 Ibid.: A40/A44 routes out of London, 8 October 1940.
135 Ibid.
136 Ibid.: Windsor and Reading. Windsor, 8 October 1940.

137 TK, MOA TC 5 Evacuation 1939–44, 1/K Miscellaneous notes and correspondence on evacuation, September–December 1939, War-time Directive, No. 3, November 1939.
138 Mass Observation, *War Begins at Home*, 3.
139 See Hinton, *The Mass Observers*, 192–5.
140 TK, MOA TC 5 Evacuation 1939–44, 1/L Printed material on evacuation 1939–41, Harrisson, 'The Third Evacuation', *The New Statesman and Nation*, 9 November 1940, 461.
141 TK, MOA TC 1 Housing, 1/A The Housing Centre 1939–40, Harrisson's notes, 24 October 1939, 6.

# 3  Lazy Dogs

1 Kean, *Animal Rights*, 193; Kean, *The Great Cat and Dog Massacre*, 4; and The Keep (TK), Mass Observation Archive (MOA) Topic Collection (TC) 79 Dogs in War Time 1939–42, 1/E Survey of non dog owners – August 1941.
2 'Dogs in War-Time: Exaggerated Reports of Destruction', *The Times*, 2 October 1939.
3 Turner, *The Phoney War*, 113. Campbell, *Bonzo's War*, x and xiii, estimates that two and a half million animal companions died over the course of the war from injury as well as the assumption that it was a kind thing to put down animals in anticipation of war.
4 TK, MOA Diarist (D) 5390, 10 May 1940, or Ashford (pseudonym) in Garfield, *We Are at War*, 218.
5 TK, MOA TC 79 Dogs in War Time 1939–42, 1/A Dog Organisations in war time. War-Time Dog Food, National Canine Defence League Leaflet No. 484, 22 September 1939.
6 Howell, 'The Dog Fancy at War', 547.
7 Hinton notes that Bob Martin joined the board in the 1950s, as Mass Observation's restructuring at the end of the 1940s saw it turn more towards commercial research. See Hinton, *The Mass Observers*, chapter 15 for elaboration of these transformations within the organization.
8 Hinton, *The Mass Observers*, 304–5.
9 See Ibid., 376–7.
10 TK, MOA TC 79 Dogs in War Time 1939–42, 1/E Survey of non dog owners – August 1941.
11 Campbell, *Bonzo's War*, 6.
12 Ibid., 13.
13 Ibid., 17.
14 The National Archives (TNA), Home Office (HO) 186/113, The Protection of Your Home Against Air Raids, Leaflet, 1938, 22.

15 TNA, HO 186.2489, ARP Handbook No. 12 Air Raid Precautions for Animals. HMSO, 1939, 1.
16 Ibid., 24.
17 Campbell, *Bonzo's War*, 21.
18 Kean, *The Great Cat and Dog Massacre*, 21.
19 Campbell, *Bonzo's War*, 49.
20 TNA, HO 186.2075, NARPAC Report on the Service for Urban Areas. 9 April 1942, 1.
21 TK, MOA File Report (FR) 2256 Dogs and Dog-Health in Wartime, 7 June 1945. Mass Observation reported that 'there are no signs of any major permanent increase or decrease in the dog-population over prewar times'.
22 Kean, *The Great Cat and Dog Massacre*, 168.
23 Ibid., 162.
24 Howell and Kean, 'The Dogs That Didn't Bark in the Blitz', 50.
25 McHugh, *Dog*, 9.
26 TK, MOA TC 79 Dogs in War Time 1939–42, 1/A Dog Organisations in war time, War-Time Dog Food, National Canine Defence League Leaflet No. 484, 22 September 1939.
27 TK, MOA TC 79 Dogs in War Time 1939–42, 1/A Dog Organisations in war time, The Animal World, November 1939.
28 'Dogs in War-Time: Exaggerated Reports of Destruction', *The Times*, 2 October 1939.
29 'Dog Breeding in War Time: Plenty of Suitable Food', *The Times*, 3 October 1938.
30 Campbell, *Bonzo's War*, 35.
31 In her book, *The Animal Estate*, Ritvo explains that pre-modern English law assigned rights and responsibilities to animals. Ritvo references the hanging of both a woman and a dog in punishment for bestiality, as both were considered guilty. She notes that Germanic jurisprudence provided provision for household animals to submit testimony in court and that their presence in the trial room granted more force to the plaintiff's charge. By the nineteenth century, animals were no longer endowed with rights and responsibilities and were demoted to instrumental property. Thus, no longer could an animal be held responsible for damages that its actions may have imposed; rather, the animal's owner was assigned that responsibility, being charged with the proper governance of the animal's actions.
32 Howell, *At Home and Astray*, 180, explains how the lucrative informal economy of dog napping in the period played an instrumental role in this development.
33 TK, MOA TC 79 Dogs in War Time 1939–42, 1/A Dog Organisations in war time, Animals and Air-Raids: Editorial Notes, 'The Animal World', November 1939.
34 Longmate, *How We Lived Then*, 154–5; Buckley, *Writing the Kitchen Front*, 25.
35 Hey, *The View from the Corner Shop*, 13. Diary entry for 18 July 1941.
36 MOA, FR 77 Gert and Daisy's BBC Talks, 23 April 1940, 4.

37 Patricia Seymour, 'How *One Person's* meat ration can make a *Meal for Five!*', Pyrex Advertisement, *Women's Illustrated*, 17 June 1944, Edinburgh: Memorabilia Pack Company.
38 Hobbs, *Don't Forget to Write*, 221–3.
39 Particularly, the vegetables from Holland and eggs from Belgium. 'Food That Came From Holland', *The Times*, 21 May 1940, 3.
40 TK, MOA TC 79 Dogs in War Time 1939–42, 1/D Dog Survey 1941 – Final questionnaire.
41 TK, MOA TC 79 Dogs in War Time 1939–42, 1/C Dog Survey 1941 – Second Pilot, Interviews and indirects with shop keepers, 30 July 1941.
42 Kean, *The Great Cat and Dog Massacre*, 90–1; Campbell, *Bonzo's War*, 225.
43 'Lord Woolton and the Poultry-Keeper', *The Times*, 13 August 1940, 2.
44 'Emergency Food Plans', *The Times*, 28 May 1940, 7.
45 Campbell, *Bonzo's War*, 92.
46 TK, East Sussex Record Office (ACC) 8068/8, Papers of Charles Elwell (1880–1956) and his son Charles John Lister Elwell. Postcard from C Elwell Esq, to [Frederick James Marquis, Lord] Woolton, Minister of Food, post stamped 18 July 1942.
47 TK, ACC 8068/8, Papers of Charles Elwell (1880–1956) and his son Charles John Lister Elwell. Letter from Lettice Cooper, Public Relations, Ministry of Food to C. Elwell, Esq., 10 August 1942.
48 'War-Time Feeding', *The Times*, 17 October 1940, 2.
49 'Dog Food or Farm Help?', *Daily Mail*, 31 May 1941, 3.
50 Campbell, *Bonzo's War*, 183.
51 Campbell, *Bonzo's War*, 185.
52 'Dogs Eat One Week's Food', *Daily Mail*, 8 April 1941, 3.
53 Letter, *Picture Post* 8.5, 3 August 1940, 3.
54 Letter, *Picture Post* 8.7, 17 August 1940, 3.
55 'Economy in Use of Food', *The Times*, 5 April 1940, 5.
56 TNA, HO 186.2075, An Animals' Rally, excerpt from *Manchester Guardian*, 17 July 1941.
57 Ostermeier, 'History of Guide Dog Use by Veterans', 588; Kirk, 'In Dogs We Trust?'.
58 TK, MOA FR 804, Dogs in London, 29 July 1941.
59 TK, MOA TC 79 Dogs in War Time 1939–42, 1/B Dog Survey 1941.
60 TK, MOA TC 79 Dogs in War Time 1939–42, 1/E Survey of non dog owners – August 1941.
61 TK, MOA TC 79 Dogs in War Time 1939–42, 1/B Dog Survey 1941.
62 TK, MOA TC 79 Dogs in War Time 1939–42, 1/E Survey of non dog owners – August 1941.
63 Ibid.
64 Ibid.

65 TK, MOA TC 79 Dogs in War Time 1939–42, 1/B Dog Survey 1941.
66 TK, MOA TC 79 Dogs in War Time 1939–42, 1/E Survey of non dog owners – August 1941.
67 TK, MOA TC 79 Dogs in War Time 1939–42, 1/D Dog Survey 1941 – Final questionnaire.
68 TK, MOA D 5390, 19 September 1940, or see Garfield, *We Are at War*, 370.
69 TK, MOA TC 79 Dogs in War Time 1939–42, 1/E Survey of non dog owners – August 1941.
70 TK, MOA TC 79 Dogs in War Time 1939–42, 1/B Dog Survey 1941.
71 TK, MOA TC 79 Dogs in War Time 1939–42, 1/E Survey of non dog owners – August 1941.
72 TK, MOA TC 79 Dogs in War Time 1939–42, 1/C Dog Survey 1941 – Second Pilot.
73 TK, MOA TC 79 Dogs in War Time 1939–42, 1/E Survey of non dog owners – August 1941.
74 Ibid.
75 TK, MOA FR 804, Dogs in London, 29 July 1941.
76 TK, MOA TC 79 Dogs in War Time 1939–42, 1/E Survey of non dog owners – August 1941.
77 TK, MOA FR 838, Provincial Dogs, 20 August 1941.
78 Haraway, *When Species Meet*, 78.
79 Woolgar, 'Configuring the User: The Case of Usability Trials', 65–6.
80 Haraway, *When Species Meet*, 78.
81 Derrida, *The Animal That Therefore I Am*, 111.
82 Haraway, *When Species Meet*, 72.
83 TK, MOA FR 838, Provincial Dogs, 20 August 1941.
84 TK, MOA TC 79 Dogs in War Time 1939–42, 1/D Dog Survey 1941 – Final questionnaire.
85 TK, MOA TC 79 Dogs in War Time 1939–42, 1/E Survey of non dog owners – August 1941.
86 Howell, 'The Dog Fancy at War', 547.
87 Ibid., 559.
88 TK, MOA FR 804, Dogs in London, 29 July 1941.
89 TK, MOA TC 79 Dogs in War Time 1939–42, 1/C Dog Survey 1941 – Second Pilot.
90 TK, MOA TC 79 Dogs in War Time 1939–42, 1/E Survey of non dog owners – August 1941.
91 Howell, *At Home and Astray*, 11.
92 Kete, *The Beast in the Boudoir*, 41.
93 Ibid., 79.
94 TK, MOA TC 79 Dogs in War Time 1939–42, 1/E Survey of non dog owners – August 1941.

95  TK, MOA FR 838, Provincial Dogs, 20 August 1941.
96  TK, MOA FR, 804, Dogs in London, 29 July 1941.
97  Ibid.
98  TK, MOA FR 838, Provincial Dogs, 20 August 1941.
99  TK, MOA FR 804 Dogs in London. 29 July 1941.
100 Pearson, '"Four-legged Poilus"', 3.
101 Alexander, 'War and its Bestiality', 103–4.
102 Irvine, 'A Model of Animal Selfhood', 9; Jerolmack, 'Animal Practices, Ethnicity, and Community', 876.
103 Jerolmack, 'Animal Practices, Ethnicity, and Community', 883. See also Irvine, 'Animals as Lifechangers and Lifesavers'.
104 Kean, *The Great Cat and Dog Massacre*, 10–22.
105 Ibid., 4.
106 Ibid., 59.
107 TK, MOA FR 20 Recording the War, 29 January, 1940.
108 TK, MOA FR 804 Dogs in London. 29 July 1941.

## 4  Confused Animacies on the Home Front

1  The autumn of 1940 brought reports that a new order had been introduced in Germany for the inspection of dog, fox and badger meat for human consumption, for instance, 'Dogs and Foxes for Food', *The Times*, 18 November 1940, 4.
2  Letter, *Picture Post* 8.3, 20 July 1940, 3.
3  Letter, *Picture Post* 8.5, 3 August 1940, 3.
4  Letter, *Picture Post* 8.7, 17 August 1940, 3.
5  Chen, *Animacies*, 29.
6  Todd, 'An Indigenous Feminist's Take On The Ontological Turn', 7–8. See also Coulthard's *Red Skin White Masks* for discussion of the meaning of land in Indigenous metaphysics and how grounded normativity crucially underlines this, and Simpson's book *As We Have Always Done*.
7  Ritvo, *Animal Estate*, 39–42.
8  Taylor, *Beasts of Burden*, 87–8.
9  Ibid., 103.
10 Ibid., 87.
11 Ibid., 88.
12 Orwell, *The Road to Wigan Pier*, 23.
13 Wolfe, *What is Posthumanism?*, 136.
14 Chen, *Animacies*, 91.
15 Ibid., 105.

16 Ibid., 90.
17 Seshadri, *HumAnimal*, ix–x.
18 Derrida, *The Animal That Therefore I Am*, 28.
19 Tuan, *Dominance and Affection*, 78.
20 Lin, 'National Identity and Social Mobility', 335.
21 Mayall and Morrow, *You Can Help Your Country*, 88.
22 Farley, '"Operation Pied Piper"', 32.
23 Ibid., 34.
24 Ibid., 40.
25 Chen, *Animacies*, 89.
26 'Fewer Dogs, More Eggs', *Dundee Courier*, 8 August, 1940, 3.
27 'Destroy Grey Squirrels', *Exeter Plymouth Gazette*, 8 October 1943, 5.
28 Ritvo, *Animal Estate*, 18.
29 Ibid., 21.
30 McHugh, *Animal Stories*, 3.
31 Williams, 'Inappropriate/d Others', 93.
32 Turner, *The Phoney War*, 114.
33 'Dog Breeding in War Time', *The Times*, 3 October 1938, 20.
34 Campbell, *Bonzo's War*, 46.
35 'Dog Breeding in War Time', *The Times*, 3 October 1938, 20.
36 The Keep (TK), Mass Observation Archive (MOA) Topic Collection (TC) 79 Dogs in War Time 1939–42, 1/E Survey of non dog owners – August 1941.
37 TK, MOA File Report (FR) 804, Dogs in London, 29 July 1941, appendix ii.
38 McLaine, *Ministry of Morale*, 64.
39 I am indebted to Lucy Curzon for this observation.
40 TK, MOA TC 79 Dogs in War Time 1939–42, 1/E Survey of non dog owners – August 1941.
41 Haraway, *When Species Meet*, 80.
42 Hey, *The View From the Corner Shop*, 84.
43 Seshadri, *HumAnimal*, 143–4.
44 TK, MOA TC 5 Evacuation 1939–44, 1/E General comments on success of evacuation scheme, September–December 1939.
45 MOA, Receiving Evacuees September 1939. TC 5/1/B.
46 TK, MOA TC 5 Evacuation 1939–44, 1/E General comments on success of evacuation scheme, September–December 1939.
47 TK, MOA TC 5 Evacuation 1939–44, 1/M Press Cuttings, 'The Lighter Side of Evacuation: Scores of Amazing and Amusing Incidents', *Northampton Independent*, 8 September 1939.
48 Peter Conway quoted in Bell, *London Was Ours*, 114–15.
49 Paneth, *Branch Street*, 19–20.

50 Ibid., 27.
51 Ibid., 53.
52 Ibid., 103.
53 Ibid., 73.
54 Ibid., 87.
55 Miller, *The Anatomy of Disgust*, x.
56 Ibid., xi.
57 Ibid.
58 TK, MOA TC 5 Evacuation 1939–44, 1/E General comments on success of evacuation scheme, September–December 1939.
59 Quoted in Moore, '"A Band of Public-spirited Women"', 154.
60 Miller, *The Anatomy of Disgust*, 206.
61 Ibid., 251.
62 Moore, '"A Band of Public-spirited Women"', 154.

## 5  Careless Homes Cost Lives

1 Quoted in Garfield, *We Are At War*, 30.
2 Hobbs, *Don't Forget to Write*, 141.
3 Ibid., 128.
4 Ibid., 145.
5 Ibid., 144.
6 Warren T. Reich, 'History of the Notion of Care', The History of Care, Georgetown University. Available online: http://care.georgetown.edu/Classic%20Article.html (accessed 21 June 2018).
7 Ibid.
8 Tuan, *Dominance and Affection*, 163.
9 Ibid., 5.
10 Hamilton, *Security*, 4.
11 Ibid., 10.
12 Mass Observation, *War Begins at Home*, 43.
13 Noakes, '"Serve to Save"', 735.
14 Purcell, *Domestic Soldiers*, 3.
15 Mort, 'Fantasies of Metropolitan Life', 127.
16 Ibid., 145.
17 Isaacs et al., *The Cambridge Evacuation Survey*, 2; Wagner, 'Evacuation', 98–9; Padley and Cole, *Evacuation Survey*, 3.
18 Giles, *The Parlour and the Suburb*, 132.
19 Soloway, *Demography and Degeneration*, 313.

20 Welshman, 'The Social History of Social Work', 458.
21 Ibid., 458–9.
22 Welshman, 'Evacuation, Hygiene, and Social Policy', 786.
23 *Our Towns*, xiii.
24 Ibid., xiv.
25 Welshman, 'The Social History of Social Work', 458. See also Hilton et al., *The Politics of Expertise*.
26 Tebbutt, *Women's Talk?*, 152.
27 Welshman, 'The Social History of Social Work', 463. The Lancet article responded to Tom Stephens on the work being done by the Pacifist Service Units.
28 Hollow, 'Utopian Urges', 571.
29 *Our Towns*, 103–4.
30 Ibid., xiv.
31 Ibid., 105. The phrase 'cutting the slum mind off at its root' also appears in appendix VIII in Elizabeth Denby's summary of *Europe Rehoused*.
32 Moran, 'Imagining the Street in Post-war Britain', 181.
33 Hollow, 'Utopian Urges', 571.
34 Ibid., 572.
35 Moore, '"A Band of Public-spirited Women"', 151; Pomfret, 'The City of Evil and the Great Outdoors', 410.
36 Overy, *The Twilight Years*, 99.
37 Rose, *Governing the Soul*, 180.
38 Schuller, *The Biopolitics of Feeling*, 7.
39 Ibid., 6.
40 Merricks, 'Should Such a Faith Offend?', 356.
41 Ibid., 102–3.
42 Lemke, *Biopolitics*, 9–15.
43 Kushner, *We Europeans?*, 49.
44 Huxley et al., *We Europeans*, 27–8.
45 Barken, *The Retreat of Scientific Racism*, 241–2, 276.
46 Cannadine, *Ornamentalism*, 6.
47 Kushner, *We Europeans?*, 48.
48 Hinton, *The Mass Observers*, 314–16: 'of MO's books this was probably the one most in need of editorial pruning. It was also the most polemical, "frankly partisan" in its advocacy of larger families.'
49 Quoted in Hollow, 'Utopian Urges', 579.
50 Mass Observation, *Britain and Her Birth-rate*, 24.
51 Kushner, *We Europeans?*, 24–5.
52 The Keep (TK), Mass Observation (MOA), File Report (FR) 360 US 18, 1 August 1940, 1.

53 TK, MOA, FR 1683 Harrisson. 'Notes on Class Consciousness and Class Unconsciousness'. *Sociological Review* 34, no. 3–4 (1942): 147–64.
54 TK, MOA TC 1 Housing, 1/A The Housing Centre 1939–40, Harrisson's notes, 24 October 1939, 5.
55 TK, MOA FR 874 Human Planning, 15 Sept 1941, 8.
56 TK, MOA TC 1 Housing, 1/A The Housing Centre 1939–40, Harrisson's notes, 24 October 1939, 5.
57 TK, MOA Worktown Box 44/A Social Conditions and Housing, The Housing Estate: Top o' th' Brow.
58 TK, MOA FR 873–4 Human Planning, 9.
59 Lewis, 'So Clean', 130–1.
60 TK, MOA TC 1 Housing, 1/A The Housing Centre 1939–40, Harrisson's notes, 24 October 1939, 5.
61 Quoted in Lewis, 'So Clean', 110.
62 Mass Observation, *Britain*, 217.
63 Hinton, *The Mass Observers*, 245, quotes a letter from Harrisson to Richard Fitter, 20 March 1941.
64 Mass Observation, *People's Homes*, 5.
65 Ibid., 3.
66 Ibid., 107.
67 Tebbutt, *Women's Talk?*, 146–7.
68 Mass Observation, *People's Homes*, 121.
69 Ibid., 69.
70 TK, MOA, FR 1948 'The Tube Dwellers', *The Saturday Book*, 1943, 102.
71 TK, MOA, FR 459 Third Weekly Report to Home Intelligence, 18 October 1940, 20.
72 TK, MOA, FR 1948 'The Tube Dwellers', *The Saturday Book*, 1943, 107.
73 Ibid., 106.
74 Ibid., 107.
75 Ibid., 109.
76 Sayer, *Making Trouble*, 65–6.

# Bibliography

Addison, Paul. *The Road to 1945: British Politics and the Second World War.* London: Pimlico, [1975] 1994.

Addison, Paul and Jeremy A. Crang, eds. *Listening to Britain: Home Intelligence Reports on Britain's Finest Hour – May to September 1940.* London: Vintage Books, 2011.

Alexander, Martin S. 'War and its Bestiality: Animals and their Fate during the Fighting in France, 1940'. *Rural History* 25, no. 1 (2014): 101–24.

Arendt, Hannah. *The Origins of Totalitarianism.* Orlando: Harcourt Brace Jovanovich, 1976 [1966].

Bailey, Jenna. *Can Any Mother Help Me?: The True Story of Motherhood, Friendship and a Secret Magazine.* London: Faber and Faber, 2007.

Barkan, Elazar. 1992. *The Retreat of Scientific Racism: Changing Concepts of Race in Britain and the United States between the World Wars.* Cambridge: Cambridge University Press.

Bell, Amy. 'Landscapes of Fear: Wartime London, 1939–1945'. *Journal of British Studies* 48, no. 1 (2009): 153–75.

Bell, Amy Helen. *London Was Ours: Diaries and Memoirs of the London Blitz*, New York: I.B. Tauris & Co Ltd, 2011.

Briggs, Asa. *The History of Broadcasting in the United Kingdom, Volume II: The Golden Age of Wireless.* Oxford and New York: Oxford University Press, 1995.

Brooke, Stephen, ed. *Reform and Reconstruction: Britain after the War, 1945–51.* Manchester and New York: Manchester University Press, 1995.

Brown, Andrew. *J.D. Bernal: The Sage of Science.* Oxford and New York: Oxford University Press, 2005.

Buckley, Ariel. 'Writing the Kitchen Front: Food Rationing and Propaganda in British Fiction of the Second World War'. MA diss., McGill University, Montreal, 2010.

Burns, Tom. *The BBC: Public Institution and Private World.* London: Macmillan, 1977.

Calder, Angus. *The People's War: Britain 1939–1945.* New York: Pantheon Books, 1969.

Campbell, Clare. *Bonzo's War: Animals Under Fire 1939–1945.* London: Constable & Robinson Ltd, 2013.

Campbell, Timothy, C. *Improper Life: Technology and Biopolitics from Heidegger to Agamben.* Minneapolis and London: University of Minnesota Press, 2011.

Cannadine, David. *Aspects of Aristocracy.* London: Penguin, 1995.

Cannadine, David. *Ornamentalism: How the British Saw Their Empire.* New York: Oxford University Press, 2011.

Chen, Mel Y. *Animacies: Biopolitics, Racial Mattering, and Queer Affect.* Durham and London: Duke University Press, 2012.

Coast, David and Jo Fox, 'Rumour and Politics'. *History Compass* 13, no. 5 (2015): 222–34.

Coulthard, Glen Sean. *Red Skin White Masks: Rejecting the Colonial Politics of Recognition.* Minneapolis and London: University of Minnesota Press, 2014.

Cox, Daniel, Rachel Lienesch and Robert P. Jones. 'Beyond Economics: Fears of Cultural Displacement Pushed the White Working Class to Trump'. Public Religion Research Institute/The Atlantic Report, 2017. Available online: https://www.prri.org/research/white-working-class-attitudes-economy-trade-immigration-election-donald-trump/ (accessed 10 February 2018).

Crosby, Travis. *The Impact of Civilian Evacuation in the Second World War.* London: Croom Helm, 1986.

Cunningham, Peter and Philip Gardner. '"Saving the Nation's Children": Teachers, Wartime Evacuation in England and Wales and the Construction of National Identity'. *History of Education* 28, no. 3 (1999): 327–37.

Curzon, Lucy D. *Mass-Observation and Visual Culture: Depicting Everyday Lives in Britain.* London and New York: Routledge, 2017.

Derrida, Jacques. *The Animal That Therefore I Am*, edited by Marie-Louise Mallet and translated by David Willis. New York: Fordham University Press, 2008.

Esposito, Roberto. 'Community, Immunity, Biopolitics'. *Angelaki: Journal of the Theoretical Humanities* 18, no. 3 (2013): 83–90.

Farley, Lisa. '"Operation Pied Piper": A Psychoanalytic Narrative of Authority in a Time of War'. *Psychoanalysis and History* 14, no. 1 (2012): 29–52.

Fassin, Didier. 'The Biopolitics of Otherness: Undocumented Foreigners and Racial Discrimination in French Public Debate'. *Anthropology Today* 17, no.1 (2001): 3–7.

Fassin, Didier. 'Compassion and Repression: The Moral Economy of Immigration Policies in France'. *Cultural Anthropology* 20, no. 3 (2005): 362–87.

Fassin, Didier. *Humanitarian Reason: A Moral History of the Present.* Berkeley and Los Angeles: University of California Press, 2012.

Foucault, Michel. *History of Sexuality: An Introduction. Volume 1*, translated by Robert Hurley. New York: Vintage Books, [1978] 1990.

Foucault, Michel. '"Omnes et Singulatim": Toward a Critique of Political Reason'. In *Power: Essential Works of Foucault 1954–1984, vol. 3*, edited by Paul Rabinow, 298–325. New York: The New Press, 1994.

Foucault, Michel. *Abnormal: Lectures at the Collège de France 1974–1975*, edited by Valerio Marchetti and Antonella Salomoni and translated by Graham Burchell. New York: Picador, 2003.

Foucault, Michel. *'Society Must Be Defended': Lectures at the Collège de France, 1975–76*, edited by M. Bertani and A. Fontana and translated by David Macey. New York: Picador, 2003.

Foucault, Michel. *Security, Territory, Population: Lectures at the Collège de France 1977–1978*, edited by Michael Sennellart and translated by Graham Burchell. New York: Picador, 2007.

Foucault, Michel. *The Birth of Biopolitics: Lectures at the Collège de France 1978–1979*, edited by Michael Sennellart and translated by Graham Burchell. New York: Picador, 2008.

Fox, Jo. 'Careless Talk: Tensions within British Domestic Propaganda during the Second World War'. *Journal of British Studies* 51.4 (2012): 936–66.

Freedman, Jean R. (1999), *Whistling in the Dark: Memory and Culture in Wartime London*, Lexington: The University Press of Kentucky.

Garfield, Simon, ed. *We Are at War: The Diaries for Five Ordinary People in Extraordinary Times*. London: Ebury Press, 2006.

Giles, Judy. *The Parlour and the Suburb: Domestic Identities, Class, Femininity and Modernity*. Oxford: Berg, 2004.

Grayzel, Susan R. *At Home and Under Fire: Air Raids and Culture in Britain from the Great War to the Blitz*. Cambridge: Cambridge University Press, 2012.

Greene, Graham. *The Ministry of Fear*. London: Vintage Books, [1943] 2001.

Hajkowski, Thomas. *The BBC and National Identity in Britain, 1922–53*. Manchester and New York: Manchester University Press, 2010.

Hall, David. *Worktown: The Astonishing Story of the 1930s Project that Launched Mass-Observation*. London: Weidenfeld & Nicolson, 2016.

Hall, Stuart. 'The Social Eye of the *Picture Post*'. *Working Papers in Cultural Studies* 2 (1972): 71–120.

Hamilton, Cicely. *Theodore Savage*. Boston and Brooklyn: HiLoBooks, [1922] 2013.

Hamilton, John T. *Security: Politics, Humanity, and the Philology of Care*. Princeton and Oxford: Princeton University Press, 2013.

Haraway, Donna. 'Situated Knowledges: The Science Question in Feminism and the Privilege of Partial Perspective'. *Feminist Studies* 14, no. 3 (1988): 575–99.

Haraway, Donna. *When Species Meet*. Minneapolis and London: University of Minnesota Press, 2008.

Harris, Jose. 'War and Social History: Britain and the Home Front during the Second World War'. *Contemporary European History* 1, no. 1 (1992): 17–35.

Harrisson, Tom. *Living through the Blitz*. London: Faber and Faber, [1976] 2010.

Heimann, Judith M. *The Most Offending Soul Alive: Tom Harrisson and His Remarkable Life*. Honolulu: University of Hawai'i Press, 1998.

Hey, Kathleen. *The View from the Corner Shop: The Diary of a Yorkshire Shop Assistant in Wartime*, edited by Patricia and Robert Malcolmson, London and New York: Simon and Schuster, 2016.

Highmore, Ben. *Everyday Life and Cultural Theory: An Introduction*. London and New York: Routledge, 2002.

Highmore, Ben. *Ordinary Lives: Studies in the Everyday*. London and New York: Routledge, 2011.

Hilton, Matthew, James MacKay, Nicholas Crowson and Jean-François Mouhot. *The Politics of Expertise: How NGOs Shaped Modern Britain*. Oxford: Oxford University Press, 2013.

Hinton, James. *Nine Wartime Lives: Mass-Observation and the Making of the Modern Self.* New York: Oxford University Press, 2010.
Hinton, James. *The Mass Observers: A History, 1937–1949.* Oxford: Oxford University Press, 2013.
Hobbs, Pam. *Don't Forget to Write: The true story of an evacuee and her family.* London: Ebury Press, 2009.
Hollow, Matthew. 'Utopian Urges: Visions for Reconstruction in Britain, 1940–1950'. *Planning Perspectives* 27, no, 4 (2012): 569–85.
Holman, Brett. '"Bomb Back, and Bomb Hard": Debating Reprisals During the Blitz'. *Australian Journal of Politics and History* 58, no. 3 (2012): 394–407.
Holman, Brett. 'The Shadow of the Airliner: Commercial Bombers and the Rhetorical Destruction of Britain, 1917–35'. *Twentieth Century British History* 24, no. 4 (2013): 495–517.
Howell, Philip. 'The Dog Fancy at War: Breeds, Breeding, and Britishness, 1914–1918'. *Society & Animals* 21 (2013): 546–67.
Howell, Philip. *At Home and Astray: The Domestic Dog in Victorian Britain.* Charlottesville and London: University of Virginia Press, 2015.
Howell, Philip and Hilda Kean. 'The Dogs That Didn't Bark in the Blitz: Transpecies and Transpersonal Emotional Geographies on the British Home Front'. *Journal of Historical Geography* 61 (2018): 44–52.
Hubble, Nick. *Mass Observation and Everyday Life. Culture, History, Theory.* New York: Palgrave Macmillan, 2010.
Huxley, Julian and A.C. Haddon. *We Europeans: A Survey of 'Racial' Problems*, New York and London: Harper and Brothers, 1935.
Irvine, Leslie. 'A Model of Animal Selfhood: Expanding Interactionist Possibilities'. *Symbolic Interaction* 27, no. 1 (2004): 3–21.
Irvine, Leslie. 'Animals as Lifechangers and Lifesavers: Pets in the Redemption Narratives of Homeless People'. *Journal of Contemporary Ethnography* 42, no. 3 (2013): 3.30.
Irving, Henry. 'Paper Salvage in Britain during the Second World War'. *Historical Research* 89, no. 244 (2016): 373–93.
Issacs, Susan and Sybil Clement Brown. *The Cambridge Evacuation Survey: A Wartime Study in Social Welfare and Education.* London: Methuen & Company Ltd, 1941.
Jerolmack, Colin. 'Animal Practices, Ethnicity, and Community: The Turkish Pigeon Handlers of Berlin'. *American Sociological Review* 72, no. 6 (2007): 874–94.
Kean, Hilda. *Animal Rights: Political and Social Change in Britain since 1800.* London: Reaktion Books Ltd., 1998.
Kean, Hilda. *The Great Cat and Dog Massacre: The Real Story of World War II's Unknown Tragedy.* Chicago and London: Chicago University Press, 2017.
Kete, Kathleen. *The Beast in the Boudoir: Petkeeping in Nineteenth-Century Paris.* Berkeley, Los Angeles, London: University of California Press, 1995.

King, Laura. 'Future Citizens: Cultural and Political Conceptions of Children in Britain, 1930s–1950s'. *Twentieth Century British History* 27, no. 3 (2016): 389–411.

Kirk, Robert G. 'In Dogs We Trust?: Intersubjectivity, Response-able Relations, and the Making of Mine Detector Dogs'. *Journal of the History of the Behavioral Sciences* 50, no. 1 (2014): 1–36.

Kushner, Antony Robin Jeremy. *We Europeans?: Mass-Observation, 'Race' and British Identity in the Twentieth Century*. Aldershot and Burlington: Ashgate, 2004.

Langhamer, Claire. '"A Public House Is for All Classes, Men and Women Alike": Women, Leisure and Drink in Second World War England'. *Women's History Review* 12, no. 3 (2003): 423–43.

Lemke, Thomas. *Biopolitics: An Advanced Introduction*, translated by E. F. Trump. New York and London: New York University Press, 2011.

Lewis, Brian. *'So Clean': Lord Leverhulme, Soap and Civilization*. Manchester and New York: Manchester University Press, 2008.

Lin, Patricia Y. 'National Identity and Social Mobility: Class, Empire and the British Government Overseas Evacuation of Children during the Second World War'. *Twentieth Century British History* 7, no. 3 (1996): 310–44.

Lindqvist, Sven. *A History of Bombing*, translated by Linda Haverty Rugg. New York: The New Press, 2001.

Longmate, Norman. *How We Lived Then: A History of Everyday Life During the Second World War*. London: Pimlico, [1971] 2002.

Lowe, Rodney. 'The Second World War, Consensus, and the Foundation of the Welfare State'. *Twentieth Century British History* 1, no. 2 (1990): 152–82.

Mackay, Robert. *Half the Battle: Civilian Morale in Britain during the Second World War*. Manchester and New York: Manchester University Press, 2002.

Marcus, Laura. 'Introduction: The Project of Mass Observation'. *New Formations* 44 (2001): 5–20.

Mass Observation. *First Year's Work: 1937–1938*, edited by Charles Madge and Tom Harrisson. London: Faber and Faber, [1938] 2009.

Mass Observation. *Britain*, arranged and written by Charles Madge and Tom Harrisson. London: Faber and Faber, [1939] 2009.

Mass Observation. *War Begins at Home*, compiled by Tom Harrisson and Charles Madge. London: Faber and Faber, [1940] 2009.

Mass Observation. *An Enquiry into People's Homes: A Report by Mass-Observation for the Advertising Service Guild*. London: John Murray, 1943.

Mass Observation. *Britain and Her Birth-rate: A Report by Mass-Observation for the Advertising Service Guild*. London: John Murray, 1945.

Mayall, Berry and Virginia Morrow, *You Can Help Your Country: English children's work during the Second World War*. London: University of London, 2011.

McHugh, Susan. *Dog*. London: Reaktion Books, 2004.

McHugh, Susan. *Animal Stories: Narrating Across Species Lines*. Minneapolis and London: University of Minnesota Press, 2011.

McLaine, Ian. *Ministry of Morale: Home Front Morale and the Ministry of Information in World War II*. London: George Allen & Unwin, 1979.

Merricks, Patrick T. 'Should Such a Faith Offend? Bishop Barnes and the British Eugenics Movement, c. 1924–1953'. PhD diss., Oxford Brookes University, Oxford, 2014.

Miller, Dan E. '"Snakes in the Greens" and Rumor in the Innercity'. *Social Science* 29 (1992), 381–93.

Miller, Dan E. 'Rumor: An Examination of Some Stereotypes'. *Symbolic Interaction*, 28 (2005), 505–19.

Miller, William Ian. *The Anatomy of Disgust*. Cambridge and London: Harvard University Press, 1997.

Moore, Francesca. '"A Band of Public-spirited Women": Middle-class Female Philanthropy and Citizenship in Bolton, Lancashire before 1918'. *Transactions* 41 (2016): 149–62.

Moran, Joe. 'Imagining the Street in Post-war Britain'. *Urban History* 39, no. 1 (2012): 166–86.

Morgan, David and Mary Evans. *The Battle for Britain: Citizenship and Ideology in the Second World War.* London and New York: Routledge, 1993.

Mort, Frank. 'Fantasies of Metropolitan Life: Planning London in the 1940s'. *Journal of British Studies* 43, no. 1 (2004): 120–51.

Myers, Kevin. 'The Ambiguities of Aid and Agency'. *Cultural and Social History* 6, no. 1 (2009): 29–46.

Nicolson, Harold. *Diaries and Letters 1939–1945*, edited by Nigel Nicolson. London: Collins, 1967.

Noakes, Lucy. '"Serve to Save": Gender, Citizenship and Civil Defence in Britain, 1937–41'. *Journal of Contemporary History* 47, no.4 (2012): 734–53.

Orwell, George. *The Road to Wigan Pier*. London: Penguin Books, [1937] 2001.

Orwell, George. *Coming Up for Air*. London: Penguin Books, [1939] 1990.

Ostermeier, Mark. 'History of Guide Dog Use by Veterans'. *Military Medicine* 175, no. 8 (2010): 587–93.

*Our Towns: A Close-Up*. A study made in 1939–42 with certain recommendations by the Hygiene Committee of the Women's Group on Public Welfare (in association with the National Council of Social Service), 2nd edn, London, New York, Toronto: Oxford University Press, [1943] 1944.

Overy, Richard. *The Twilight Years: The Paradox of Britain between the Wars*. New York: Penguin, Ebook edition, 2009.

Padley, Richard and Margaret Cole, eds. *Evacuation Survey: A Report to the Fabian Society*, London: Routledge, 1940.

Paneth, Marie. *Branch Street: A Sociological Study*, London: George Allen & Unwin Ltd, 1944.

Pearson, Chris. '"Four-Legged *Poilus*": French Army Dogs, Emotional Practices and the Creation of Militarized Human-Dog Bonds, 1871–1918'. *Journal of Social History* 52, no.3 (2019): 731–60.

Pomfret, David. 'The City of Evil and the Great Outdoors: The Modern Health Movement and the Urban Young, 1918-40'. *Urban History* 28, no. 3 (2001): 405-27.

Purcell, Jennifer. 'The Domestic Soldier: British Housewives and the Nation in the Second World War'. *History Compass* 4, no. 1 (2006): 153-60.

Purcell, Jennifer. *Domestic Soldiers: Six Women's Lives in the Second World War*. London: Constable, [2010] 2011.

Repo, Jemima. *The Biopolitics of Gender*. New York: University of Oxford Press, 2016.

Repo, Jemima. 'Governing Juridical Sex: Gender Recognition and the Biopolitics of Trans Sterilization in Finland'. *Politics & Gender* 15, no. 1 (2019): 83-106.

Ritvo, Harriet. *The Animal Estate: The English and Other Creatures in the Victorian Age*. Cambridge: Harvard University Press, 1987.

Robinson, James Philip. 'Invisible Targets, Strengthened Morale: Static Camouflage as a "Weapon of the Weak"'. *Space and Polity* 16, no. 3 (2012): 351-68.

Rose, Nikolas. *Governing the Soul: The Shaping of the Private Self*, 2nd edn, London: Free Association Books, 1999.

Rose, Sonya O. 'Women's Rights, Women's Obligations: Contradictions of Citizenship in World War II Britain'. *European Review of History: Revue européenne d'histoire* 7, no. 2 (2000): 277-89.

Rose, Sonya O. *Which People's War? National Identity and Citizenship in Wartime Britain 1939-1945*. Oxford University Press, 2003.

Saint-Amour, Paul K. *Tense Future: Modernism, Total War, Encyclopedic Form*. Oxford and New York: Oxford University Press, 2015.

Sayer, Derek. *Making Trouble: Surrealism and the Human Sciences*. Chicago: Prickly Paradigm Press, 2017.

Sayer, Derek. 'White Riot – Brexit, Trump, and Post-factual Politics'. *Journal of Historical Sociology* 30 (2017): 92-106.

Schuller, Kyla. *The Biopolitics of Feeling: Race, Sex and Science in the Nineteenth Century*. Durham and London: Duke University Press, 2018.

Seshadri, Kalpana Rahita. *HumAnimal: Race, Law, Language*. Minneapolis and London: University of Minnesota Press, 2012.

Shapira, Michal. *The War Inside: Psychoanalysis, Total War, and the Making of the Democratic Self in Postwar Britain*. Cambridge: Cambridge University Press, 2013.

Sheridan, Dorothy, ed. *Wartime Women: An Anthology of Women's Wartime Writing for Mass Observation 1937-45*. Heinemann: London, 1990.

Sheridan, Dorothy, Brian Street and David Bloome. *Writing Ourselves: Mass-Observation and Literacy Practices*. Cresskill, Hampton Press, 2000.

Shibutani, Tamotsu. *Improvised News: A Sociological Study of Rumor*. New York: Bobbs-Merrill, 1966.

Shukin, Nicole. *Animal Capital: Rendering Life in Biopolitical Times*. Minneapolis and London: University of Minnesota Press, 2009.

Shukin, Nicole. 'Transfections of Animal Touch, Techniques of Biosecurity'. *Social Semiotics* 21, no. 4 (2011): 483-501.

Simpson, Leanne Betasamosake. *As We Have Always Done: Indigenous Freedom through Radical Resistance*. Minneapolis and London: University of Minnesota Press, 2017.

Slocombe, Richard. *British Posters of the Second World War*. London: Imperial War Museum, 2014.

Soloway, Richard A. *Demography and Degeneration: Eugenics and the Declining Birthrate in Twentieth-Century Britain*. University of North Carolina Press, [1990] 1995.

Stevenson, Lisa. *Life Beside Itself: Imagining Care in the Canadian Arctic*. Oakland: University of California Press, 2014.

Stradling, Robert. *Your Children Will Be Next: Bombing and Propaganda in the Spanish Civil War, 1936–1939*. Cardiff: University of Wales Press, 2008.

Summerfield, Penny. 'Mass-Observation: Social Research or Social Movement?' *Journal of Contemporary History* 20, no. 3, (1985): 439–52.

Summerfield, Penny. 'The "Levelling of Class"'. In *War and Social Change: British Society in the Second World War*, edited by Harold L. Smith, 179–207. Manchester: Manchester University Press, 1990.

Summerfield, Penny and Corinna Peniston-Bird. 'Women in the Firing Line: The Home Guard and the Defence of Gender Boundaries in Britain in the Second World War'. *Women's History Review* 9 no. 2 (2000): 231–55.

Taylor, Sunaura. *Beasts of Burden: Animal and Disability Liberation.* New York and London: The New Press, 2017.

Tebbutt, Melanie. *Women's Talk?: A Social History of 'Gossip' in Working Class Neighbourhoods, 1880–1980*, Aldershot and Burlington: Scholar Press and Ashgate Publishing, 1997.

Tebbutt, Melanie. 'Listening to Youth?: BBC Youth Broadcasts during the 1930s and the Second World War'. *History Workshop Journal* 84 (2017): 214–33.

Titmuss, Richard M. *Social Welfare and Health Care in World War II, Vol 1*, London: HMSO, 232 Celsius Ebook edition, 1950.

Todd, Selina. *The People: The Rise and Fall of the Working Class.* London: John Murray, 2015.

Todd, Zoe. 'An Indigenous Feminist's Take On The Ontological Turn: "Ontology" Is Just Another Word for Colonialism'. *Journal of Historical Sociology* 29, no. 1 (2016).

Trevelyan, Julian. *Indigo Days: The Art and Memoirs of Julian Trevelyan.* Aldershot: Scolar Press, [1957] 1996.

Tuan, Yi-Fu. *Dominance and Affection: The Making of Pets*. New Haven and London: Yale University Press, 1984.

Turner, E. S. *The Phoney War on the Home Front.* London: Faber and Faber, [1961] 2012.

University of Liverpool Social Science Department. *Preliminary Report on the Problems of Evacuation*. University of Liverpool Press, 1939.

University of Liverpool Social Science Department. *Our Wartime Guests – Opportunity or Menace?: A Psychological Approach to Evacuation*. London: The University Press of Liverpool and Hodder & Stoughton Ltd, 1940.

Visser, Margaret. *The Rituals of Dinner: The Origins, Evolution, Eccentricities, and Meaning of Table Manners.* Toronto: HarperCollins Canada, ebook, [1991] 2008.

Wagner, Gertrude. 'Evacuation'. *Social Welfare* 4, no. 6 (1940): 98–107.
Walters, William. 'Foucault and Frontiers: Notes on the Birth of the Humanitarian Border'. In *Governmentality: Current Issues and Future Challenges,* edited by U. Bröckling, Susanne Krasmann and Thomas Lemke, 138–64. New York: Routledge, 2011.
Wells, H.G. 'The Shape of Things to Come'. In *H. G. Wells: The Complete Novels*, 171699–171701. Book House Publishing, ebook, 2017.
Welshman, John. 'Evacuation and Social Policy during the Second World War: Myth and Reality'. *Twentieth Century British History* 9, no. 1 (1998): 28–53.
Welshman, John. 'The Social History of Social Work: The Issue of the "Problem Family", 1940–70'. *The British Journal of Social Work* 29, no. 3 (1999): 457–76.
Welshman, John. 'Evacuation, Hygiene, and Social Policy: The Our Towns Report of 1943'. *The Historical Journal* 42, no. 3 (1999): 781–807.
Wiggam, Marc. *The Blackout in Britain and Germany, 1939–1945.* Palgrave Pivot, 2018.
Williams, David. 'Inappropriate/d Others or, The Difficulty of Being a Dog'. *The Drama Review* 51, no. 1 (2007): 92–118.
Wolfe, Cary. *Animal Rites. American Culture, the Discourse of Species, and Posthumanist Theory.* Chicago and London: The University of Chicago Press, 2003.
Wolfe, Cary. *What is Posthumanism?*. Minneapolis, London: University of Minnesota Press, 2010.
Woolgar, Steve. 'Configuring the User: The Case of Usability Trials'. In *A Sociology of Monsters: Essays on Power, Technology and* Domination, edited by John Law, 57–99. London and New York: Routledge, 1991.

## Archival collections

**The Keep, Brighton, UK (TK)**
*Mass Observation Archive (MOA)*
 Diaries (D)
 File Reports (FR)
 Topic Collections (TC)
*Charles Madge Archive*
 Autobiographical Papers (SxMS)
*East Sussex Record Office*
 Papers of Charles Elwell (1880–1956) and his son Charles John Lister Elwell (ACC)

**The National Archives, Kew, London, UK (TNA)**
Board of Education (ED)
Home Office (HO)
Ministry of Information (INF)

# Index

The letter *f* after an entry indicates a page that includes a figure.

ableism 138, 139
Adams, Mary 43, 44, 45, 62, 63
Addison, Paul
   *Road to 1945, The* 6, 8
affect theory 50
Air Raid Precaution (ARP). *See* ARP
*Air Raid Precautions for Animals* (ARP) 113
air raids viii–x, xi–xii, xviii, xix, 153
   blitz, the 159, 160
   damage/destruction xx
   dogs 116, 129, 131–2
   fear xix
   Mumford, Lewis xvi
   pets 112–13, 117–18
   planning vii–viii, xii–xiii
   security 156–8
   tube dwelling 167–9
airplanes viii–x
*Anatomy of Disgust, The* (Miller, William Ian) 151–2
animacy hierarchies 36–8, 136–7, 142, 147
   language 139–40
animal-human distinction 137–42
*Animal-Human War, The* 115
animalization 148–50, 151
animals 4 *see also* pets
   air raid precautions 112–3
   companion. *See* pets
   comparative worth 142–7
   destruction 113, 116, 140, 144
   domestic. *See* pets
   food 120
   hierarchies 122, 144–6
   Kean, Hilda 115, 132
   laboratory 36, 127
   livestock 113, 118–19, 120
   productivity 5, 110, 120
   response 140
   responsibilities/rights 193 n. 31
   utility 5, 34–5, 36, 120–1, 143*f*–4
'Animals and Air Raids' (RSPCA) 116
anonymous care 3, 29, 68
anti-war conflict xi–xii
anticipation xvi, xvii–xviii, xx
antisemitism 8, 53, 106–7, 163, 164–5
architecture 150, 160, 165 *see also* slums
ARP (Air Raid Precaution) xiii, 1, 2, 109
   instructions xiii–xiv, xv–xvi
   *Air Raid Precautions for Animals* 113
Ashford, Pam xvii, 56, 125–6
attentiveness 154–5

Barthes, Roland 14, 15
BBC 54
Bell, Amy 11
Beveridge, William
   'Social Insurance and Allied Services' 6, 27
biopolitics 29–38, 48–9, 156
   eugenics 162
   governance 40
biopower 47–8
birth-rate 164
'Black-out: A Symbol of the War Which Mustn't be Photographed' feature 54
blackout measures 9
blitz, the 159, 160, 167–8 *see also* air raids
'Blitz Information – The Lifeline of Civil Defence' (Harrisson, Tom) 39–40
Bob Martin's Ltd 111, 117–18
Bolton Queen Street Mission 152
*Branch Street* (Paneth, Marie) 149–51
Brexit 26
*Britain* (Harrisson, Tom and Madge, Charles) 14, 22, 23

*Britain and Her Birth-rate* (Mass Observation) 164
'Butcher Boys of Birmingham' letter 100

Calder, Angus
    *People's War, The* 7
Cambridge 83
Cambridge Evacuation Survey 83–4
Cambridge Scientists Anti-War Group (CSAWG). *See* CSAWG
Capa, Robert xii
care 3, 40–2, 104, 154–6
    animals 110
    anonymous 3, 29, 68
    everyday 3, 68
    priorities 136
    security and 156–8
careless homes 158–63
careless talk 59–61
carelessness 157
categorization 33–4
cats 4
    destruction 4, 109, 114
    food 120
    productivity 120
    selfhood 132
    utility 34–5, 36, 120
censorship 54
Chamberlain, Neville 177 n. 58
Chen, Mel Y. 36, 38, 136, 139, 142
children 10–11, 135
    animalizing 141–2, 148–50, 151
    charity 152
    disapproval 148
    environment/heredity 160–2
    evacuation 74, 75, 83–4, 140
    evil 150–1
    as vermin 151
    wartime duty 102
    wild 148–51
citizenship 8–9 *see also* good citizens
    children 10
    dogs 145
    politics 28
city, the 96
civic duty xii–xiv, xviii, 102
civic virtue 9
civil defence vii–viii, 1, 12, 156–7, 169

civilian protection plans vii–viii, xii–xiii, 171 n. 11
class. *See* social class
clothing 82
*Coming Up for Air* (Orwell, George) xvii
communication xiii, xiv–xix, 19, 40, 59, 139–40
    gossip 58
    media, the 18–19
    propaganda 54–6
    rumours 56–64 *see also* evacuation stories
    wartime instructions vii–viii, xiii–xx
companion animals. *See* pets
compassion 25, 27, 41
consensus 6
contempt 150–1
Cooper, Duff 62, 64
cooperation 6, 12
    individual 30
Cooper's Snoopers scandal 62, 63–4
countryside, the 96
Cox Commission on Loneliness 26–7
CSAWG (Cambridge Scientists Anti-War Group) xii
    *Protection of the Public from Aerial Attack, The* xii
culture
    race and 163
*Culture of Cities, The* (Mumford, Lewis) xvi
cultural displacement 26
cultural studies 14–15
Cura, myth of 155, 156
Curzon, Lucy 17

Darwin, Charles 137
death 32, 147–8,
    Cura, myth of 155, 156
defendism 53
Derrida, Jacques 127–8, 140
desertion 141
disgust 151, 152
domestic animals. *See* pets
domestic work 9, 10
dogs 4, 115
    affection for 121
    air raids 116, 129, 131–2
    breeding 129

citizenship 145
comparative worth 142–7
dangerous 34, 35
destruction 4, 109, 114, 121, 124, 126, 135
disapproval 4, 34–5, 125–6, 127
feelings 131
food 110, 116, 119–20, 125, 126–7, 128, 135, 146–7
geography 123–5
mongrels 129
morale 130–1
names 133
nationalism 129, 145
pro-dogism 131
productivity 120, 122
racism 145
responsibility 117
sacrifice 126–8
selfhood 132
service 144
status 117
surveys 110, 111, 122–33
tax on 130
utility 36, 121, 126, 128–31, 135–6, 142, 144
Dunn, Denis 62–3
Durkheim, Émile 24

education 95, 159–60
emotion 11, 151–2 *see also* feelings
  evacuation 71–2, 98
emotional socialization 11
*Enquiry into People's Homes* (Mass Observation) 166–7
environment 160–2
equality 3, 7
eugenics 103, 158, 159, 160–4
evacuation 2, 3, 38, 103–4, 140–1, 158 *see also* evacuation stories
  advertisers 76
  desertion 141
  distribution 74–5
  emotion 71–2, 98
  homesickness 97–8
  hosts 6–7
  housing 157
  implementation 71–6
  neglect 6
  opposition to 141
  pets 34–5, 112–13, 114
  planning viii
  returning/running away 93–6, 141
  social divide 2, 3, 7
  studies 157
  Titmuss, Richard 12, 76–7
  wartime duty 102
  Welshman, John 177 n. 59
'Evacuation and Social Policy During the Second World War' (Welshman, John) 177 n. 59
evacuation stories 2, 67–8, 69–70, 75–9, 104–8
  affectionate/amusing 97–8
  authority 86–7
  boundaries 87
  categorization and separation 102–3
  cleanliness 83–4
  contamination threats 79–88, 100, 102, 103
  disorientation 82–3
  food 82
  good citizens 90–2, 96–100
  gratitude 88–92, 98, 106
  health 81, 86–7
  Hobbs, Pam 153–4
  hosts 74–5, 78, 79, 82, 84, 89, 92, 98–9
  kind warden's wife, the 98–9
  politics 100–1, 102
  Potter, Eileen 153
  problems 72–3, 74, 76–7, 79–85, 106–7
  racism 98–100, 106–7
  religion 100–1, 102
  returning/running away 93–6
  social divide 67–8, 73–5, 81–2, 84–5, 87
  Spanish 100–1, 102
  sympathy 106
  table etiquette 85, 86
  wild children 148–9, 151
  women 90–2
Eve, fall of 93–6
everyday care 3, 68
everyday writing 16
evolutionary theory 137–8
exclusion 25–6

Farley, Lisa 141–2
Fassin, Dider 25–6, 27, 28, 29

fear xix–xx
feckless mothers 92
feelings 50, 131 *see also* emotion *and* morale
  public feeling experiment 49
fifth column 18–10, 57
  Silent Column campaign 59–62
food
  cooking 118
  dogs 110, 116, 119–20, 125, 126–7, 128, 135, 146–7
  efficient use 120–1, 126–7
  evacuation 82
  hoarding 57
  Kitchen Front 109–10
  livestock 120–1, 127
  pets 4, 116
  poultry keeping 118–19, 120, 121
  propaganda 55–6
  Racehorses 120–1
  rationing 4, 118, 119
  social prestige 55–6
Foucault, Michel 29, 30, 32
  biopower 47–8
  governmentality 104
  individuals 64
  pastoralism 46, 47, 48
  power 46
  state racialization 102–3, 104
Fox, Jo 61–2
Frank-Heaton Protective Enclosure 117–18
'Freedom is in Peril, Defend it with All Your Might' poster xiv–xv
Fremlin, Celia 44, 106
Freud, Sigmund 15
'From the Slum to the Sea' initiative 152
functional penetration 17
future, the xix, 10, 24

gender 33
Germany 135
good citizens 9, 11, 30
  civic duty xii–xiv, xviii, 102
  evacuation 90–2, 96–100
  pets 114, 117
gossip 58
government 19, 39
  biopolitical 29–30

biopolitics 29–38, 40, 48–9, 156, 162
children 10
citizen groups 28–9
decentralization 27–8
humanitarian 25, 28
intelligence. *See* Home Intelligence
state racialization 102–3, 104
wartime instructions vii–viii, xiii–xx
wartime planning vii–viii, xii–xx, 171 n. 11
welfare state 6, 177 n. 59
governmentality 104
*Grab, Grab, Grab* poster 53
Grandin, Temple 139
Grayzel, Susan ix, xii, 2
*Great Cat and Dog Massacre, The* (Kean, Hilda) 132
Greene, Graham ix
Groves, P.R.C.
  'Our Future in the Air' ix–x

Hamilton, Cecily
  *Theodore Savage* x–xi, xvi
Hamilton, John T. 156
hand sanitation 30
Haraway, Donna 127–8, 147–8
Harris, Jose 6, 7
Harrisson, Tom 13, 16–17, 18–19, 22
  Adams, Mary 44
  'Blitz Information – The Lifeline of Civil Defence' 39–40
  defendism 53
  evacuation 105, 106, 108
  fear xix–xx
  food 54–5
  funding 21
  government advice, providing 55
  Helpful Warden post 40–1
  Home Intelligence 46
  housing 165, 166
  'I Married a Cannibal' 21
  Madge, Charles, disagreement with 23–4, 46
  morale 50–4
  *Savage Civilisation* 13
  war 53
Harrisson, Tom and Madge, Charles
  *Britain* 14, 22, 23
  *War Begins at Home* 22–3, 45

health 30–1f
Helpful Warden post 40–1
heredity 160–2
Hey, Kathleen 118, 148
Highmore, Ben 14–15, 24
Hilton, Matthew, MacKay, James, Crowson, Nicholas and Mouhot, Jean-François 12, 29
Hinton, James 23, 111
history 24
hoarding xvii, 57
Hobbs, Pam 118–19, 153–4
Hollow, Matthew 159, 160
Holman, Brett ix–x
home front 2, 115, 156–7
    blackout measures 9
    civic duty xii–xiv, xviii
    governance 27–8
    humanitarian reason 25–9
Home Intelligence 21, 22, 43–6, 48
    morale 51
homes 10, 156–8
    careless homes 158–63
    civil defence vii–viii
    problem families 159
    slums 157, 159–60
    state, relationship with 2
    tube dwelling 167–9
*Homo Sylvestris* (Tyson, Edward) 138
horses 120–1, 142, 144
housewives 166–7
housing 157, 160, 164, 165–7
Howell, Philip 129
Hubble, Nick 14, 15, 19, 22–3
human/non-human 37
humanitarian governance 25, 28
humanitarian reason 12, 25–9
humans 137
    animal-human distinction 137–42
    Cura, myth of 155, 156
    labour 138
    language 139–40
    as pets 140
    posture 137–9
    response 140
    vision 139
Huxley, Julian and Haddon, Alfred C. *We Europeans: A Survey in 'Racial' Problems* 162–3

'I Married a Cannibal' (Harrisson, Tom) 21
identity 8–9 *see also* national identity
    dogs 129
    selfhood 132
impressibility 162
impressionability 162
indirects 123
individual, the 64–5
individual cooperation 30
individualism 7
inequality 3, 7, 89–90, 155–6
information, dissemination of 40
informative rumours 58
intelligence gathering 65
internment 18–19
*It's That Man Again* radio show 62

Jahoda, Marie 20–1
Jennings, Humphrey 13

Kean, Hilda 115
    *Great Cat and Dog Massacre, The* 132
'Keep Calm and Carry On' poster xiv
Kete, Kathleen 129–30
kind warden's wife, the 98–9
King, Laura 10
Kitchen Front 109–10
Kushner, Tony 164

laboratory animals 36, 127
Lamarckism 162
Langhamer, Claire 9
language 37, 139–40
leisure 9–10, 65
Letchworth 165–6
Lever Brothers 166
life 29–32
    Cura, myth of 155, 156
    pets 110
    relative value 103, 121, 126, 136, 142–7
    *see also* animacy hierarchies *and* eugenics
'Lighter Side of Evacuation: Scores of Amazing and Amusing Incidents, The' feature 97
Lin, Patricia Y. 141
Lindqvist, Sven viii, ix
livestock 113, 118–19, 120

London xii
   dogs 124–5
   reputation 73
loneliness 26–7
Lowe, Rodney
   'Second World War, The' 176 n. 23

McHugh, Susan 115, 145
McLaine, Ian 49, 62
Madge, Charles 13, 22, 44 see also *Britain and War Begins at Home*
   Harrisson, Tom, disagreement with 23–4, 46
   morale 50
   rumours 57
'Madrid – The "Military" Practice of the Rebels' poster xi
Malinowski, Bronislaw
   'Nation-wide Intelligence Service, A' 56
*March of Progress, The* image 138
marriage 47
   fidelity 47
Mass Observation 1–2, 42, 45, 164–9
   bias 20–1
   biopolitics of care 38–42
   *Britain and Her Birth-rate* 164
   care 68
   commercial commissions 111
   communication 59
   criticism 20–3, 111
   definition 15
   'Dogs in London' survey 111
   dog surveys 110, 111, 122–33
   *Enquiry into People's Homes* 166–7
   eugenics 164
   evacuation 3, 68–73, 104–8
   functional penetration 17
   funding 21
   goals 18, 19, 23, 24, 105
   government contracts 21, 22–3, 43–6
   government, recommendations to 39–41, 46, 53, 68
   history, recording 24, 105
   Home Intelligence 21, 22, 43–6, 48, 51
   housing 165–7
   Hubble, Nick 19
   indirects 123
   influence 19
   interviews 63–4, 123
   Jahoda, Marie 20–1
   leisure 65
   Malinowski, Bronislaw 56
   *May the Twelfth* 169
   methodologies 16–17
   morale 50–2, 53, 56–64, 65
   news 55
   panel 20–1, 25
   politics 24–5, 44
   'Provincial Dogs' survey 111
   public caregiving 21
   public feeling experiment 49
   rumours 56–64
   séances 65
   social class 165
   as source and agent 13–25
   subjectivity-objectivity dichotomy 20–1
   subversion 44
   suspicion of 62–3
   Trevelyan, Julian 21
   'Tube Dwellers, The' 167, 168
   tube dwelling 167–9
   visual work 17
Mass Observation Archive (MOA) 16
*May the Twelfth* (Mass Observation) 169
media, the 18–19
   propaganda 54–6
Miller, William Ian
   *Anatomy of Disgust, The* 151–2
Ministry of Information (MOI). *See* MOI
MOA (Mass Observation Archive) 16
modern racism 103
MOI (Ministry of Information) 22, 43
   BBC 54
   *Grab, Grab, Grab* poster 53
   Home Intelligence 21, 22, 43, 43–6, 48, 51
   legitimacy/ridicule 62
   morale 49–50, 51
   posters xiv–xv
morale 49–54, 65
   Home Intelligence 43–5, 48, 51
   individual, the 64
   news 55
   pets 4, 5, 130–1
   psychoanalysis 51–2
   rumours 56–64
   sensorial resocialization 11

wishful thinking 51–2
morale barometer 44–5
Mort, Frank 157
mothers 92, 94f–6
Mumford, Lewis
    *Culture of Cities, The* xvi
Myers, Kevin 100–1

NARPAC (National Air Raid Precautions for Animals Committee) 115, 122
'Nation-wide Intelligence Service, A' (Malinowski, Bronislaw) 56
National Air Raid Precautions for Animals Committee (NARPAC) 115, 122
National Canine Defence League (NCDL) 110, 112
national identity 8–9, 163
    dogs 129, 145
nationalism 145
NCDL (National Canine Defence League) 110, 112
news 55
newsletters 54–5
NGOs (non-governmental organizations) 12, 29
Nicolson, Harold 8
noise 11
non-governmental organizations (NGOs) 12, 29
non-human/human 37

Operation Pied Piper 3, 67, 141–2, 157
opinion 18
Orwell, George
    *Coming Up for Air* xvii
    *Road to Wigan Pier, The* 138
'Our Future in the Air' (Groves, P.R.C.) ix–x
*Our Towns: A Close Up* report 38, 158, 159–60
*Our Wartime Guests* evacuation study 75

Paneth, Marie
    *Branch Street* 149–51
pastoralism 46, 47, 48–9
People's War 2
*People's War, The* (Calder, Angus) 7
pets 3, 4 *see also* cats *and* dogs
    affection for 121

air raids 112–13, 117–18
    comparative worth 142–7
    destruction of 4, 109, 112, 113–16, 121, 126, 132–3, 140
    disapproval 4–5, 6, 34
    essential 34
    evacuation 34–5, 112–13, 114
    food rationing 4, 116, 119
    humans as 140
    instructive literature 115–16
    morale 4, 5
    poultry 118–19, 120
    protective devices 117–18
    refugee 112
    sacrifice 5, 110, 126–8, 133
Phoney War, the xviii, 67, 132
photography xii, 54
*Picture Post* 54, 62, xii
    evacuation 71, 77, 100
*Pied Piper of Hamelin, The* 141–2
political consensus 6
politics
    privatization of 12, 28
    professionalization of 28–9
politics of life 29, 36
politics of resentment 26
popular culture 14–15
    propaganda 55
population, the 29–32
    biopower 47–8
    individual, the 64
    racism 102–3
Port Sunlight 166
post-humanism 37, 137
posture 137–9
Potter, Eileen 153
poultry 118–19, 120
power
    biopower 47–8
    mechanisms of 46–7
    pastoralism 46, 47, 48–9
private opinion 18, 50
problem families 158–63
propaganda 54–6
*Protection of the Public from Aerial Attack, The* (CSAWG) xii
psychoanalysis 51–2, 141–2
'Public Defence: Some Things You Should Know if War Should Come' leaflet xiii

Public Information Leaflets xvi–xvii
public opinion 50 *see also* morale
Purcell, Jennifer 10
*Put Out More Flags* (Waugh, Evelyn) 62

race/racism 37–8, 162–3, 164 *see also* eugenics
  antisemitism 8, 53, 106–7, 163, 164–5
  dogs 145
  evacuation 98–100, 106–7
  Foucault, Michel 32, 102–3, 104
  kind warden's wife, the 98–9
  *March of Progress, The* image 138
  Schuller, Kyla 33
racehorses 120–1
radio 54, 57, 62, 118
rats 35, 36, 141–2
Reeves, Rachel 27
reform 7–8
Regional Information Officers (RIOs) 43
Reich, Warren T. 155
resilience 6, 12
resources *see also* food
  efficient use 120–1
response 140
RIOs (Regional Information Officers) 43
Ritvo, Harriet 137, 142, 144
*Road to 1945, The* (Addison, Paul) 6, 8
Rose, Sonia O. 11, 90, 92, 104
  *Which People's War* 8–9, 176 n. 23
RSPCA
  'Animals and Air Raids' 116
rumours 56–64 *see also* evacuation stories

sacrifice 5, 110, 126–8, 133, 147–8
Saint-Amour, Paul K. xvi
*Savage Civilisation* (Harrisson, Tom) 13
Sayer, Derek 24, 26, 169
Schuller, Kyla 33
séances 65
second-person pronoun xv–xvi
'Second World War, The' (Lowe, Rodney) 176 n. 23
secular sacrifice 5, 126–8, 133, 147–8
security 156–8
self-help 40–1
self-sacrifice 5
selfhood 132
Seligman, Charles 162–3

sensorial resocialization 11
Seshadri, Kalpana Rahita 37–8, 148
sex 33
*Shape of Things to Come, The* (Wells, H.G.) viii
silence 37, 132–3, 140
Silent Column campaign 59–62
Singer, Charles 162–3
slums 157, 159–60
social change 16–17, 156
social class 149, 165 *see also* social divides
  clothing 82
  dogs 147
  equality 3, 7–8, 89–90
  food 55–6, 82
  Harris, Jose 7
  housing 166
  judgement 74
  Letchworth 166
  Nicolson, Harold 8
  table etiquette 85, 86
  Todd, Selina 7
social differentiation 25–6
social divides 155–6, 163
  animalization 149
  evacuation 3, 7
  evacuation stories 2, 67–8, 73–5, 81–2, 84–5, 87
  problem families 158–63
'Social Insurance and Allied Services' (Beveridge, William) 6, 27
social policy 6, 12, 27, 157, 167
  welfare state 6, 177 n. 59
Spanish Civil War xi, xii
species, hierarchy of 136, 137, 147 *see also* animacy hierarchies
spying 57, 62–4
squirrels 144
state, the. *See* government
state racism 32
Stevenson, Lisa 3
subjectivity-objectivity dichotomy 20–1
suffering xx, 25–6
Summerfield, Penny 8
Summerfield, Penny and Peniston-Bird, Corinna 9, 10
surveillance 46 *see also* spying
survey research 63

table etiquette 85, 86
Taylor, Sunaura 137, 138
Tebbutt, Melanie 57
*Theodore Savage* (Hamilton, Cecily) x–xi, xvi
Titmuss, Richard 76–7
Todd, Selina 7
Trevelyan, Julian xviii, 21
Trump, Donald 26
Tuan, Yi-Fu 3, 140, 155–6
'Tube Dwellers, The' (Mass Observation) 167, 168
tube dwelling 167–9
Tyson, Edward
    *Homo Sylvestris* 138

unimpressibility 162
utility 5, 126, 128–31, 147

vision 139
Visser, Margaret 85, 86

war 53
    anticipation of xvi, xvii–xviii, xx
    planning vii–viii, xii–xx, 171 n. 11
    suffering xx
*War Begins at Home* (Harrisson, Tom and Madge, Charles) 22–3, 45
'War-Time Dog Food' leaflet 110
wartime instructions vii–viii, xiii–xx
Wartime Social Survey (WSS) 43, 62, 63
Waters, Doris 118
Waters, Elsie 118
Waugh, Evelyn
    *Put Out More Flags* 62

*We Europeans: A Survey in 'Racial' Problems* (Huxley, Julian and Haddon, Alfred C.) 162–3
welfare state 6
    evacuation 177 n. 59
Wells, H.G.
    *Shape of Things to Come, The* viii
Welshman, John 158–9
    'Evacuation and Social Policy During the Second World War' 177 n. 59
*Which People's War* (Rose, Sonia O.) 8–9, 176 n. 23
Wiggam, Marc 9
Williams, David 145
wishful thinking 51–2
Wolfe, Cary 139
women 9–10, 146
    adultery 47
    dogs 131
    evacuation 90–2, 95
    Eve, fall of 93–6
    feckless mothers 92
    as good citizens 90–2, 96–100
    housewives 166–7
    kind warden's wife, the 98–9
    leisure 65
    mothers 92, 94f–6
    nursing 90
    posture 138
    wartime obligations 90–2
worries 155
WSS (Wartime Social Survey) 43, 62, 63

you xv–xvi
'Your Courage, Your Cheerfulness, Your Resolution Will Bring Us Victory' poster xiv–xv

www.ingramcontent.com/pod-product-compliance
Lightning Source LLC
Chambersburg PA
CBHW062148300426
44115CB00012BA/2047